THE SHORT AMERICAN CENTURY

THE SHORT AMERICAN CENTURY

A Postmortem

Edited by

ANDREW J. BACEVICH

Harvard University Press

Cambridge, Massachusetts

London, England

2012

Library of Congress Cataloging-in-Publication Data

The short American century : a postmortem / edited by Andrew J. Bacevich.
p. cm.
Includes bibliographical references and index.
ISBN 978-0-674-06445-4 (alk. paper)
1. United States—Civilization—20th century. 2. United States—Social conditions—
20th century. 3. United States—Economic conditions—20th century. 4. National
characteristics, American. 5. Civilization, Modern—American influences. 6. United
States—Foreign relations—20th century. 7. Politics and culture—United States.
8. Social values—United States—History—20th century. 9. Luce, Henry Robinson,
1898–1967 American century. I. Bacevich, Andrew J.
E169.12.S5152   2012
973.91—dc23   2011034058

Contents

THE SHORT AMERICAN CENTURY

CHAPTER 1

Life at the Dawn of the American Century

Andrew J. Bacevich

As contemplated by average Americans, sitting in their living rooms and leafing through their favorite magazine, the outside world in mid-February 1941 seemed nothing if not troubled. Occupying the center of attention was Great Britain, its people stoic in the face of a widely expected invasion. Although the intensity of German air raids had diminished in recent weeks (a pause that some called the "Lullablitz"), Londoners were still spending their nights in underground shelters. Fleet Street speculated endlessly about what the Nazis might be planning, British newspapers buzzing with stories "of gas clouds to be blown across the Channel, of paralyzing gas, of inaudible sound waves that make people sick, of 40,000 troop gliders, of air-troop landings in 500 places at once." Although small numbers of demonstrators, "alleged to be Communists," were complaining that food rationing arrangements favored the privileged and well-to-do, the British upper lip remained admirably stiff.

Emissaries from Washington bore witness to the travails of the British people and "absorbed every detail of Britain's war effort." One such visitor was Harry Hopkins, President Franklin D. Roosevelt's "personal unofficial envoy," who "stuck close to Winston Churchill" as he set about discerning "tactfully and discreetly, from every possible source, the nature of Britain's post-war aims." Making a far greater impression on the locals was the ebullient Wendell Willkie. Defeated by FDR for the presidency the previous November, Willkie had embarked for London on a fact-finding trip that became a "triumphant invasion of England" and "a personal triumph of fabulous proportions." Offering words of "cheer and encouragement," Willkie visited pubs, rode double-decker buses, surveyed the damage done by the Blitz, and joined George VI for tea. The American left "no doubt that he was 100% for Britain and the cause for which it fought." As an immediate consequence, his standing "in the eyes of millions of friends of freedom on both shores of the sea" skyrocketed.

Meanwhile, in France, the Vichy government of Marshal Philippe Pétain was maneuvering vainly to preserve some shred of autonomy even as it collaborated with Adolf Hitler. Berlin was demanding that France hand over its fleet and a base at Bizerte, along the coast of Tunisia. The French navy rejected the former, the French army the latter, "but neither refusal had teeth in it." The Nazis seemed likely to have their way. Evidence of just how supine the French had become came from the Near East. Touring the region as a "special observer" for President Roosevelt, Colonel William J. ("Wild Bill") Donovan had finished consulting with officials in Bulgaria, Yugoslavia, and Turkey and was headed next to French-controlled Syria. In Ankara, Donovan was about to board his Damascus-bound train "when a secretary of the French Embassy rushed up with a cable from Vichy cancelling his visa."

Battlefield developments in North Africa offered a modest glimmer of hope. There, British and Australian troops under the command of General Archibald Wavell had captured Bardia in eastern Libya, and with it over forty thousand Italian prisoners. Immense stores of equipment fell into British hands. With Italian forces in headlong retreat, their commander, General Rodolfo Graziani, told local residents as he decamped, "You stay here. The British are coming but they are gentlemen. They will treat you kindly."

For Finns, war had ended altogether. By valiantly defending itself against a 1939 Soviet invasion, Finland "had secured its position as America's favorite nation on the continent of Europe." Popular esteem did not translate into substantive assistance, however, as Washington refused a request for aid because "Finland is under suspicion of letting food trickle through to Germany." Meanwhile, much closer to home,

Cuban President Fulgencio Batista had unearthed and foiled another coup attempt. Suspending the constitution and banishing the principal coup plotters—the chiefs of Cuba's army, navy, and national police—to Miami, Batista declared, "Democracy has been saved."

All of these reports, gathered from "the newsfronts of the world," appeared—along with much else—in the issue of *Life* magazine bearing the cover date February 17, 1941.[1] The brainchild of Henry R. Luce, *Life* had first seen the light of day just slightly more than four years earlier. With sales and subscriptions far exceeding initial projections, it had already proven a smashing success. Arguably the most influential popular periodical in American history, *Life* owed its existence to Luce's long-standing ambition to create a high-quality "picture magazine." Yet the magazine's prospectus, drafted well before the publication of volume I, number 1, suggests a grander purpose: "To see life; to see the world; to eyewitness great events," employing photography not simply to record a moment but to explain, interpret, and influence.[2]

Life was the latest franchise in Time Inc., the journalistic juggernaut that had vaulted Luce while still a young man to a position of wealth and power. Yet for Luce, Time Inc.'s self-described editor in chief, power implied obligation. Raised in China as the son of missionaries, he retained throughout his life a missionary inclination, determined to have a hand in great deeds. This determination found expression in various enthusiasms, the promotion of Wendell Willkie's political prospects prominent among them. Yet by 1941, one cause took precedence over all others: supporting Great Britain in its lonely struggle against Nazi Germany.

Like Willkie, Luce was 100 percent for Britain. At the time, many of his countrymen were not so sure. The course of events in Europe had divided U.S. public opinion—some Americans favored all-out assistance to Britain, while others were intent on keeping the United States out of war. In early 1941, with Roosevelt proceeding by half steps—offering the British help but stopping short of outright intervention—Luce sought to force the issue. He had grown impatient with Washington's shilly-shallying. He wanted the United States all in.

The result, a lengthy editorial appearing in that same issue of *Life,* went far beyond simply advocating greater U.S. support for Great

Britain, however. It called instead for the United States to assume unequivocally and permanently the mantle of global leadership. Easily the most famous essay ever to appear under Luce's own byline, it carried the evocative title "The American Century."

The Summons

Luce began his essay by putting his fellow citizens on the couch and assuming the role of national shrink. His diagnosis: a case of rampant malaise was afflicting the country. "We Americans are unhappy," he wrote. "We are nervous—or gloomy—or apathetic." When they looked to the future, the people of the United States were "filled with foreboding."

For Luce, the contrast between Americans and Britons was striking. Fighting for their very existence, the people of Great Britain "are profoundly calm. There seems to be a complete absence of nervousness." With the onset of war, "all the neuroses of modern life had vanished from England."

Why were Americans feeling so out of sorts? The role that the United States had come to play in the ongoing European war—involved yet less than fully committed—offered a clue. The times called for action, yet Americans persisted in dithering. Everywhere, the good, the vulnerable, and the innocent looked expectantly to the United States for aid and assistance. Yet the inhabitants of "the most powerful and most vital nation in the world" remained on the sidelines or responded at most with half measures.

To Luce, the moment had arrived for the United States to answer history's call. As he put it, "the complete opportunity of leadership is *ours.*" Americans simply needed to seize that opportunity, guiding others toward salvation. "What we want will be okay with them." Yet Americans stubbornly and knowingly seemed intent on dodging their obligations. Here lay the taproot of the nation's current maladies.

The "cure" was self-evident. Luce summoned his countrymen "to accept wholeheartedly our duty and our opportunity . . . to exert upon the world the full impact of our influence for such purposes as we see fit and by such means as we see fit." In an immediate sense, duty required the United States to ally itself with Great Britain as a full-fledged belligerent in the European war. Yet this amounted to hardly more than a necessary first step. Duty implied a mission of transforming the entire global order. In the course of performing that duty, Luce fully expected the United States to transform—and perfect—itself.

Implicit in Luce's diagnosis was this premise: America itself could no longer provide the wherewithal enabling Americans to realize their aspirations. "Freedom requires and will require far greater living space than Tyranny," he observed in passing. When it came to cultivating freedom, a landscape extending from sea to shining sea no longer sufficed. A pioneering people needed new frontiers to conquer.

Franklin Roosevelt's New Deal, Luce opined, had tried "to make American democracy work successfully on a narrow, materialistic and nationalistic basis" and had failed abysmally. Roosevelt had fallen short, as Luce saw it, because he had not aimed high enough. To define America's purposes in national or material terms was to sell democracy short. "Our only chance now to make it work is in terms of a vital international economy and in terms of an international moral order."

Fortunately, perhaps even providentially, the world itself was changing in ways that appeared to accommodate America's requirement for a larger canvas upon which to work. Revolutionary changes were afoot and "for the first time in history" the prospect of "one world, fundamentally indivisible" was presenting itself. No nation was better positioned to determine the character of this new world than the United States. As "the inheritors of all the great principles of Western civilization—above all Justice, the love of Truth, the ideal of Charity"—Americans already embodied what an indivisible global society might eventually become.

"American jazz, Hollywood movies, American slang, American machines and patented products"—according to Luce, "the only things that every community in the world, from Zanzibar to Hamburg recognizes in common"—already constituted the basis for "an immense American internationalism." Yet this was only the beginning. Luce insisted that any American internationalism worthy of the name would necessarily incorporate the nation's distinctive ideals as well. "It must be a sharing with all peoples of our Bill of Rights, our Declaration of

Independence, [and] our Constitution. . . . It must be an internationalism of the people, by the people and for the people."

By rising to this challenge, Luce hoped the United States might become "the Good Samaritan of the entire world." As Good Samaritan, "really believing again that it is more blessed to give than to receive," America would share with others its "technical and artistic skills" and accept its "manifest duty" to feed the hungry everywhere. Rather than merely serving as "the sanctuary of the ideals of civilization," the United States would become "the powerhouse from which [those] ideals spread throughout the world," thereby accomplishing "their mysterious work of lifting the life of mankind from the level of the beasts to what the Psalmist called a little lower than the angels."

This described what Luce foresaw as the probable achievements of "the first great American Century," a cause in which he urged *Life*'s readers to enlist with "joy and gladness and vigor and enthusiasm."

Visions of Abundance

Apart from Luce's attention-grabbing essay, the contents of his magazine that week offered little to support the editor in chief's analysis or his prescription. To judge by *Life*'s own depiction of the country's mood, apathy and unhappiness were notable by their absence. Instead, optimism prevailed. American life was pretty good and getting better all the time.

So the front cover—by no means atypical for *Life*—featured a winsome, bare-shouldered Hollywood starlet. On the back was a full-page ad for Coca-Cola, touting "the pause that refreshes." The overall content of the pages in between was sunny and upbeat.

This predominantly cheery perspective was hardly surprising. After all, *Life* had captured the popular imagination not by trafficking in gloom and doom but by paying tribute to an idealized version of the American past, enthusing over the latest scientific and technological breakthroughs, keeping its readers abreast of fads, diversions, and cultural trends, and, above all, celebrating a middle-class, middlebrow formula for personal happiness.

Although *Life* editorials usually appeared near the front of the magazine, "The American Century" began on page 61, sandwiched between a feature on women's fashion ("Shoe Fair Features Casual Styles Inspired by U.S. Navy and Cowboys") and a profile of Betty Carstairs, oil heiress, adventuress, and speedboat racer. Known for "her mannish clothes and her tattooed arms," Carstairs had acquired a nine-mile-long island near the Bahamas, which she ruled like a private fiefdom. *Life* devoted six pages of text and photos to explaining how Carstairs had become "a living legend as the misanthropic Queen of Whale Cay."

Elsewhere the contents emphasized not distemper but a sense of things headed in the right direction. References to the economic crisis of the previous decade were nowhere to be found. The world beyond America's borders might seem stormy, but at home an atmosphere of hopeful normalcy—and fun—prevailed.

On Broadway, a new season had begun and showed signs of real promise. Among the hit musicals that had already opened were *Pal Joey,* with "gay, sly ditties" by Richard Rodgers and Moss Hart; *Panama Hattie,* featuring "sex, sumptuous sets, [and] Cole Porter songs"; and *Cabin in the Sky,* with Ethel Waters heading "an all-Negro cast." Leading the roster of notable comedies were *My Sister Eileen* and *Arsenic and Old Lace.* Other shows starred such favorites as Ethel Barrymore, Helen Hayes, Gertrude Lawrence, Al Jolson, and Ed Wynn. Broadway offerings included only a single war-related play, Elmer Rice's *Flight to the West,* which *Life* judged a disappointment, "despite some excellent anti-Nazi speeches."

On the opposite coast, "a fancy shindig that offered everything the U.S. fan ever envisaged in the way of a Hollywood party" drew *Life*'s attention. "Guests came in opulent costumes," while "champagne burbled in high tidal abundance." Although the purpose of the gathering was unclear, "virtually everybody who was anybody was there," *Life*'s photographer verifying the presence of Dorothy Lamour, Rosalind Russell, Randolph Scott, Rudy Vallee, and Walter Pidgeon, among other glamorous film figures.

There was more: an article on iceboating; an appreciation of Mahonri Young, acclaimed by *Life* as "the George Bellows of realistic American sculpture"; the unveiling of a massive relief map of the United States, sixty-three feet across and fifteen years in the making; plus a report on the latest findings on ant research, reveling in the ability of these tiny creatures to "solve complex problems."

Meanwhile, coeds at the University of Maryland—"acutely conscious of the necessity of being popular"—helped *Life* demonstrate the latest dos and don'ts of "campus etiquet" [*sic*]. Tidbits of advice included "Don't play footsie in library"; "Don't ignore a dud blind date"; "Don't dangle cigarets in mouth"; and "Don't blow on soup." This feature also provided an update on campus footwear fashion: heels were out; knee-high boots and saddle shoes were in.

Preparations for war barely left a dent on the home front. *Life* did note an innovation making its appearance at government installations and in defense plants: employee identification badges. In an accompanying photo, a nameless guard inspected the ID of General George C. Marshall, shown reporting to work in overcoat and fedora and looking more like an insurance executive than the army's chief of staff. A short feature titled "Winter at Yaphank" recounted the exertions of thirty-five hundred soldiers "marching through deep snowdrifts, drilling in near-zero temperatures, [and] shooting their guns when hands and feet ache with cold" as they endured frigid conditions on eastern Long Island. But Broadway shows, Hollywood parties, campus social mores, and ants meandering through mazes received far more attention than did military trainees on field exercises.

Then there were the advertisements, the basis of *Life*'s considerable profitability. Featured inside the front cover was a full-color ad for Libby's "family" of canned juices (which included loganberry and kraut). Dad in coat and tie, grandma in a flower-print dress, and sis, hair neatly braided, had gathered around the breakfast table to choose from among Libby's ten different varieties.

Gadgets promised improvements in everyday life: electric irons; electric coffeemakers; automatic clothes washers ("Easy as turning on a light"); and electric sunlamps ("You too can have that winter vacation look"). Packaged foods offered both convenience and nutrition: frozen succotash; processed meats; cellophane-wrapped donuts, "dated for freshness"; canned chicken noodle soup ("a favorite among the simple homey dishes that built the men who built the nation"); and Dromedary-brand gingerbread mix, "made from the original recipe of

George Washington's mother." Promoting the down-home goodness of Cream of Wheat and Aunt Jemima pancakes were grinning images of African Americans, otherwise absent from the advertisements appearing in *Life*.

For men, there were several brands of whiskey; for women, slips, girdles, bras, hosiery, face powder, and diamonds; for everyone, mouthwash and tobacco, with Lucky Strike proudly declaring that it was paying top dollar "for the finer, lighter, the more naturally mild tobaccos."

Testifying most alluringly to the promise of American life were the car ads, each one a full page, most in vivid color: a Chrysler in cerulean blue (with plaid interior), featuring a Spitfire engine and Vacamatic transmission; a dashing red Mercury roadster, "built according to aviation principles"; an Oldsmobile "Special" Town Sedan, available in gleaming yellow; and a Chevrolet, with its Victory engine, "unisteel turret top," and "tip-toematic clutch," all offered at no extra cost. With more than 10 million female drivers cruising America's highways and byways, a Ford ad announced that "it is the women of this country who determine what needs the engineers must meet" and depicted a sturdy green four-door as the tangible response to those needs.

Here was life, liberty, and the pursuit of happiness made manifest.

Petering Out

The vision of American global leadership that Luce advanced in his essay and the vision of personal gratification and fulfillment that his magazine extolled from one week to the next shared this much in common: each represented an aspiration, not to be confused with an actually existing reality. Yet those aspirations, even if coexisting in *Life*'s pages, were not self-evidentially congruent or even compatible. Put bluntly, Luce might yearn to see the United States become the world's Good Samaritan, but the millions who subscribed to his magazine had their sights set on goals that were considerably more mundane: they wanted a bigger piece of all that *Life* itself promised.

The events of the next several years camouflaged the disparity between what *Life*'s proprietor was seeking and what *Life* itself was selling. In December the Japanese attack on Pearl Harbor ended any lingering American ambivalence about getting in the game. Luce embraced war. Most Americans accepted it, willing to postpone paradise, but only for the duration.

The European war morphed into a much larger global crusade, the scope of the ensuing conflict fostering outsized expectations of a world made new. Americans saw their own fighting troops making that new world possible. On the home front, all-out mobilization meant that gizmos, gadgets, and many consumer goods disappeared. The government imposed, and Americans mostly accepted, a mild form of rationing. In *Life,* the ads shifted their focus from present to future, showcasing new and improved products currently on the drawing board but just waiting for peace to appear in stores.

When first unveiled, Luce's concept of an American Century amounted to little more than the venting of an overwrought publishing tycoon. By the time World War II ended, observers surveying the extraordinarily favorable position in which the United States found itself concluded that something akin to an American Century had in fact commenced. Claims that in 1941 sounded grandiose became after 1945 unexceptionable. The phrase coined by Luce infiltrated the political vernacular, adopted by both defenders and critics of U.S. policy as shorthand for an era of putative American dominion.

For those like Luce who hankered for the United States to take on the responsibilities of global leadership, the American Century soon found expression in a Pax Americana, Washington wielding broad authority throughout the "Free World." For those like *Life*'s readers who hankered for benefits closer to home, the American Century found expression in plentiful jobs, proliferating leisure activities, cheap energy readily available from domestic sources, and a cornucopia of consumer goods, almost all of them bearing the label "Made in the USA." Briefly, that is, Americans seemed to have it both ways. Exercising power abroad appeared perfectly compatible with pursuing the good life at home.

But only briefly: The very unpopular Korean War first hinted at the tension between these two visions of an American Century. A decade later, the Vietnam War brought that tension fully into the open, revealing the limits of both Washington's capacity to police the American

Century and the American people's willingness to underwrite that effort. More or less simultaneously, the foundations of U.S. economic primacy began to erode. The terms of trade tipped from black to red and stayed there. The oil needed to sustain the personal mobility that Americans prized came increasingly from abroad. So too did the manufactures—including automobiles—that Americans coveted, acquired, used, and discarded with abandon.

The decline and eventual collapse of the Soviet Empire—interpreted in Washington as vindicating and renewing the American Century—disguised the significance of these developments. As the Cold War wound down, politicians and pundits vied with one another to replicate Luce's earlier feat, attempting to capture in a single phrase what "victory" over communism signified. In a tacit salute to Luce, the most ardent exponents of deploying U.S. power "for such purposes as we see fit and by such means as we see fit" called their enterprise simply the Project for a New American Century (PNAC). While PNAC agitated for the more aggressive use of U.S. military muscle (thought to be unassailable), the advocates of globalization (said to guarantee wealth generation on a scale without precedent) unleashed rhetorical flourishes that would have made Luce himself blush. Few observers paid much attention to the fact that when the United States now employed armed force, it rarely achieved decisive results, or that globalization, while making some people very rich indeed, found many ordinary Americans left behind and hurting.

Rather than deflating this post–Cold War triumphalism, the events of September 11, 2001, had precisely the opposite effect. After 9/11, President George W. Bush launched an all-out effort to realize the American Century throughout the Islamic world, articulating his aims with a religious fervor that outdid Luce himself. To eliminate the conditions giving rise to violent jihadism, Bush vowed to transform the entire Greater Middle East. Making an end to evil: that defined the nation's purpose. Waging open-ended war on a global scale: that defined its chosen means. Supremely confident in the prowess of U.S. military forces, Bush embarked upon his war without mobilizing the country or even adjusting its domestic priorities. Rather than collective sacrifice, uninhibited consumption, encouraged by reduced taxes, defined the wartime role allotted to the American public. This effort proved a costly failure. Rather than eliminating evil, the forces operating under President Bush's command became ensnared in it, committing acts of torture and abuse, killing innocents, and, in general, creating chaos. Campaigns launched in Afghanistan and then Iraq with expectations of achieving quick, decisive outcomes turned out to be long, bloody, and inconclusive. Hopes that U.S. military action would trigger a wave of democratic change sweeping the Middle East were stillborn. Change did eventually come, but as a result of spontaneous popular uprisings directed from within, not as a result of Western military campaigns organized in Washington. Meanwhile, the costs, fiscal as well as human, absorbed by the American people turned out to be vastly greater than anticipated.

During the interval between the off-year elections of November 2006 and the presidential election of November 2008, the bottom fell out. Without giving up on war, U.S. military and political leaders gave up on victory. Rather than transforming the Middle East, simply extricating the United States from Iraq with some semblance of dignity now became the Bush administration's ranking priority. Perhaps worse, the economy went into a tailspin, producing a crisis not seen since the Great Depression of the 1930s. For its part, PNAC quietly closed up shop.

Put simply, the conditions that once lent plausibility to visions of an American Century had ceased to exist. It was not so much that the United States itself was experiencing decline—although plenty of evidence existed to suggest that was the case—or that a Chinese, Indian, Brazilian, or European Century loomed on the horizon. Rather, it was that the world itself had changed. Contemporary reality no longer accommodated the notion of a single nation arrogating to itself the role of global Good Samaritan, especially a nation with dirty hands. To take seriously Washington's professions of good intentions in Iraq or Afghanistan or Pakistan required a shorter memory than the subjects of America's post-9/11 ministrations possessed.

Meanwhile, shenanigans on Wall Street exposed as fraudulent the economic utopianism that the United States had promoted during the

1990s. As a blueprint for assured global prosperity, the so-called Washington Consensus turned out to be bogus. In parallel fashion, events on the field of battle put paid to the notion that the Pentagon had mastered the art of war. "Shock-and-awe" turned out to be smoke and mirrors. In the realm of popular and commercial culture, American products no longer defined the one thing Zanzibar and Hamburg shared in common. Whether the hedonistic, consumer-oriented definition of freedom that America represented was sustainable or even desirable was itself becoming the subject of debate.

Politicians and ideologues insisted otherwise, continuing to identify themselves with Luce's dream. As a candidate for the presidency, for example, Senator Barack Obama summoned his followers "to unite in common purpose, to make this century the next American century."[3] Yet this was akin to promising that world peace or a cure for cancer lies just around the corner: a pleasant thought with little basis in reality. Were there any doubts in that regard, the disappointments associated with Obama's own presidency soon quashed them. Economic stagnation, high unemployment, trillion-dollar deficits, deep-seated political dysfunction, and the perpetuation (even expansion) of costly, inchoate armed conflicts did not herald the dawn of a new era of American dominion. In short, by the time the seventieth anniversary of Luce's famous essay rolled around in 2011, the gap between what he had summoned Americans to do back in 1941 and what they were actually willing or able to do had become unbridgeable.

The era of wishful thinking was drawing to a close. Contemplating the implications of President Obama's decision to begin withdrawing U.S. troops from Afghanistan during the summer of 2011, *Washington Post* columnist Richard Cohen observed that "the American Century just ended." For Cohen, the president's announcement marked a watershed. "We are not Henry Luce's America," he wrote, "not because we no longer want to be, but because we no longer can be."[4]

In Retrospect

Although like most Washington-based observers Cohen lagged considerably behind events, his basic verdict is likely to stand. To the extent

that an American Century ever did exist—a point on which the contributors to this collection are *not* in unanimous agreement—that moment has now definitively passed. The utility of Luce's formulation as
a description of the contemporary international order or as a guide to
future U.S. policy has been exhausted. What comes next may not be
entirely clear, but a return to the heyday of U.S. political, economic,
and military supremacy does not figure among the likely alternatives.

This book accepts that outcome. Its purpose is neither to decry nor
to mourn the passing of the Short American Century (much less to
promote its resurrection) but to assess its significance. Consigning the
abbreviated period of supposed American dominion to the past cre-
ates fresh opportunities to discern what that period was all about. If
the United States at the zenith of its power and influence never succeeded in lifting humankind to a level approximating that of the an-
gelic hosts, as Luce had predicted, what exactly are we to make of this
brief interval of history? How should inhabitants of what Fareed
Zakaria has called the present-day "post-American world" assess the
considerable achievements, large disappointments, and missed opportunities of the era just past?[5] In short, what did the effort to forge an
American Century—satisfying the ambitions expressed by Luce and
the appetites of the millions who read his magazine—ultimately yield?

The essays that follow, offered from a variety of vantage points, reflect
on these questions. Surveying a considerable swath of U.S. history—in
some cases reaching back well before the publication date of Luce's
essay—they are, for the most part, critical rather than celebratory. The
aim here is not to prop up American self-esteem. Before history can
teach, it must challenge and even discomfit. This collection takes stock
of U.S. achievements and failures over several crucial decades. It ac-
knowledges the nation's penchant for oversized aspirations—for attempting big things in a big way—but also confronts evidence of severe
myopia and even blindness. And it assesses the consequences that ensued, both intended and unforeseen, for the United States and for the
rest of the world. Taken as a whole, the result serves as a sort of dis-
senter's guide to the American Century.

CHAPTER 2

The Origins and Uses of American Hyperpower

David M. Kennedy

The concept of inevitability is the assassin of the historical imagination. In Sir Arthur Conan Doyle's "Silver Blaze," a dog that did not bark provided Sherlock Holmes with the telltale clue. Unlike Doyle, historians do not write fiction; but like him, they rely on their imaginations to reconstruct the past. And like Holmes, they often find it useful to inquire about what did not happen as a way to illuminate what did. Asking "what if?" can be a powerful tool to reveal the contingencies of history and to sort out the often baffling welter of both causes and consequences. It also serves as a reminder that while history is remembered backward, it is lived forward, by men and women for whom what is our settled past was their unknowable future—men and women who necessarily interrogated that future with their own urgent "what ifs."

So here is a particularly probative "what if" question about one of the most apparently inevitable, foreordained facts of the modern era: What if the United States had lost World War II? How in that event would the world of the last seven decades have been different? That is the strongest form of the question. A more manageable version might be: What if the United States had fought a different kind of war, on a different timetable, governed by different strategic assumptions, deploying a different scale and mix of armed forces, with a different mobilization program, and therefore achieving a substantially different kind of victory? What then would have been the character of the postwar era, for Americans and for others? Would Henry Luce's conceit of an "American Century" even have been imaginable?

A premise informs these thoughts about World War II, one aimed at establishing a proposition. The proposition, in turn, is meant to serve as a platform for a conclusion about the role that the United States played in the post–World War II era, and for a question about whether that era can now be said to have closed.

The premise is that World War II constituted a massively transformative event, for both the United States and the world—that it set the stage for the so-called American Century, or at least half century. The proposition is that the United States *chose*—I use that word deliberately—to fight a certain kind of war. In doing so, it succeeded, to a degree unmatched by virtually all other combatants in that or any other war, in fighting on its own terms.

The peculiar character of American belligerency, in short, did not just happen. It owed, rather, to certain key decisions. And the conclusion is that the United States exercised the power that World War II bestowed upon it to effect a revolution in international affairs—one that the Founders had dreamt and Woodrow Wilson had tried but failed to implement. It was a revolution marked at times by setbacks, failures, and follies, but it succeeded sufficiently in the latter half of the twentieth century to define an era in the long history of the international order.

So just how transformative was World War II? For the Americans themselves, the war marked a great historical cadence. It conclusively banished the Great Depression and ushered in what the novelist Philip Roth has called "the greatest moment of collective inebriation in American history," characterized by "an explosion of self-assertion," a contagious "upsurge of energy," with "the clock of history reset and a whole people's aims limited no longer by the past."[1] More summarily, Winston Churchill declared in 1945 that "the United States stand at this moment at the summit of the world."[2]

Uniquely prosperous and formidably powerful, America bestrode the postwar world like a colossus. Yet these developments could not have been confidently predicted before the war. Indeed, when Henry

Luce laid out his vision for the "American Century" in a February 1941 issue of *Life,* he gave solitary voice to a singular, almost laughably idiosyncratic vision, with nothing but the most dreamily aspirational basis in fact. Maybe that is why he cast his hortatory piece in such egregiously millennial and chauvinistic terms.

To understand the full scope of the war's transformative agency, one need only glance at the contrast between America's situation in its last full peacetime year—1940—and its situation at the war's end in 1945, when Churchill offered that telling assessment about standing at the summit of the world. Nineteen-forty was the eleventh year of the Great Depression. Neither Herbert Hoover nor Franklin Roosevelt had managed to find an exit from the seemingly permanent economic crisis whose onset had been heralded by the great stock market collapse in October 1929. Unemployment had averaged 17 percent throughout the 1930s, and still stood at 14.6 percent as the decade of the 1940s opened.[3] More than 40 percent of all white households and 95 percent of all African American households lived in poverty in 1940.

On the international stage, the contrast between America's prewar and postwar situations is even more dramatic. In the two decades before 1940, the United States had rejected membership in the League of Nations, even though the League was the brainchild of an American president, Woodrow Wilson. It had erected the highest tariff barriers in its history—the Fordney-McCumber Tariff in 1922, followed by the notoriously trade-strangling Hawley-Smoot Tariff in 1930. In the same spirit of economic nationalism, Franklin Roosevelt had declared in his first inaugural address that "our international trade relations are secondary to the establishment of a sound national economy"—one of just four sentences that he devoted to foreign affairs—and he persisted for some time thereafter in pursuing economically isolationist policies.[4]

Successive American administrations in the 1920s had bedeviled European exchequers and raised hob with international capital flows by insisting that Allied governments repay in full the war debts to the U.S. Treasury contracted during the First World War. ("They hired the money, didn't they," said dour New England skinflint President Calvin Coolidge.) The Immigration Act of 1924 had placed numerical caps on immigration for the first time in American history, reducing the pre–World War I immigrant flood to a trickle; the nation proved to be in no mood in the ensuing Depression decade to change that restrictionist regime, even to accommodate refugees from Nazism. Congress had passed no fewer than five neutrality statutes during the 1930s, designed to restrain the executive from the kind of mischief that Wilson had worked by taking the United States into battle in 1917—widely understood as a tragic mistake in the First World War's disillusioned aftermath. And while it is true that in that same year of 1940 Congress enacted the nation's first peacetime military conscription law, it envisioned an army of fewer than 1 million men, held them to service for only one year, and forbade their deployment outside the Western Hemisphere. Politically, economically, morally, and militarily, America in the interwar decades did not merely re-embrace its historic policies of isolationism. It amplified them to unprecedented intensities.

Now imagine if a street-corner speaker in some American city in 1940 had said the following:

> My fellow Americans! I'm here to tell you that just over the horizon of the future, only five years hence, this stricken land of ours, blighted by more than a decade of depression and unemployment, will provide work for all who seek it. What is more, we will then be embarking upon a half century-long economic expansion of phenomenal proportions. The size of the middle class will increase by 50 percent within less than a generation. By century's end, poverty will be all but unknown among the elderly and will afflict less than one in ten Americans overall. Black Americans will share conspicuously in this bounty, as our nation will at last, after nearly a century of broken promises, make good on the pledges of racial equality tendered in the Civil War and Reconstruction Era.
>
> What is more, our isolationist country—the country that in our lifetimes turned its back on the League of Nations, closed its domestic markets to importers, insisted, Scrooge-like, on World War I debt repayment, effectively barred its doors to refugees from the Nazi menace, repeatedly declared its own neutrality in the struggle to contain that menace, and dithered about re-armament—this same

country, in just a few years' time, will field a 16-million-man armed force that in conjunction with its allies will defeat Germany as well as Japan; will maintain thereafter the most formidable military machine in the world's history; will found a successor body to the League, called the United Nations (UN); will take in some 700,000 refugees in just fifteen years, and another 30 million immigrants before the century's close; and will give birth to an array of institutions that will underwrite trade-liberating and investment-enhancing changes in the international order so sweeping that ultimately a new word—"globalization"—will be coined to describe them.

Anyone voicing such views in 1940 would have been rightly regarded as a lunatic, which is why Luce's piece, published just a few months after this hypothetical harangue, seemed so impossibly utopian to so many readers at the time. Yet in fact our mad ranter in 1940 accurately prophesied both the domestic and the international orders that crystallized in the second half of the twentieth century. How did this come about?

In general, and emphatically in this case, history is not just a matter of one damn thing after another. Both the domestic and foreign-policy transformations that World War II occasioned in the United States did not simply befall the country. They issued, rather, from a set of deliberate policy decisions made both before and during the war. Taken together, those decisions deposited the United States at Churchill's summit of the world in 1945, a position it occupied for the remainder of the century, and to which—though ever more tenuously—it still clings.

Even as late as the Japanese attack on Pearl Harbor on December 7, 1941, the pattern that those decisions would limn was not yet clear. The disparate reactions of Adolf Hitler and Winston Churchill to the Pearl Harbor attack illustrate the opacity with which America's precise war intentions were still cloaked. "Now it is impossible for us to lose the war," Hitler crowed when he heard the news from Hawaii. "We now have an ally [Japan] who has never been vanquished in three thousand years."[5] Yet Winston Churchill, hearing the same news at almost the same moment, came to precisely the opposite conclusion.

As he later recalled: "I could not foretell the course of events. . . . [B]ut now at this very moment I knew the United States was in the war, up to the neck and in to the death. So we had won after all . . . ! England would live. . . . Being saturated and satiated with emotion and sensation, I went to bed and slept the sleep of the saved and thankful."[6]

Events would of course prove Churchill right and Hitler disastrously mistaken. But that their opinions should differ so widely in December 1941 is a reminder that history at that moment was still pregnant with many different futures, conspicuously including the prospect of a protracted war enabling the United States to bring to bear the stupendous weight of its momentarily crippled but still behemoth economy. The United States was like "a gigantic boiler," the British diplomatist Sir Edward Grey had once told Churchill. "Once the fire is lighted under it there is no limit to the power it can generate."[7] Hitler's foreign minister, Joachim von Ribbentrop, made a similar point in a strategic advisory he submitted to Hitler after the initial exhilaration of the Pearl Harbor news had given way to more sober second thoughts: "We have just one year," Ribbentrop warned his führer in mid-December 1941, "to cut off Russia from her American supplies. . . . If we don't succeed and the munitions potential of the United States joins up with the manpower potential of the Russians, the war will enter a phase in which we shall only be able to win it with difficulty."[8] Similarly, Admiral Isoroku Yamamoto, commander in chief of Japan's Combined Fleet, had warned his government as early as September 1940 that "if I am told to fight regardless of the consequences, I shall run wild for the first six months or a year, but I have utterly no confidence for the second or third year. . . . I hope," he concluded, "that you will endeavor to avoid a Japanese-American war."[9]

Unlike Hitler, crazed by fanatical visions and deluded by his early and easy military triumphs, both Ribbentrop and Yamamoto held fast to the cardinal rule of warfare laid down centuries earlier by Sun-Tzu: know your enemy. They understood the full implications of Roosevelt's declaration that the United States intended to be "the great arsenal of democracy"—not principally the sword of democracy, nor even its shield, but its workshop and munitions depot, its forges and fields and factories unleashing an avalanche of the implements of war. Roosevelt, of course, made that declaration in December 1940 when he was still trying to persuade his reluctant countrymen to face the challenges of German and Japanese aggression. He dared not at that juncture allude to the further military measures that would eventually prove necessary. But, in fact, Roosevelt's phrase on that occasion described the essence of American war-fighting doctrine throughout the conflict. With only modest qualifications, "arsenal of democracy" defined the foundational principle and the distinguishing feature of America's grand strategy for the war's entirety.

To grasp that point, and to comprehend how America succeeded in hewing so consistently to the arsenal of democracy policy, consider a parable entitled "A Tale of Three Cities." It is a tale that unfolded in a relatively brief compass of time, between August 1942 and February 1943. During those six months a series of decisions, either implemented or made, imparted to the American war effort its distinctive character and led to that summit to which the United States ascended by 1945.

The three cities are all located on historic rivers: Rouen, on the Seine; Washington, D.C., on the Potomac; and a third city that was thrice named over the course of the century. It began as Tsaritsyn; today we know it as Volgograd, after the river on whose right bank it lies; and, at the time of this tale, it was called Stalingrad.

Chapter 1 of this parable opened in Rouen, France, on August 17, 1942, when a dozen B-17 bombers lifted off their airfield in southern England and transited the Channel accompanied by a swarm of British Spitfire fighters. The squadron dropped its bomb load on a railroad marshaling yard, just a few hundred meters from Rouen's historic Gothic cathedral and not far from the site where Joan of Arc had been burned at the stake some five centuries earlier. The planes returned to base without loss to aircraft or crew. By the usual measures of such things, it was a successful raid. But its true significance becomes apparent only in the larger context of history.

That raid on Rouen marked the first assault on Nazi-occupied Europe by heavy—or "strategic"—bombers under the sole command of the United States Army Air Forces. The din from those lumbering, four-engine aircraft announced a revolution in American war-fighting doctrine. Envisioned at least a decade earlier, that revolution lay at the core of American military planning in World War II, and its legacy endures to the present day.

The revolution had many fathers, including the colorful American general Billy Mitchell, but its principal creator was an Italian, Giulio Douhet. In company with other military analysts who had been appalled by the carnage of stalemated trench warfare in World War I, Douhet cast about for some means to fight the next war in a less costly and more effective fashion. He found his answer in the airplane, and he laid out his new doctrine of "strategic bombing" in his seminal 1921 treatise *The Command of the Air*.[10] The new technology of mechanized flight, Douhet argued, could render the traditional battlefield obsolete. It was now possible to overfly the point where armed forces had clashed in combat since time immemorial and to deliver a decisive blow not against the adversary's troops in the field but against the enemy heartland. By crippling his economic base, and, not incidentally, by simultaneously terrorizing his civilian population, such deep-penetration, or "strategic," bombing would at once deprive the enemy of his capacity to support a force in the field, as well as break his people's will to continue fighting. For those who could carry it off, strategic bombing promised rich rewards: a brief war, with relatively few casualties, and minimum disruption of one's own social and economic structure.

Seizing on those ideas, the United States Army, of which the air arm was then—and would continue to be throughout the war—a part, sponsored a design competition in 1933 to develop the means by which the heady ambitions of strategic bombing might be realized. The winner was the Boeing Corporation's Model 299. By 1937 it was in production as the B-17, known colloquially as the "Flying Fortress." Those "Forts" that bombed Rouen on August 17, 1942, were the first American planes to undertake the kind of strategic mission for which they had been designed. From that time forward, the United States carried the battle to its German adversary primarily from the air. D-day, when American ground troops were committed to action for the first time against a major German force in a crucial theater of the war, came only two years later, and just eleven months before the European war's conclusion. For most of that conflict—as well as in the historic endgame of the Pacific War—America preferred to fight not on the earth but from the heavens.

For the remainder of the century, the commitment to strategic bombing dominated American war-fighting doctrine—the preferred military instrument of the American Century. (Not incidentally, that preoccupation with waging strategic warfare from the air ultimately rendered U.S. forces less fit for counterinsurgency operations, or "wars among the people.") The B-17 and its companion workhorse of World War II, the B-24, yielded to a successor generation of longer-range, larger-payload B-29s even before the war's conclusion, and eventually, in the decades that followed, to B-52s, intercontinental ballistic missiles, stealth bombers, and unmanned aerial vehicles. All of those later weapons delivery systems, together with the precision-guided munitions that became such intimidating features of the American arsenal in the twenty-first century, shared with their World War II progenitors the hallmarks of Douhet's original strategic doctrine: their primary purpose was to attack the enemy's infrastructure, civilian population, and state of mind and morale, not the enemy's armed forces in the field. They also leveraged two assets that worked then and now vastly in America's favor: enormous productive capacity and technological superiority.

In an almost Gothic coincidence, the lead pilot on that Rouen raid in 1942 was Paul Tibbets, the pilot on a no less historic mission almost precisely three years later—the flight of the *Enola Gay* to deliver history's first atomic bomb on Hiroshima on August 6, 1945. It might be said that the arc of this one man's World War II military career traces the cardinal tenets of American strategy in that war: to fight from the air to the maximum extent possible; to minimize or delay or perhaps even to avoid entirely (as happened in the case of Japan) the commitment of ground troops; and to exploit to the maximum possible American industrial and scientific dominance.

So the commitment to develop a heavy-fisted air arm, with all that implied for force composition, industrial mobilization, and campaign planning, constituted one key component of the American way of war in World War II, as initiated on August 17, 1942, in the skies over Rouen.

Other components came into clear view just weeks later, as chapter 2 of this parable reveals. Its setting—Washington, D.C.—could boast a history less rich than Rouen's, its principals were less anointed by fate than Paul Tibbets, and its action was less dramatic than an aerial bombing attack—though scarcely less consequential. Just weeks after that initial B-17 raid, on October 6, 1942, the civilian head of the American War Production Board, Donald Nelson, met in his office with War Department Undersecretary Robert Patterson and Lieutenant General Brehon B. Somervell, commander of Army Service Forces. They were there to resolve the "Feasibility Dispute," a long-forgotten controversy but one that had plagued America's mobilization program through 1942 and generated seething antagonism between military and civilian mobilization officials. The terms of the agreement grudgingly reached on that day would all but complete the peculiar pattern of America's distinctive war.[11]

Before the war Nelson had headed one of the nation's largest retailers, Sears Roebuck. Perhaps his long career serving consumers made him especially sensitive to anything that might encroach on civilian standards of living. Nelson might also have worried that asking too much of the American people ran the risk of rekindling their notorious isolationist inclination. He was in any case reflexively supportive of an analysis prepared by the noted economist Simon Kuznets, who claimed that the scale and pace of mobilization as pursued in the first half of 1942 were simply not feasible. In trying to meet the ambitious goals laid out in the comprehensive 1941 planning document known as the "Victory Program," Kuznets argued, the United States was endangering civilian living standards and inflicting extravagant inefficiencies on the economy.

Patterson, who sported a belt allegedly stripped from the body of a German soldier he had killed in 1918, and Somervell, a no-nonsense professional warrior decorated in the Battle of the Meuse-Argonne in the same year, had little patience with Nelson's insistence on scaling back mobilization targets. (The trouble with civilian administrators like Nelson, Somervell later said, was that "they have never been bombed. They have little appreciation of the horrors of war and only in a small percentage of instances do they have enough hate.")[12] But with political support from the White House (Vice President Henry Wallace was also present in Nelson's office on October 6), Nelson prevailed. The helter-skelter, chaotic mobilization effort of early 1942 slowed down. Its gigantic military manpower drafts were drastically downsized.

Two fateful consequences followed.

First, the target date for the cross-Channel amphibious invasion of northwestern France, the event that history knows as D-day, originally scheduled for July 1, 1943, slipped to May 1, 1944 (in the event, it took place some five weeks later, on June 6). Second, the Victory Program's goal of conscripting, outfitting, training, transporting, and deploying 215 ground divisions was ratcheted down to just ninety divisions.

At the time, and in the history books, the result of the October 6 meeting became known as the "90-Division Gamble."[13] Why was it a gamble?

To answer that question, we turn to our parable's third chapter, and Stalingrad. As much as any single engagement could, Stalingrad constituted the pivot of World War II. Here, on the site of an exceptionally cruel and costly siege that slaughtered tens of thousands of German and Soviet troops, the war turned. The German capitulation at Stalingrad in February 1943 broke the back of the Wehrmacht's eighteen-month-old Russian offensive. The Red Army now seized the initiative and began the grisly task of pushing the Nazi invader out of the Soviet homeland, through Poland, and eventually into the streets of Berlin in the spring of 1945.

The Soviet victory at Stalingrad laid to rest a fear that had gnawed at British and American leaders since Hitler's initial assault on the Soviet Union in June 1941—that the Russians, like every other adversary that had faced the Wehrmacht, could not withstand the shock of heavily armored, fast-moving, blitzkrieg warfare. Surely the Russians too would go down in defeat, like the Poles, Dutch, Belgians, Norwegians, and French. That assumption had provided the basis for the original American decision to draft manpower sufficient to form 215 divisions. But the Soviets had demonstrated their willingness to pay a huge price to resist the German attack—3 million lost to wounds, death, or capture in the first six months alone, and far more than that through the awful fighting of 1942. The Russians thus bought the crucial, priceless asset of time, time to develop fully what Britain's Lord Beaverbrook called "the immense possibilities of American industry."[14]

Stalingrad, and the Battle of Kursk some months later, also substantially laid to rest (without entirely eliminating), a second fear that had plagued the Western members of the Grand Alliance: that their Soviet partner, though still able to hold the field militarily, might be so badly bloodied that Josef Stalin would seek a political exit from the war. There were ample precedents for such a Nazi-Soviet deal: the notorious Molotov-Ribbentrop Pact of 1939, by which Moscow and Berlin agreed to divide Poland and the Baltic states, and behind that the Brest-Litovsk Treaty of 1918, when the fledgling Bolshevik regime had taken the newborn Soviet Union out of World War I, releasing millions of the kaiser's troops for a final assault in the West.

In the wake of Stalingrad, the likelihood of any recurrence of these episodes dwindled. The Soviets passed from defensive to offensive warfare and waged it with ruthless effect. Their actions made evident their commitment to eradicating the Nazi regime.

These developments ratified the viability of decisions the Americans had made earlier. The full dimensions and logic of America's war-fighting doctrine now lay revealed. The principal guarantor of that doctrine, wrote official U.S. Army historian Maurice Matloff, was "the demonstration by the Soviet armies of their ability to check the German advance. Another significant factor brightening the strategic picture was the improving prospect of gaining air superiority over the Continent. These developments finally made obsolete the initial Victory Program estimates of 1941."[15]

The economic basis for that doctrine was the sense of physical limits the Feasibility Dispute had brought to the fore. With the so-called 90-Division Gamble, Roosevelt's "arsenal of democracy" strategy now fully matured. American military planners henceforward irrevocably embraced the concept of a war of machines rather than men. As Matloff noted, the Soviet victory at Stalingrad transformed from hopeful aspiration to firm reality the key assumption on which American grand strategy rested: "that the single greatest tangible asset the United States brought to the coalition in World War II was the productive capacity of its industry."[16] The United States now aimed not to field a numerically overwhelming ground force but a relatively small one, and to deploy it only in the conflict's final stage. That force would count for its battle weight not on masses of manpower but on maximum possible firepower, mechanization, and mobility. Compensating for that smaller army would be a gigantic strategic air arm—bombers in fantastic numbers that would ultimately deliver bombs of previously unimaginable destructive power.

Josef Stalin had his own description for this uniquely American way of war. The United States, he commented bitterly, had decided to fight with American money, American machines, and Russian men. Characteristically hard-bitten, Stalin's formulation was also indisputably accurate.

This war-fighting pattern had far-reaching and lasting consequences. Among other things, it made the United States the only true victor in the war—the only belligerent to emerge at war's end in a position superior to that occupied at war's onset. Ironically, but not unrelatedly, the United States paid the smallest price in both blood and treasure for the victory that it so singularly achieved. If one asks, "Who made the weightiest contribution to the defeat of Nazi Germany?" the answer is unarguably the Soviet Union. But the Soviets were not the ones who reaped the richest rewards from their own sacrifices. Franklin Roosevelt's "arsenal of democracy" strategy, in short, with its teeming implications for the scale, configuration, and timing of the American war effort and its consequences for Americans at home and for postwar foreign and military policies, rested on the successful navigation of a shrewdly calculated "least-cost pathway" to victory for the United States.

Some of the implications of following that pathway were evident even before the war's conclusion. Most notably, the United States became the only major belligerent that managed to expand its civilian economy while waging war. That achievement was unique in World War II and all but unprecedented in the entire history of warfare. Among the partner nations in the Grand Alliance, Britain saw personal consumption shrink by 22 percent. In the Soviet Union the home front experience was nearly the opposite of that in the United States—massive invasion, followed by a crash mobilization program that inflicted a harshly regulated scarcity rather than the Americans' loosely supervised abundance. The Americans fought the war from an ever-expanding economic base. The Russians fought from a remorselessly contracting one, which forced punishing resource reallocations from the civilian to the military sector. Russian food output fell to one-third of prewar levels. Russians by the millions slid into agonies of squalor and deprivation. In Germany, civilian consumption shrank by almost 20 percent during the war; in Japan, by 26 percent.[17]

Only in America was it different. The United States, alone among all the combatant states, enjoyed guns *and* butter, and both in prodigious quantities. Retail sales ascended to a record high in 1943 and then went higher still in 1944. Toward the end of that year, one of the nation's largest retailers, Macy's department store chain, organized an event that speaks volumes about the singular character of America's war.

Casting about for an appropriate occasion on which to promote a chain-wide sale, Macy's marketing team hit upon the poignantly symbolic date of December 7. Only in America, some might say, would a vendor seek commercial advantage by commemorating the date of the nation's most humiliating military disaster. But more to the point, only in wartime America could Macy's gambit have actually paid off. The date chosen for the sale—December 7, 1944—fell just six months after D-day, little more than a week before the onset of the Battle of the Bulge, less than two months after the Battle of Leyte Gulf, and about one month before the landings at Lingayen Gulf in the Philippine Islands—at the very moment, in short, when American forces were engaged in their most ferocious fighting of the war, on land and sea, in both the European and Pacific theaters. Yet on that day Macy's cash registers rang up a higher volume of sales than on any previous day in the giant retailer's history. There was not another country engaged in World War II where such a thing could have happened.[18] The war, in short, ignited the great engines of economic growth fueled by high levels of mass consumption, the formula that propelled the American people to such intoxicating heights of affluence in the postwar years.

The nation's war-fighting strategy had another implication often overlooked in American national mythology but less easily forgotten by other peoples: the war's toll in human life. Great Britain, America's first partner in what became the Grand Alliance, lost some 350,000 people to enemy action, of whom about 100,000 were civilians. China, a country whose involvement in the war is often neglected in the West, may have lost as many as 10 million people, about 6 million of them civilians. Eight million Poles perished in the war, 6 million of them civilians (of whom perhaps 4 million were Jews). Six and a half million Germans died, about 1 million of whom were civilians, most of them the victims of Anglo-American strategic bombing attacks. Japan lost some 3 million people, 1 million of them civilians, most killed not by the two atomic explosions of August 1945 but by the so-called conventional B-29 firebombing raids that commenced in late 1944 and continued even after Paul Tibbets's *Enola Gay* dropped the first atomic bomb. In the Soviet Union, it is estimated that the war took some 24 million lives, including 16 million civilians.

As for the United States, official records list 405,399 military dead in all branches of service—land, air, and sea. That is not a negligible number. But placed in the scales with the sacrifices that the war compelled other peoples to endure, it dramatically reveals the implications of America's uniquely fortunate engagement in World War II.

Even more vividly revealing are the deaths recorded on the civilian side of the ledger. In the forty-eight contiguous states of that era—the states that then had a star on the flag—the death toll attributable to enemy action was just six persons. They all died together, on the fir-clad shoulder of Gearhart Mountain, near the tiny hamlet of Bly, in south-central Oregon. On May 5, 1945, the Reverend Archie Mitchell and his twenty-six-year-old wife, Elsie, were leading a Sunday school outing in the woods near Bly. While the Reverend Mitchell was parking their vehicle, Mrs. Mitchell and five children, ages eleven to fourteen, began to tug at a strange object they had discovered in the underbrush. It exploded and killed them all—the only mainland civilian American casualties of World War II.

What Elsie Mitchell and the children had found was a Japanese firebomb. At precisely the same time the United States commenced its B-29-borne firebombing raids against the Japanese home islands, Japanese technicians in November 1944 had launched their own decidedly low-technology strategic aerial campaign against the United States. It consisted of high-altitude balloons designed to carry small incendiary bombs across the Pacific Ocean. The balloons had no on-board means of propulsion. They relied instead on the aerial currents of the jet stream to float them across the ocean. Japanese schoolchildren assembled the balloons in large indoor spaces like sumo wrestling arenas, theaters, and school assembly halls. They painstakingly laminated the four-ply mulberry paper that formed the balloons' skin and sealed the seams of each balloon's six hundred joined panels with a potato-flour paste that many of the desperately hungry pupils surreptitiously ate. Beneath the balloons' thirty-two-foot-diameter inflated sphere was suspended a small gondola basket containing the incendiary device and ringed by thirty-two sandbags. Prompted by a signal from a simple altimeter, a battery-powered mechanism released hydrogen from the balloon at an altitude of thirty-eight thousand feet and jettisoned two counterbalanced sandbags at thirty thousand feet, keeping the balloon stable within the jet stream's vertical envelope through sixteen trans-Pacific up-and-down cycles. When the last sandbags fell, a demolition charge detonated and detached the firebomb, presumably over the United States. The ultimate objective was to ignite forest fires on such a scale as to compel the Americans to redirect resources from fighting the Pacific war to firefighting in the heavily timbered coastal and Rocky Mountain West.[19]

Ninety-three hundred Japanese firebomb balloons wafted mutely eastward in the jet stream's embrace during the winter and early spring of 1945. Those that made it across the Pacific dropped their fiery loads to earth all across North America, from Mexico's Baja Peninsula to Canada's Yukon Territory, though most landed, as intended, in the northwestern corner of the United States. Arriving mostly in the wet winter season, they ignited but a few minor forest fires, which were promptly and easily extinguished. A voluntary American news blackout denied the Japanese any confirmation that their desperate scheme had any effect whatsoever.

Comparing the instrumentalities and results of the respective Japanese and American strategic bombing campaigns provides a summary illustration of the unique means by which the United States waged and won World War II. While Japan in the first half of 1945 adapted a primitive wind-driven technology in a last desperate effort to strike at the Americans in their heartland, huge B-29 bomber streams flew nightly to Japan from the Mariana Islands. Each powered by four 2,200 horsepower Wright eighteen-cylinder radial air-cooled magnesium alloy engines, fitted with two General Electric exhaust-driven turbo super-chargers, the B-29s eventually razed sixty-six of Japan's principal cities, rendered some 8 million people homeless, and killed more than 800,000 of them. Just two of those B-29s, the *Enola Gay* and *Bock's Car*, which dropped the second bomb on Nagasaki on August 9, 1945, effectively ended the Japanese-American war. The contrast with Japan's ultimately futile balloon bombs, motorlessly and passively drifting toward North America in the arms of the jet stream, could not have been starker.

That formidably intimidating American high-technology armamentarium, so deliberately conceived and so painstakingly assembled, amounted to a realization of Admiral Yamamoto's worst nightmare and the ultimate fruit of Franklin Roosevelt's "arsenal of democracy" strategy. That strategy cost relatively little but yielded enormous economic and social benefits as well as military triumph. It served as a prophylaxis against resurgent isolationism and a prelude to continuing international engagement. And it launched the United States into what became the American Century.

Understanding the nature of that pivotal historical moment is essential to comprehending the character of the international regime that flowed from it, to appreciating why that regime was on balance so successful, for Americans and others, and to acknowledging how much it matters that it is now at risk.

America's power at the end of World War II, both absolute and relative, not only military, financial, and economic but also cultural and technological, was exponentially greater than what Woodrow Wilson had wielded at the end of another world war in 1918. It arguably exceeded even the dimensions of America's allegedly "hyperpower" status at the dawn of the twenty-first century.

The United States at that formative moment had a monopoly, albeit one that proved short-lived, on nuclear weapons. It boasted both the world's largest navy and a massive long-range strategic air force. It commanded more than half the planet's manufacturing capacity and a like share of merchant shipping bottoms. It held most of the world's gold stocks and foreign currency reserves. It was the leading petroleum producer and a major oil exporter. It possessed the only intact large-scale advanced industrial economy on the globe, robustly invigorated by the war. The fighting had meanwhile devastated all other belligerents, including even America's fellow victors, the Soviet Union and the United Kingdom. Furthermore, the war incubated in Americans a new national self-confidence, infused with a sense of moral rectitude, missionary zeal, and the duty to lead.

A notable cohort of American leaders now at last gave its answer to a pointed question that Woodrow Wilson had posed some three decades earlier. "What are we going to do with the influence and power of this great nation?" Wilson had asked in a Fourth of July address in 1914. "Are we going to play the old role of using that power to our aggrandizement and material benefit only?"[20] In the wake of World War II, American leaders set out to use U. S. power in ways that finally set in motion the transformation Wilson had sought in vain. They effected nothing less than what Princeton political scientist John Ikenberry rightly calls "America's distinctive contribution to world politics."[21] It was a transformation that had been envisioned at the Republic's birth but had long lain beyond reach.

On the occasion of the first gathering of the UN in San Francisco on April 25, 1945, President Harry S Truman used words that could have been Wilson's—or Thomas Jefferson's or Thomas Paine's: "The responsibility of great states is to serve, and not dominate the peoples of the world."[22] And while it is undeniable that the United States continued to pursue what Wilson had scorned as its own "aggrandizement and material benefit" (considerations never absent from American foreign policy, nor should they be), what is most remarkable is the way that Washington exerted itself to build what the Norwegian scholar Geir Lundestad has called an "empire by invitation."[23]

At its best, that unconventional "empire" paid notable deference to inherited norms of Westphalian sovereignty even while artfully modifying them. Its first instinct was not to compel peremptory subordination but, rather, to provide incentives—and resources—for willing participation. Its architects knew, as Robert Kagan has written, that "predominance is not the same thing as omnipotence."[24] They appreciated that this was the moment to use America's unrivaled power to shape an international order that would, among other things, provide a hedge against the inevitable moment when America's power began to wane.

Ikenberry has catalogued the array of institutions created in that transmogrifying end-of-war moment: the UN, with its headquarters welcomed on the soil of America's principal city; the International Monetary Fund (IMF), designed to stabilize international exchange rates and encourage fiscal discipline; the International Bank for Reconstruction and Development, better known as the World Bank, to finance postwar reconstruction and foster worldwide economic growth; and the General Agreement on Tariffs and Trade, which would later evolve into the World Trade Organization (WTO), to reduce tariff barriers and liberalize world commerce. It is worth emphasizing that membership in those institutions was generally open to all, at least to nations outside the Cold War Communist bloc, and after the Cold War's conclusion even to former Communist adversaries. To be sure, participating states ceded to the new organizations only modest and marginal elements of their own sovereignty to secure the benefits of order and reciprocity. The UN in particular, held in check by the veto power of each of the five permanent members of the Security Council, could not plausibly be described as a proto-world government. (Indeed, it had intellectual antecedents in John C. Calhoun's fanciful concept of a "concurrent majority," which was designed to frustrate the exercise of power, not facilitate it.) But taken together these innovative institutions brought to the historically contentious arena of international politics at least a measure of lawful order and shared commitments to peaceful cooperation.

The framework provided by this innovative international regime began subtly, incrementally, to fulfill the Founders' promise of a new world order, one that would be densely populated by transnational institutions and accords and would thereby breed new norms of interstate behavior. The Marshall Plan, announced in 1947, offered further assistance for the rebuilding of Europe and strongly catalyzed the process that eventually yielded the European Union (EU). The North Atlantic Treaty Organization (NATO), formed in 1949, provided strong security guarantees for Western Europe throughout the Cold War and sustained the framework of peace that made the maturation of the EU possible (and eventually empowered the EU, in turn, to challenge America's own sovereign prerogatives when European regulators in 2001 barred the merger of two American firms, General Electric and Honeywell—a dramatic instance of grudging but eventually gracious submission by the United States to the rule of an international entity it had helped create). The International Atomic Energy Agency, dating from 1957, played a major if not fully successful role in limiting nuclear proliferation. The Nuremberg and Tokyo war crimes trials, along with the UN Declarations on Human Rights and on Genocide (a word coined in this intellectually and institutionally fecund era), established at least a minimal basis in international law for superseding a state's sovereign authority in the face of egregious crimes against humanity—though even those precedents provided but feeble support against the likes of Pol Pot, Slobodan Milosevic, or the murderous predators of Rwanda and Darfur.

Most of those institutions are now more than a half century old—a long span in the history of international regimes. Many, perhaps all, need substantial reform, of the sort that Kofi Annan tried to effect in his final years as UN secretary-general. Faced with an unexampled financial crisis in 2008, the IMF as well as the World Bank proved less than wholly adequate to the task of global stabilization and had to be buttressed by a number of ad-hoc provisions on the part of various governments. And just as U.S. forces configured for World War II and the Cold War have proven ill-suited for the counterinsurgency warfare that has become the modern military's principal assignment, the shortcomings of these institutions in dealing with the threat posed by radical Islamist terrorism have become painfully apparent. But international institutions suited to the needs of the dawning century can only arise on the foundations of mutual trust that a half century of multilateral life engendered, and that U.S. policies of the past decade have put in grave jeopardy.

Whatever their limitations, for nearly three generations those institutions sustained a remarkable passage in the world's history. They constituted the major pillars underlying an international economic expansion of unprecedented reach. They underwrote the advance of self-determination and democracy, as the colonial powers withdrew from Africa and Asia, the Soviet Empire disintegrated, and open, contested elections became the norm in countries that had not seen them in generations, if ever. And they enhanced global security. No *grand guerre* erupted on anything remotely approximating the scales of the two world wars. Barbarous, bloody Europe was pacified after centuries of conflict—itself a historic accomplishment sufficient to distinguish the age.

In this same era Americans enjoyed economic prosperity and personal security to a degree unmatched even in their enviably fortunate history while finding the confidence and courage at last to make racial equality a legally enforceable reality, lengthening life spans and raising living standards, and lifting educational levels and widening the spectrum of opportunity for tens of millions of citizens. As international regimes go, much of the American Century, despite the chronic tensions and occasional blunders of the Cold War (and especially the tragedy of Vietnam), was on the whole a laudably successful affair.

The keys to this broadly successful era for American statecraft were three: honoring inherited notions of sovereignty; seeking multilateral cooperation where it could while acting unilaterally only *in extremis;* and deploying America power, enormous but finite, to shape a world in which all states, not only the powerful, had a stake. When the United States departed from those principles, foreign policy failed, sometimes catastrophically, as in Iran, Cuba, Vietnam, and Iraq, sometimes with displays of sheer orneriness, as illustrated by American indifference to the Kyoto Protocol, diffidence about the Biological Weapons Accord, and refusal to join the International Criminal Court. But when policy makers hewed to those principles, they achieved markedly positive results and, not incidentally, bolstered America's moral stature in the eyes of the world.

For all its might and occasional swagger, the United States during the American Century preferred not to rule in solitary, preemptive

Olympian majesty. It became not a traditional imperial power but a hegemon, a word whose Greek roots denote a guide or leader—and leadership has been well defined as a relationship based on consent, not an arrangement between a capricious master and sullen vassals (nor between a president and a public manipulated into apathy or irrelevance).

Here is where the full meaning of Wilson's call that "the world must be made safe for democracy" becomes clear and compelling. Wilson had tempered his diplomatic ideals with a highly pragmatic comprehension of the nature of the modern world and both the promises and the dangers it held. He had respected the pride and the prerogatives of other peoples. He had shrewdly calculated the reach as well as the limits of American power. Perhaps most importantly, he had been keenly attentive to what kind of foreign policy, resting on principles of moral legitimacy, the American public would reliably support.

Franklin Roosevelt and Harry Truman made Wilson's aspirations their own while learning from his disappointments. They asked only that the world be made *safe* for democracy, not that the entire world forcibly be made democratic. They would have gagged on the George W. Bush administration's sweeping insistence that there is but "a single sustainable model for national success: freedom, democracy, and free enterprise." They would have bridled at the claim that the primary goal of U.S. policy should be "to bring the hope of democracy, development, free markets, and free trade to every corner of the world."[25]

The presidents who created the American Century understood the danger of seeking even laudable goals unilaterally in the modern world—a danger amply illustrated by a preventive war against Iraq that ignored the depth of Iraqi tribalism and the tenacity of Iraq's sovereign pride, convinced states in the Middle Eastern region and beyond to undertake heroic measures, including the acquisition of nuclear arms, to defend themselves against the prospect of American intervention, and alienated even traditionally reliable allies like the core members of NATO.

The damage done by this willful trashing of Wilson's, Roosevelt's, and Truman's legacy remains incalculable. Future historians will take its measure not only in the worldwide surge of anti-Americanism but also in the palpable erosion of trust in the very multinational institutions—including NATO, the UN (and its subagencies like the World Health Organization and the World Food Program), the IMF, the World Bank, and the WTO—that the United States itself so painstakingly nurtured over many decades. In an age awakening to the global dimensions of pandemics, environmental degradation, the fungibility of employment across national frontiers, massive international migrant and refugee flows, the unprecedented scale of international capital transactions, the contagious volatility of financial markets, the planetary menace of nuclear proliferation, not to mention the threat of terrorism, that erosion threatens to deny the world the very tools it needs most to manage the ever more interdependent global order of the twenty-first century. To abandon those tools or to let them rust through inanition and neglect into irretrievable disrepair would constitute the height of folly. To do so would leave all nations, conspicuously including the United States, markedly less secure. And it would dishonor the legacies of America's victory in World War II and the subsequent American Century that made the world safer, healthier, and happier.

CHAPTER 3

Consuming the American Century

Emily S. Rosenberg

Henry Luce's famous 1941 vision for the American Century laid out vast claims of power and prerogatives. Nestled within this discussion, Luce paid particular attention to what he called "an immense American internationalism." In strikingly varied forms, American influence already extended far and wide.

> American jazz, Hollywood movies, American slang, American machines and patented products, are in fact the only things that every community in the world, from Zanzibar to Hamburg, recognizes in common. Blindly, unintentionally, accidentally and really in spite of ourselves, we are already a world power in all the trivial ways—in very human ways.

In intimating that the American Century foreshadowed a Consumer Century, Luce proved remarkably prescient. If the United States never quite fulfilled his expectations of serving as a global Good Samaritan, the world's first truly mass consumerist society did transform mass consumerism into a worldwide phenomenon. Rather than creating an "immense *American* internationalism," however, the American Century radiated into a globalized culture of consumption, in which an alluring variety of consumer products and entertainments served ultimately to undermine American power and influence. Consumerism constituted the hallmark of the American Century and ultimately became its undoing.

The World's First Mass Consumerist Society

The basis for mass consumerism arose within the unique circumstances of the United States during the late nineteenth and early twentieth centuries. At that time, perhaps America's most distinguishing characteristic—and its most intractable problem—seemed to be abundance.

The sources of that abundance were varied, but two deserve special emphasis. First, America's mass consumption rested on an intensive exploitation of the continent's seemingly inexhaustible natural resources. American entrepreneurs in the late nineteenth century demonstrated an astonishing knack for turning the country's natural bounty into commodities: timber barons converted vast forests into lumber and thereby amassed immense fortunes; agriculturalists cleared the wilderness to grow wheat and corn and other crops; mining companies extracted iron, copper, and other metals; railroad moguls opened "new" lands and shipped out an amazing array of extractive products.[1] By channeling extractive wealth into capitalization for industrial ventures, Americans avoided the fate of some other nineteenth-century extractive economies. Through protective tariffs, a vigorous program of government-assisted internal improvements, and the nurturing of a strong domestic financial system, America's primary commodity sectors stimulated broad-based, diversified economic growth.

Second, American entrepreneurs sought technological solutions to overcome the country's vast continental distances and its relative scarcity of labor. The emerging consumer society rested upon the innovative technologies that spurred revolutions in transportation, communication, and mass production. By the 1890s the transportation (and thus marketing) revolution and labor-saving processes in agriculture and industry had created many of the huge U.S. companies whose names and products remained household words over the next century—Hormel, Singer, Westinghouse.[2] The far-flung domestic market spurred a distribution system and organizational sophistication that easily became international in scope.

U.S. productive capacity became so vast by the 1890s that, when a global economic contraction sent the domestic economy into a decline, business groups, politicians, and journalists all agreed that overproduction (not a scarcity of goods) was emerging as the major problem of the age. Abundance had become a burden of sorts; easing that burden required the opening of new markets. U.S. exporters and politicians became preoccupied with finding new buyers abroad, so much so that the allure of potential foreign markets shaped U.S. foreign policy at the turn of the twentieth century.[3]

Higher wages at home provided another way of boosting purchasing. In the 1920s Henry Ford famously proclaimed that mass consumption needed to be the necessary twin of his innovative mass production techniques. Ford used assembly line technology to ruthlessly lower costs while, at the same time, he raised wages so that workers could afford to buy his cars. Consumer-led growth was becoming a fixed feature of American economic practice.

The term "American standard of living" became a widely used, if ill-defined, source of national pride. It connoted a merger between a robust productive capacity and a wide availability of consumer goods. Growing numbers of people considered themselves middle class.[4]

In this sense, the United States seemed to be overturning Europe's "dismal science" based on the idea of economic scarcity. In *The New Basis of Civilization* (1907), the eminent economist Simon Nelson Patten identified abundance as the engine of a global civilizing process. Patten postulated that the "era of scarcity" had been supplanted by an "era of abundance" in which workers would enjoy upward mobility and use their new prosperity to broaden their intellectual horizons.[5]

The rise of consumerism, however, was not simply an economic story shaped by natural bounty, technological innovation, and a consumer market revolution. It also reflected America's singular social milieu. The absence of hereditary nobility and a rigid class structure facilitated an ethos in which material acquisition could become the dominant index of social standing. In countries with greater disparities in wealth and less economic mobility, ostentatious acquisition and display of mass-produced commodities by lower or middle classes often prompted charges of pretentiousness or bad taste. By contrast, commodities in America generally served as visible signs of personal advancement. Entrepreneurs in the media, entertainment, and advertising industries, often drawing on and targeting America's immigrant subcultures, transformed purchasing and acquisition into acts of self-fashioning and social belonging. Consumer goods seemed to confer glamour, leisure, and respect. This style of consumerism, so in tune with a highly diverse and mobile society, became intertwined with particular characterizations of personal "freedom" and with the political culture of "democracy." Mass consumption and mass entertainment fashioned an "American Dream" of upward mobility.

American-style consumerism thus fostered an "imagined community" out of a population divided by language, history, and customs. During the half century between 1880 and 1930, 27 million immigrants entered the United States. In the face of this cultural multiplicity, mass production and consumption, which flowered in the generation that came of age after the First World War, presented commodities as markers of national as well as personal identity. A consumer society offered a set of common referents around which people living in the United States could bond as "Americans." Especially for first- and second-generation blue-collar ethnic immigrants, consumption provided a powerful Americanizing agent, with the rituals of shopping constituting a style of "consumer citizenship" that rivaled older definitions of civic participation.[6]

An expanding array of consumer goods and entertainments offered ways to shape communities of identification around comfort, leisure, and personal interests rather than around the regional, ethnic, or familial associations that had once organized social life. Between 1900 and 1930, amusement parks, movie theaters, and dance halls brought urban villagers, especially the young, out of their own neighborhoods, onto streetcars, and, increasingly, into automobiles. New dating rituals and new kinds of workplaces accompanied the relaxation of parental supervision. Women's lives, in particular, changed dramatically. In 1920 women gained the constitutional right to vote, long a goal of women's rights activists. Just as significant as this revolution, however, were the new opportunities for women's independence associated with the enticements of self-fashioning through clothes and cosmetics. Mobility, mixing, and leisure—with accompanying hazards and opportunities— became hallmarks of a burgeoning consumer society in which women played key roles.[7] Retailers tempted buyers with splendid establishments, and new prepackaged foods promised better hygiene and easier preparation. Brand identification—Coca-Cola, Kellogg cereals, Swift meats, White Castle hamburgers—forged communities of consumption.[8]

Twentieth-century consumerism created an imagined community that included some and excluded others. The amusements and the products of American consumer culture redefined democracy and continually rearranged ethnic and class divisions. In the first half of the twentieth century, through their participation in the consumer republic, Irish, Italians, Eastern Europeans, and Jews slowly became "white" and "American." The entertainers and advertisers who helped fuse the trinity of whiteness, nationality, and consumption into one compelling imaginary also created categories of outsiders who appeared as colored and as un- (or even anti-) American. People from African, Asian, Spanish-speaking, or Native heritage often found themselves largely excluded from the performances and displays of upward mobility and consumer nationalism. Advertisements featured these consumer outsiders as adornments for consumer products but rarely targeted them as purchasers.[9]

Especially after World War II, however, the images of national community gradually changed. As the vision of consumer nationalism expanded, groups once marked as different slowly became welcome participants. In the arena of consumer culture, the process of racial integration, prominently contested in areas such as education and housing, went forward more smoothly and completely. Consumerism, in short, gradually played a key role in expanding the definition of the nation and in changing the categories of people who might claim equal treatment as citizens recognized within the marketplace. Entrance into the market was tantamount to inclusion in the national community.

Innovations in the profession of advertising, directed to the domestic market and then also employed overseas, played a growing role in promoting mass consumerism's economic and cultural appeal. Especially after World War I, advertisers began to voice a refrain that soon became a hallmark of their profession: the prosperity and stability of the nation (and then of the world) depended upon their skill in stimulating ever higher levels of purchasing and consuming and therefore of jobs and prosperity. "Buy More, Prosper More" became their unofficial motto.[10]

Over the course of the twentieth century, advertisers refined the art of psychological suggestion and played key roles in shaping and reshaping ideas about identity. Under the influence of pioneers such as Edward Bernays, marketers from the 1920s on embraced emerging techniques of psychology and survey research to construct groups of buyers whose attention and loyalties could then be sold to producers. During the 1930s through the 1960s, companies increasingly perfected strategies of "public relations" and "branding"—practices that aimed to create enduring and positive media symbols based more on a company's supposed ideals than on its specific products. During the last third of the twentieth century, an emphasis on "lifestyle advertising" developed associations between brands and the social behavior of particular groups of people with whom the buyer might have an aspirational affinity.[11] David Ogilvy and others developed complex advertising symbols that relied less on the attributes of goods than on creating identities and affiliations that the consumer might wish to purchase. In the ethnically diverse United States, advertisers sometimes carefully constructed ethnic appeals to invite, for example, Irish Americans to fly to Ireland or African Americans to buy black Barbies. In a blending of national and international imagery, such practices advanced the notion that being "American" in the late twentieth century meant consumer displays suggesting one's special localistic "roots."[12] By the 1980s advertisers had thus refined subtle strategies of market segmentation in order to appeal to a diverse nation and world; they learned to appeal locally in order to market globally—a practice that business theorists called "glocalization."

In addition to augmenting emotional bonds between buyers and certain products and brands, marketers from the 1920s on developed strategies to increase the volume of purchasing. To enhance present-giving, they reworked familiar national holidays (Christmas, Easter, Valentine's Day) and invented new ones (Mother's Day, Father's Day, and Presidents' Day). Holidays, like leisure time itself, increasingly became associated with shopping. In addition, concepts of planned obsolescence and frequent style changes encouraged buyers to replace their consumer goods more rapidly. For many products, durability and timeless style became less important than inexpensive price and transient appeal. Carefully designed disposability became a hallmark of the new mass consumer economy. Perhaps most importantly, buying on credit and through installments spread throughout the economy, as increasingly lucrative lending practices tempted individuals to allow their consumer desires to exceed their incomes. Individual savings rates declined as debt loads increased.[13]

Consumerism, stimulated by advertising and marketing practices, thus became finely knit into American economic, social, cultural, and political institutions—and, as we will see, into foreign policy as well. American advertisers, business executives, and labor leaders generally endorsed ever higher levels of consumption and mass production as the economic counterparts to American democracy. They touted a system of broad-based participation in which purchasers, in effect, possessed the power to elect and to reject products—a system in which the right to buy seemed as fundamental to civic life as the right to vote. Appealing within and across lines of ethnicity, region, gender, and class, consumerism forged communities around rituals of purchase and of leisure. It became the terrain upon which personal identities and rituals of belonging could be performed and reinforced. Within this "democracy of goods," by the second half of the twentieth century most Americans, regardless of their actual incomes, could imagine themselves as "middle class" and "free."

In this sense, the "American Way" of mass consumerism had both an economic and a cultural dimension. As an *economic* system, consumerism commodified the natural bounty of the rich North American continent and used technology to mass-produce goods. From a *cultural* perspective, it stoked always-elusive desires for self-fashioning and belonging within a highly diverse nation. Here was the American Century, which began to emerge decades before Henry Luce coined the phrase and reached its zenith and global reach in the decades following World War II: *a mass production and mass-marketing system that imagined an ever-widening abundance of goods within a culture that emphasized buying and selling, desire, glamour, and flexible, purchase-driven identities.*

Consumerism and American Global Power

During the Cold War, U.S. strategy exported to the world the assumptions and practices of America's consumer republic. Spreading the practices of mass consumerism became central to claims that the United States was leading a civilizing mission in the world. Mistaking America's specific historical circumstances for generalizable laws of development, U.S. business, governmental, and labor elites promoted the idea that a mass production/mass consumer system on the American model would lift living standards everywhere and counter the appeal of communism.

During the first half of the twentieth century, of course, the United States had already begun to export its standardized consumer products, movies, and advertising as part of a general policy of vigorous commercial expansion. During the Cold War, private and public sectors promoted the consumer revolution with even greater vigor. Export expansion meshed neatly with the new global battle against communism. America's Advertising Council (a body made up of major advertising agencies), for example, issued a booklet in 1948 called "Advertising: A New Weapon in the World Wide Fight for Freedom." Disseminated globally by the U.S. Department of State, it portrayed American advertising techniques as critical to the stimulation of consumer demand and, therefore, to the restoration of productive capacity worldwide. It touted consumer choice within a marketplace characterized by private ownership and informed by advertising as virtually synonymous with a highly exportable "American Way of Life."[14]

As part of this initiative, the Advertising Council helped U.S. businesses develop overseas public relations programs that explained how capitalism accommodated a wide range of workers' needs. Attempting to counter arguments favoring a government-run welfare state, America's large employers and insurance companies developed and then bragged about their corporate-provided health care, recreational programs, and pension plans for workers.[15] Celebrants of consumerism used this U.S. model to refute claims that capitalism exploited workers and provided no long-term security. Messages touting the advantages of capitalism connected American-style mass consumerism to higher standards of living for ordinary workers. U.S. practices were generally represented as universal in their application to other countries. Other Cold War cultural offensives also sold America as a consumer haven and a model easily exportable abroad. The European Economic Plan's counterpart funds, for example, financed traveling displays featuring America's high wages and bulging shops—this against the backdrop of postwar privation in Europe. The distribution of Hollywood movies—boosted by U.S. government pressure on other countries to repeal quota restrictions—similarly advertised consumer abundance.[16] Moreover, as Marshall Plan money became a major source of advertising revenue for some European media, it nudged Europe toward greater acceptance of commercial radio advertising, a trend that, in turn, encouraged consumer spending on both foreign and domestic products.[17]

The new United States Information Agency (USIA), formed in 1953, made consumerism a major part of its Cold War offensives. One USIA campaign, which emerged in 1956 from a Yale University-Advertising Council roundtable, advocated a campaign called "people's capitalism." The goal was to counter the appeal of Communist rhetoric claiming that workers lived better under socialism.[18] The major Cold War international expositions during the 1950s reflected the consumerist emphasis on "people's capitalism."

At the 1958 Brussels Universal and International Exhibition, for example, the American pavilion displayed washing machines, dishwashers, a Sears Roebuck catalog, frozen food packages, TV and recording studios, and a pink built-in oven. *Vogue* magazine, which staged a daily fashion show at the center of the circular building, featured a "Young America Look." It showcased affordable apparel such as jeans and plaid shirts, tennis outfits, evening gowns, and inexpensive sack dresses. American women, this show implied, already enjoyed abundant leisure time and easy access to such mass-produced clothing. They could slip easily among a variety of social roles simply by changing clothes.[19] Imagery designed to appeal to women pervaded Cold War displays of consumerism.[20]

The American National Exhibition in Sokolniki Park in Moscow in 1959 took such messages into the heart of the Communist world. Ordinary factory workers in America, Russian audiences were told, could afford the six-room ranch house that proved to be the exhibition's most popular exhibit. No less than three model kitchens boasted appliances, convenience foods, and gadgets of all sorts. Fashion shows again displayed stylish but inexpensive attire. Helena Rubinstein and Coty Cosmetics offered free samples and beauty shop demonstrations to Soviet women until Soviet authorities intervened with a ban. The famous "kitchen debate" between Vice President Richard Nixon and Premier Nikita Khrushchev occurred against this backdrop of consumerism.[21]

U.S. information officers were careful to portray consumerism as more than mere materialism. The themes of "people's capitalism" portrayed a high standard of living as flowing from the values of hard work, spiritual fulfillment, and commitment to family and community. The USIA's Office of Religious Information proposed that Eisenhower initiate days of prayer and often mention prayer in public remarks in order to portray the Cold War as a spiritual, not just a material, struggle. Within this construction, consumer abundance served to confirm Americans' piety and their providential mission in the world.[22]

On both sides of the Cold War, consumer abundance became widely accepted as an indicator of national power and virtue—and as a test of each system's claims on the future. In this contest, leaders throughout the Communist bloc tried to enhance their legitimacy by emphasizing that consumerism would follow close upon necessary sacrifice. This appeal worked for a while. In the immediate postwar era, people in the Eastern bloc measured their well-being in comparison to the low living standards that prevailed during the war. By the mid-1950s, however, a new generation increasingly looked toward international comparisons with Western Europe and even with Tito's Yugoslavia, which became a shopping destination for people in other socialist nations. Yugoslavia embraced a "socialist consumerism" that rhetorically upheld Communist goals but, in practice, adapted the advertising methods of American companies and embraced the idea that stimulating consumer demand would drive greater production.[23] Khrushchev, attempting to demonstrate Soviet socialism's ability to redefine consumerism in ways that would outpace the appeal of capitalist models, launched plans for housing projects that featured greater personal privacy and diverted resources toward socialist versions of consumer goods. Similarly, East Germany's leaders, feeling pressure from rising living standards in West Germany and the flood of refugees fleeing to the West, expanded consumer credit, introduced mail-order catalogues, and planned new self-service retail stores. In 1956 Khrushchev pledged that the German Democratic Republic would become a "showcase" of the Cold War, and the East German Communist Party subsequently vowed to surpass West Germany in productivity and personal consumption by 1962. The erection of the Berlin Wall in 1961, a desperate attempt to staunch the growing flood of migration to the West, signaled a failure to achieve these goals.[24]

The dreams and realities of consumer abundance increasingly marked the terrain of Cold War rivalry in Asia as well. After the People's Republic of China was established in 1949, American cold warriors sought to contrast the poverty and repression in "Red China" with the economic revitalization of America's allies in Japan and Taiwan. In hosting the Olympics Games in 1964, for example, Japan made its debut on the world scene as an American-guided, modernized nation. Even more impressively, the Expo '70 exhibition in Osaka, Japan, showcased the new prosperity and power of America's Asian ally. Held between March and September 1970 and attended by 64 million people, this world's fair—the first in Asia—celebrated a modernity marked by technological achievement and abundance. Space-age designs—especially the innovative air-supported cable roof that billowed over the dome of the U.S. exhibition—were omnipresent, and the United States featured rocks brought from the moon in addition to its usual displays of consumer products. Japan foreshadowed its own growing specialization in new consumer electronics and computers, introducing an early type of cell phone and other communication devices. Moreover, Expo '70's extravagant corporate pavilions helped promote America's Cold War message that equated capitalism with an ever-rising standard of living linked to a surge of industrial, artistic, and architectural innovation.[25]

Not everyone, of course, welcomed the American mass production/consumption model. Even as consumerist practices spread, critics from both the Left and the Right waged anti-Americanization campaigns.

They portrayed "Americanization" as materialistic, conformist, feminized, and immature. In France and elsewhere, they protested against American products, especially the heavily advertised Coca-Cola, which became a symbol of unwanted (and also of wanted) "Americanization." Just as consumerism's celebrants tended to equate the American Way with the spread of mass consumerism, so did the critics of both.

Scholarship on the postwar spread of consumerism, however, complicates any claim that consumer revolutions simply converged toward a homogenized "Americanization." Especially from the mid-1950s on, the robust and diverse growth of mass consumer societies, drawing from American models as well as from national traditions, transformed most countries of Western Europe and Japan. Even Communist nations adopted and adapted consumerist practices. The spread of differentiated and locally assembled consumer societies may have been influenced by some version of the standardized production methods and images often associated with the United States. Over time, however, consumerism and Americanization seemed less and less closely associated. Several factors account for the ease with which mass consumerist appeals and practices went global through local adaptation.

First, aspects of American mass culture, as Richard Pells has pointed out, "never felt all that foreign" to many people outside the United States because American commercial culture drew from a "transnational America." The United States was a nation of immigrants whose consumer goods, images, and leisure-time innovations often emerged from elsewhere, then adapted to the broad diversity of American life, before reemerging again as exports to world markets. The world had thus been transforming America even as American culture also influenced desires across the globe. In this sense, "Americanization" was not some singular influence but a process marked by hybridity and selective accommodation.[26]

Second, countries and people embraced mass consumerism within the context of their own traditions. Even before World War II, an accelerated pace of standardization in production and mass marketing had already ushered in a variety of mass consumerist practices across Western Europe.[27] Clearly, Americans offered distinctive practices and sensibilities, but the influence of American advertising and consumer practices promoted cultural diffusion rather than a clear-cut "Americanization." In the period of postwar reconstruction, consumerism and its appeals continued to develop nationally distinctive characteristics. Most people outside of the United States, for example, remained ambivalent about American-style mass marketing and consumerism. The desirability of personal spending presented especially contested terrain. People in postwar Japan and Europe retained deep traditions that associated frugality with building a strong national and personal economic future. They therefore approached ideas about personal consumption with an ambivalence that reflected both a yearning for affluence and individualism yet also a respect for frugality and community. Despite postwar influences from the United States, many of the governments faced with postwar reconstruction encouraged citizens to save rather than spend.[28] With distinctive mixes of practices related to spending and saving, every country (including the United States) exhibited its own unique patterns of consumerism.

In addition, the managerial style, the labor policies, and the resource- and technology-intensive qualities of American corporate capitalism clearly had different valences in different places. In France and Germany, for example, internal political and economic structures made it possible for those countries to embrace America's Marshall Plan with some enthusiasm. In Italy, that enthusiasm was less pronounced. As in the interwar era, different traditions about the roles of management, labor, gender, and political economy built local versions of consumer-oriented capitalism, each country using its own filtering mechanisms to borrow from, adapt, and reject the techniques associated with American consumerism.[29] Throughout the world, then, to varying degrees, particular features of the American model both attracted and repelled.

Moreover, the notions of glamour and desire that propelled mass consumerism also grew from local contexts. Marketers created images of beauty, style, and sex appeal, often linked to "stars" and celebrities. Many of these images became broadly recognizable in the non-Communist and, increasingly, in the Communist world. But these conceptions—so important to consumerism—were continually circulated and readapted—as the films of Federico Fellini and the cultural flows between Hollywood and Paris illustrate.[30] Consumerism, accompanied by images of desire, was part of a complex circuitry modified by whatever culture it reached.

In a process akin to what linguistic anthropologists have called "code-switching," assemblages of consumerist goods and activities constructed individual and national identities in modular fashion by switching particular attributes on or off to create new combinations. Consumerism throughout the world, as in the United States, helped build imagined communities around projections of modernity expressed through consumption, but these identities had flexibility.[31] Consumerism found expression globally, nationally, and locally.

Advertising played an important role in these localized consumer revolutions. Wherever trade barriers and media regulations fell, advertising followed: it flourished within the economic integration of the European Union, with the decline of economic nationalism in the Third World, and especially after the fall of communism. At the same time, the shift to "lifestyle advertising" often bonded consumers into particular "lifestyle" groups by evoking and serving local values and traditions ("glocalization"). Large American-based chains—Coca-Cola, KFC, McDonald's, and others—altered their products to encourage local talent and accommodate regional tastes.[32] This practice could reinforce or even create "unique" characteristics associated with a specific locale. Geremie R. Barmé, for example, makes the point that "one of the central features of consumer culture is that through it shoppers are differentiated and treated as individuals via a so-called commodity self; identities and consumer profiles are melded and desires simulated and directed by the guiding hand of advertisers." Critics of consumerism had long viewed this process as manipulative. Yet being "targeted" by advertisers could also, Barmé points out, bring with it the feeling of choice, self-realization, and individual empowerment.[33]

As advertisers and producers learned to appeal individually and locally, mass consumerism broke loose from any U.S. cultural base. Globalization, a word that became more and more prominent from the late 1970s on, diffused nation-state-based power. As incomes rose, trade accelerated, and media regulations eased in many parts of the world, consumerism and advertising became ever more integral parts of daily life everywhere.[34] Visions of the goods and entertainments associated with mass consumption that had once stirred fears of "Americanization" increasingly seemed badges of pride and signs of national and personal advancement. Although debates still raged about the precise relationships between America and mass consumerism, "anti-globalization" increasingly took the place of "anti-Americanization" as the rallying cry of those who protested the spread of mass production and mass consumption.[35]

Within a few decades after the end of World War II, America had ceased to be the national home of the Consumer Century. Consumerism and its cultural codes spread and blurred global and local. As its seductions enveloped Western Europe, Japan, the Communist systems in Eastern Europe, Russia, China, and the Third World, it adopted various guises. Indeed, many countries incorporated mass consumerism into their own ideologies of national advancement by promising citizens greater access to consumer lifestyles. People on the left and on the right who still tried to denounce America because of its identification with mass consumerism—or those who sought to denounce mass consumerism by identifying it primarily with "Americanization"— found their arguments increasingly irrelevant.

Consumerism was the "ism" that "won" the ideological battles of the twentieth century. As in the United States itself, the mass consumerist-advertising complex became adept at appealing within and across lines of nationality, region, ethnicity, gender, class, and ideology. Consumerism "won" less because it implied "Americanization" than because its appeals proved so globally adaptive that it ceased to be seen as American at all.[36]

Consumerism and the End of the American Century

As the American Century morphed into an adaptive and increasingly globalized Consumer Century, it centered less and less on America's once prodigious productive capacities. An increasingly globalized system of production and distribution fed the insatiable appetite for goods everywhere, but especially in the United States. From being the world's principal producers, Americans became its central consumers.[37]

An open-trading world and global advertising expertise that had once provided American *producers* with an antidote to fears about inadequate markets now presented American *consumers* with access to cheap, attractively promoted goods made beyond their shores. Moreover, as U.S. retirement plans shifted from defined benefits to individual portfolios (such as the 401(k)), more Americans acquired a stake in the stock market and its globalized giants. An earlier emphasis on production, the role of work, and pride in Fordist-style high wages morphed into an emphasis on consumption, lower prices, and return on investment.[38]

The historian Charles Maier has analyzed how, in the late 1960s and 1970s, America's "empire of production," which had sought exports for the nation's vigorous productive capacity, became an "empire of consumption," accumulating larger and larger trade imbalances by consuming an ever greater percentage of goods made elsewhere. As an "empire of production," the United States had run trade surpluses and was a capital lender in the world economy. As an "empire of consumption," the United States increasingly ran trade deficits. To feed its appetite for less expensive imported goods—and growing quantities of imported oil—it slowly, but inexorably, became the world's greatest debtor.[39] America's citizens, for whom consumerism seemed by now almost a birthright, gradually stoked lower-cost production and oil-based energy sectors elsewhere. The market that the world had once been to America, America now became to the world.

Accompanying this trend, of course, the very largest firms became globalized and relocated operations, and even management, to widely scattered and often mobile locations. This globalization of production, accompanied by flexible manufacturing techniques, accelerated during and after the 1970s, as businesses reduced costs by exporting production and jobs. On the domestic front, the globalization of production and increasing energy dependence yielded unsettling effects. During the 1970s, stagflation and deindustrialization became signatures of how the "shock of the global" might transform the lives of middle-class Americans: lower prices for many consumer goods would be linked to downward pressure on wages.[40]

To keep America's empire of consumption afloat, advertising and financial industries grew rapidly. Even as jobs in manufacturing capacities in the United States declined, these industries continued to stoke mass consumer demand and to extend credit, pushing both to ever higher levels and eclipsing the core strengths once associated with the American Century.

The emphasis on maintaining high levels of consumption at home through lower prices shaped U.S. international economic policies and drove American politics. With robust consumerism now figuring so prominently in the commonplace understanding of the "American Way of Life," any proposal to put the brakes on the escalating cycle of ever cheaper imports and lower prices was politically risky. Even as incomes languished, the appetite among consumer-citizens for cheaper products and greater credit only increased. For their part, politicians shaped economic policy in ways intended to accommodate both global businesses and consumer desires. The ability of Americans to consume (and to borrow in order to consume) had become so connected to nationalist themes that political leaders largely ignored the deficits in national and personal savings that accompanied its sharply deteriorating terms of trade.

America's growing import imbalance, of course, had a flip side: the flourishing export sectors especially in China and in oil-producing nations. Nations that had once been net borrowers in global capital markets became lenders. This shift, reinforced by a continued penchant for savings in countries such as Germany and Japan, produced a global savings glut, arguably contributing to successive credit bubbles in the United States, first in equities in the 1990s and then in housing after 2000.[41]

Yet specific U.S. policies exacerbated the problem. Financial deregulation catered to financial companies and consumer-citizens by boosting buying power through credit, even as other policies related to minimum wage rates and labor unions eroded incomes. The repeal of the

Depression-era Glass-Steagall regulatory system, especially in the Financial Services Modernization Act of 1999, freed commercial banks, investment banks, securities firms, and insurance companies to consolidate and develop more "innovative" forms of credit. The Commodity Futures Modernization Act of 2000 placed an increasingly inscrutable but lucrative derivatives market outside of effective government regulation. Funding for regulatory oversight of the financial sector dropped, as did the will to make it effective. During the Republican ascendancy of the early twenty-first century, the pressures in the United States to maximize credit availability for its consumer-citizens became especially pronounced—even as the nation's productive capacities shrank and the costs of the off-budget wars in Iraq and Afghanistan soared.

The result was dramatic. Over little more than a decade after the deregulatory "modernization" acts, the twenty largest U.S. financial institutions grew from controlling 35 percent of America's financial assets to 70 percent. In the 1990s the nation's six largest banks had owned assets of less than 20 percent of GNP. A decade later that figure had jumped to 60 percent.[42] The political and economic dominance of the financial industry, the biggest lobby within both political parties, powered the consumer spending-and-debt complex in the United States. A new gilded age emerged not from producing goods but from conjuring up innovative ways to lend money to consumers already deeply in hock. Before the reckoning that came in the Great Recession of 2008–2009, consumption in the United States hit a record high of 71 percent of GDP. Net domestic savings had sunk into negative territory.[43]

Debt seemed to lose its significance during the opening decade of the twenty-first century. If middle-class wages for the broad working class had been the American system's claim to fame at the beginning of the American Century, credit cards became the central symbol of the Consumer Century. Credit funded America's deteriorating trade balances; it also funded the gap between the wages most people could earn and their continued, indeed, escalating, desires for consumer products. Facilitating while helping camouflage the ever greater accumulation of debt, politicians looked the other way, eager to please both the financial industry and consumer constituencies, while credit instruments became ever more profitable, more abstract, and less transparent. Credit-based consumer citizenship triumphed; the Consumer Century reigned unchallenged; the American Century withered.

Force-feeding consumer desire, initially designed to solve the problem of abundance but now increasingly a driver of debt and deficit, undermined the American Century in other ways as well. The American emphasis on advertising and credit availability as the keys to sustaining economic growth ended up exacting unanticipated long-term costs in the form of environmental damage and dependence on resources located outside of the United States.[44]

Global warming and a heightened competition for resources are only two indicators suggesting that the resource-intensive American model of mass production and mass consumption is of questionable long-term viability. This is true for both the United States and the rest of the world. More importantly, stubborn adherence to the U.S. model is significantly undermining American power by augmenting rivalries and resentments over access to distant resources and over how to tackle climate change.[45] In sum, as the American Century gave way to the Consumer Century, it brought daunting new global challenges in the environmental, as well as the financial, realm.

Conclusion

Mass consumerism in America grew from late nineteenth-century efforts to manage abundance. It took shape alongside several related factors: the commoditization of the country's rich natural endowments; revolutions in productivity stimulated by the technological innovation; labor shortages and vast geographical distances; a relatively fluid social structure in which commodities became indexes of status and mobility; and an immigrant-based society that found in consumerist rituals paths to Americanization. Advertising came to occupy center stage in this new demand-driven consumer republic. Woven tightly into institutions and identities during the twentieth century, mass consumerism became central to—and even defined—the American Way of Life.

The American Century, the period of maximum U.S. power and influence in the world, served as a precursor to a global Consumer Century—something that Henry Luce himself seemingly glimpsed without fully understanding. During the immediate post–World War II period, American exports dominated world markets for goods and entertainments, and both American elites and America's critics abroad portrayed this spread of mass consumerism as "Americanization." Mass production, mass consumption, advertising, and credit buying, however, proved highly adaptive to local cultural variation and gradually became both globalized and localized. By the late twentieth century, the Consumer Century no longer had its national home in the United States. In every region of the globe, including once-Communist states, consumer revolutions altered older social and cultural forms. Out of the ideological battles of the twentieth century, consumerism emerged triumphant. Yet even before it had finished unraveling the Communist systems, consumerism had begun to undermine the seemingly preeminent position of the United States itself.

Whereas the institutions and desire-making technologies of mass consumerism had once stimulated America's productive capacities and helped solidify its national cohesion and its middle class, the increasingly globalized system of mass production, mass consumerism, and credit "innovations" began to prey on America's consumer-citizens. The central logic of postwar mass production became driving down prices by driving down costs of production, and Americans, as the world's most reliable consumers, became buyers of last resort in a global economy that inexorably spread productive capacity to ever less expensive areas. As advertisers stoked demand, financial institutions, enabled by deregulation, sought higher profits in ever more elaborate schemes to expand credit, papering over the gap between what Americans produced and what they purchased. Especially after the turn of the twenty-first century, the glut of savings that piled up in export-rich countries helped further drive down costs for credit and loosen standards. Moreover, a consumerist system in which abundance had once seemed a central problem increasingly strained an environment beset by climate change and natural resource scarcity. Through debt and environmental abuse, then, the Consumer Century that was once identified with the American Century became its undoing.

CHAPTER 4

The Problem of Color and Democracy

Nikhil Pal Singh

Internationally, the world is going through huge changes, but we are perfectly poised to make the 21st century again the American Century.

—*Barack Obama, March 11, 2011*

Nineteen forty-one, the year that Henry Luce published the eponymous essay that here signals the beginning of the "Short American Century," is also the year that black activist and trade unionist A. Philip Randolph launched the March on Washington Movement (MOWM), now largely heralded as the symbolic origin of the modern African American civil rights imperative. Blithely imperialist in his outlook on the world, the media mogul Luce hardly paused to imagine the burgeoning racial crisis at home becoming intertwined with and threatening to undermine the American world leadership he wanted to promote. Abler commentators like Gunnar Myrdal quickly acknowledged that white supremacy and "the Negro problem" comprised "an American dilemma" in an era that would be characterized by the rise of the darker nations.[1] More sharply, W. E. B. Du Bois called colonies "slums of the world," and pronounced "color and democracy: the colonies and peace," the real stakes in any adjudication of a just world order.[2] The color line in this way shadowed the American Century from its inception, particularly as black commentators probed and prodded at the gaps between America's democratic ideals and despotic racial practices. Some officials, particularly in the U.S. State

Department, recognized the problem by the early 1950s. The genie, however, was out of the bottle. Even as support for domestic racial reform became a hallmark of cold war liberalism, civil rights activists used race as a cipher to decode the more nefarious aspects of U.S. foreign policy. The reformist achievements of the Kennedy and Johnson administrations notwithstanding, "Selma and Saigon" became linked in the black political imagination, as the racial crisis and democratic demands at home became a way of reading the world scene.

The collective trauma of that era's political violence has receded. The moderate amelioration of affirmative action and the benign (and increasingly malign) neglect of the black poor recast the contradiction of color and democracy that roiled the Short American Century. With the passage of time, a palliative civil rights civic mythology gradually took hold. To think that the problem was either quietly resolved or simply dissolved would be a mistake, however. At the onset of the Iraq War, pundit Michael Ignatieff pronounced the American empire acceptable in the eyes of the world because it was not built on "conquest and the white man's burden." Speaking for the Bush administration, Condoleezza Rice claimed that the civil rights movement had helped the United States "find its voice" as a "champion of democracy" overseas.[3] Torture, indefinite detention, and occupation (as well as the disproportionately black refugees from Hurricane Katrina that provided the backdrop to Rice's remarks) rendered such pronouncements hollow at best. To some, the election of the nation's first black president, Barack Obama, in 2008, served to refurbish America's image and standing in the world, bringing ideals and practices supposedly wrenched apart back into alignment. Yet note the irony: Obama, whose rise was scripted as a fulfillment of civil rights teleology, has not only seen his nationality and birthright widely questioned but has also been tasked with curing the ailments of an empire that still cannot speak its name. The color line, in short, still shadows and indexes American global power.

When Martin Luther King Jr. in his fateful final year described "racism, materialism and militarism" as America's *interrelated flaws,* he was under no illusions about the distinction between democratic development and imperial policy. King viewed the Vietnam War as a con-

tinuation of colonialism by other names, thwarting popular democratic aspirations at home and around the world. Written after 9/11, a
new preface to *Dreams from My Father* illustrates Obama's own complex experiences of the world, hearkening back to this moment, as well
as to the Afro-diasporic and postcolonial sensibilities of Du Bois's
earlier pronouncement. The conflict between "worlds of plenty and
worlds of want," Obama writes arrestingly, "twists the lives of children on the streets of Jakarta or Nairobi in much the same way as it
does the lives of the children on the South Side of Chicago." Failing to
comprehend this dynamic, the powerful needlessly intensify a destructive spiral with their "dull complacency . . . unthinking applications
of force . . . longer prison sentences and more sophisticated military
hardware."[4] Here, Asia, Africa, and black Chicago are transnational
coordinates linked by shared agonies and common dreams in a world
bound and divided by ever more entrenched material inequalities.
Criticizing dominant responses to ensuing social and political crises
that privilege force and violence, this pre-presidential Obama recognizes that questions of security cannot be easily parceled into foreign
and domestic compartments. A reflexive emphasis upon military and
police power, moreover, has not only failed to achieve security abroad
but is here implicitly associated with the rise of a sprawling U.S. prison
complex vastly overpopulated by black citizens.

Indeed, this kind of statement might suggest a reengagement with
the *unfinished* dialectic of color and democracy at the origins of the
Short American Century. No such reengagement ensued, however.
Instead, Luce's conceit has proven remarkably resilient, prominently
promoted in the 1990s by the Project for a New American Century (a
group that included vociferous advocates and future planners of the
Bush administration's Iraq adventure) and now used ostentatiously
and with increasing frequency by President Obama himself.[5] With the
charge that Obama does not truly believe in American exceptionalism
employed to insinuate that he is in various and manifold ways *un-
American,* the president's embrace of the American Century may be
largely defensive. At the same time, that Obama's election fertilized
undead weeds of racism and xenophobia has not prevented the full
flowering of the self-congratulatory narrative in which his election to

the nation's highest office vindicates America's (post) racial transcendence, and thus its exceptional standing among nations. That Obama's term as U.S. president marks the occasion for this "postmortem of the short American Century" is then doubly ironic. For if the agonistic, public performance of struggles for racial equality has been a means for meditating upon and assessing the limits of American democracy at home and abroad since World War II, the supposed culmination of those projects with the election of a black president may have deprived us of this metric precisely when we need it most.

To appreciate the bipartisan staying power of the idea of an American Century, it is important to revisit Luce's original statement, and to recognize how capably it realigned older nationalist conceptions of America as a "city on a hill" and first among nations with new global imperatives. As members of "the most powerful and the most vital nation in the world," Luce called upon his fellow Americans to "play their part as a world power . . . [and] exert upon the world the full impact of our influence for such purposes as we see fit and by such means as we see fit."[6] Statements of this type ran counter to his defensive assertion that you could not "extract imperialism from 'The American Century' "—that "the internationalism America had to offer" should be an "internationalism of the people, by the people and for the people."[7] The essay's muscular celebration of America's "inheritance of all the great principles of Western Civilization," withering condemnation of "isolationist sterility," and missionary promise of tough love for the fallen and abject overseas, however, left less the impression of a world bound by consent and common purpose than the foreboding of a shotgun wedding. If anyone mistook his meaning, Luce invoked the most ancient precedent of all: the rights of settlers won by conquest— the "blood of purposes and enterprise and high resolve" that charted the "progress of man" across a continent. The American Century was an old proposal adapted for new times: the forcible betrothal of the world's peoples to the American "powerhouse."[8]

These more disturbing implications were not lost on Luce's contemporaries, many of whom at the time directly and forcibly challenged the idea of an American Century. Most notable was Vice President Henry Wallace, torchbearer of New Deal liberalism, who publicly responded to Luce with his own call for "the century-of the common-man," or "people's century."[9] Describing the war as a struggle between freedom and slavery, Wallace drew upon a different U.S. historical precedent, namely, civil war. He also attempted to temper Luce's unilateralist presumptiveness, emphasizing democracy and anti-imperialism as the non-negotiable baseline of the new behavioral norms codified by the Atlantic Charter (1941). These views found extensive support from civic organizations like the Common Council for American Unity, whose popular periodical *Common Ground* promoted the image of the United States as a "nation of nations" and advanced the idea that pluralism and diversity, especially among recent immigrant populations, were distinctive American values that augmented U.S. claims to world leadership. The most acute thinkers in this vein, such as Carey McWilliams, highlighted the global significance and imperial-colonial context of America's racial divisions: "If England is haunted by the problem of India, so are we haunted by the problem of our 12,000,000 Negroes."[10]

Despite his emphasis on the universalization of popular sovereignty, his de-emphasis of the role of force in world affairs, and his internationalist developmental vision akin to a global New Deal, Wallace no less than Luce associated widening spheres of U.S. global influence and involvement with a special national providence. In this sense, Wallace may have done less to clarify the terms of an emerging debate about future U.S. foreign policy than to rhetorically camouflage the deficiencies of Luce's vision, softening what may have appeared as chauvinist exuberance. The substitution of "immigrant" for settler nationalism, moreover, left the future standing of those whom Du Bois called "non-national" peoples mostly unremarked upon and unresolved. Luce's rewriting of "exclusive continentalism" as a narrative of global manifest destiny, in other words, remained largely unchallenged.[11] Wallace later admitted that he saw nothing fundamentally wrong with Luce's pronouncements (though he sensed that other nations might.)[12] As Dwight MacDonald caustically observed: "Although Wallace's slogan, 'The People's Century,' was evolved as a counter to Henry Luce's 'The American Century,' it is difficult to find significant differences between the two." Since he was "a reactionary . . . [Luce] put things bluntly, without the double-talk to which liberals are accustomed."[13]

MacDonald anticipated the bipartisan internationalist consensus that would characterize the development of a globe-spanning military complex as the corollary of U.S. global ascendancy. However, he overlooked enduring geopolitical and policy differences that would require continuous and assiduous adjudication. The Wallace/Luce contretemps reflected a fundamental division. On one side was the Roosevelt administration's prioritization of collective security centered on the Atlantic world that envisaged an orderly decolonization, and the development of multilateral institutions under international law. On the other was a hemispheric, "Pacificist orientation" rooted in a long history of westward expansion and characterized by unilateral, militarized encounters, particularly with peoples of color at home and overseas.[14] U.S. imperial interventions and long-term occupations had already taken place in the Caribbean and Pacific, including a long, bloody counterinsurgency war fought by U.S. forces in the Philippines at the turn of the century. Landing in Australia in 1942, commanding U.S. forces in the Southwest Pacific during World War II, General Douglas MacArthur evoked this tradition when he hailed "the indescribable consanguinity of race" that gave citizens of two British settler colonies "the same aspirations, the same hopes and desires, the same ideals and same dreams for future destiny."[15] In this view, white Australians, white New Zealanders, and white Americans were agents of a shared civilizing project, set apart from and superior to backward, potentially subversive Asian masses. The son of U.S. China missionaries, Luce embraced the centrality of Asia to U.S. "Open Door" dreams of material abundance and global preeminence through access to world markets and never doubted the primacy of force over moral suasion for the achievement of such aims in the midst of culturally and racially distinct peoples. Although imperial control and colonial acquisitions may feature only episodically in the history of U.S. foreign relations, what might be called a settler-colonial standpoint was never far from the surface in U.S. military encounters in racial and colonial contexts. From this point forward, U.S. intervention, even in nominally independent countries, rarely occurred without new territorial accretions of U.S. power overseas. The result: an empire of military bases gradually encircling the planet, with American soldiers and sailors enjoying privileged status.[16]

There was a further challenge to the grafting of internationalist and national-expansionist tendencies within a new global orientation: they not only represented different views of the world beyond U.S. borders but were also rooted in antagonistic regional and racially inflected visions of the American polity. Thus it is not surprising that black public opinion, as recorded in the black press and by intellectuals and other notables in the 1940s, exhibited a decided preference for Wallace's version of American globalism. Black commentators, however, did not just naively follow the debate; they significantly sharpened its political stakes and meaning. Whether the promise of the Atlantic Charter applied to all the world's people or merely to those under "the Nazi yoke," as Winston Churchill claimed, for example, was a major source of contention within the black press during World War II.[17] As wartime race riots rocked urban areas and workplaces pressured by new black migrants and fair employment mandates, the *Chicago Defender* went so far as to publish Axis radio reports that questioned whether under the circumstances the United States was "justified in their ambition of Americanizing the world . . . and making the 20th-century an American Century."[18] Du Bois, who hoped that World War II "might become openly and declaredly a war for racial and cultural equality," cautioned in the *New York Amsterdam News* that "the American Century" was the provenance of those who wanted to "rule mankind as heirs of decrepit England."[19] Writing just after the war, George Padmore remained convinced that U.S. business and military interests were "haunted by the threat of world revolt" and determined "to make the world safe for 'American imperialism' and to establish the 'American Century' in the five continents and seven seas."[20]

Colonial questions were at the forefront of black concerns. In their landmark ethnography of black Chicago, entitled *Black Metropolis,* St. Clair Drake and Horace Cayton argued that urban black populations were "more international-minded" than most Americans and found the problems of colonial peoples "strangely analogous" with their own.[21] Intimate familiarity with the vulnerability of rightless and stateless peoples to sovereign violence, labor exploitation, and material deprivation not only made U.S. black publics skeptical of the kind of internationalism that "the American Century" might bring but, more importantly, made them ask which *version of Americanism* would be internationalized. With its "Double-V" campaign the *Pittsburgh Courier* popularized the idea that racial despotism was akin to homegrown fascism that needed to be defeated just as surely as did the Hitlerian variety. Columnists and cartoonists asked which set of values would America export: Roosevelt's Four Freedoms or the "Nazi-minded" attitudes of "America Firsters" and southern segregationists?[22] Writing in *Negro Quarterly*, Ralph Ellison embraced Wallace's call for a "people's century" but lexically modified it into a more sharply egalitarian call for a "peoples' century," insisting that the democratic aspirations of the world's "darker peoples" constituted the war's real significance. Ellison outlined a challenge that U.S. policy makers largely failed to answer for decades: "If minority and colonial peoples are to be convinced that the statements of Wallace rather than those of Churchill embody allied intentions, and that the action of the Senate [for example, filibustering antilynching legislation] does not express the Administration's Negro Policy, then let us see convincing action."[23]

Increasingly vociferous expressions of black opinion made an impression upon public policy and upon the emerging national security complex. Black newspapers were banned on U.S. military bases, as the FBI began its Survey of Racial Conditions (RACON), an ambitious surveillance program to monitor potentially disloyal or seditious black action and sentiment. At the same time, the Roosevelt administration's accession to some MOWM demands, increasing black representation in war work, signaled the widening of reformist channels. So too did the massive, well-funded (and widely lauded) study of the "Negro problem" commissioned by the Carnegie Foundation. The Swedish economist Gunnar Myrdal, who presided over the study, sounded a cautious note that would become commonplace in the years to come: "the treatment of the Negro is America's greatest and most conspicuous scandal. It is tremendously publicized. . . . For the colored peoples all over the world, whose rising influence is axiomatic, this scandal is salt in their wounds."[24] In its sheer monumentality, *An American*

Dilemma: The Negro Problem and Modern Democracy provided the liberal establishment with a grand piece of counter-publicity. For Myrdal's genius was to reframe the global racial and colonial crisis as an opportunity: the "dream of American patriots that America should give to the entire world its own freedoms . . . would come true," he wrote, if "America can demonstrate that justice, equality and cooperation are possible between white and colored people."[25]

The Myrdal study sought to stake out a new middle ground. On the one side were restive black publics who charged that the Negro problem "forces the US to abdicate its . . . leadership of democracy in the world" and who viewed racism, colonialism, and fascism as related, perhaps even indivisible, forms of domination.[26] On the other side were U.S. foreign policy elites who shared Luce's sense of custodianship of Western civilization (including the "grand areas" of the globe controlled by Europe's crumbling empires). As heirs to a Wilsonian world-ordering vision, advocates of U.S. internationalism, such as Henry Stimson or Cordell Hull, had little difficulty combining a rhetorical emphasis upon self-determination with support for the tutelary, developmental value of colonialism for unfit, unprepared peoples.[27] The contradictions built into this temporizing position, however, had become increasingly untenable. From the 1940 Republican standard-bearer Wendell Willkie to strident New Dealers like Wallace and independent leftists like Du Bois, the idea that the war had created for the first time "one world" demanded enfranchisement of the global majority who suffered under the stigma of race and the denial of nationhood. Myrdal's lasting innovation was to identify a moral and ethical commitment to racial equality as an inherent dimension of U.S. civic culture ("an American Creed") and as something that exemplified and legitimated American exceptionalism on a global scale.

An American Dilemma might be seen as a kind of ideological midwife to an American Century. Myrdal looked upon the United States as an extension of European civilization and as the savior of a "Western" liberal tradition that was broader than America itself. In this way, his thinking strongly resonated with Atlanticist predilections. Yet by characterizing the "Negro problem" as a peculiarly American dilemma whose global significance derived from the role that the United States was destined to play as a world-ordering power, it paradoxically affirmed another aspect of American exceptionalism, one that distanced the United States from the racial and colonial crisis that engulfed European liberalism. Indeed, the Carnegie Foundation chose Myrdal as an arbiter for the study because he was allegedly impartial: from a European country "with high intellectual and scholarly standards, but with . . . no traditions of imperialism."[28] As if by design, *An American Dilemma* constructed an internal resolution to the "Negro problem" as a proxy for future U.S. attitudes and policy approaches to decolonization, which remained ambiguous and ambivalent at best during and after World War II. Doing so erased the substantive linkages between the denial of civil and political rights, exposure to sovereign violence, economic exploitation, and resource plunder that black activists argued jointly characterized racial and colonial domination across the globe. Henceforth, racism would be characterized as pathological prejudice and associated primarily with an aberrant Nazi regime rather than seen as part of the warp and woof of Western civilization itself. The *real* racists were the despised and defeated Germans, not the Americans who, after all, liberated an enslaved Europe.

Much of this, in any case, was anticipatory. In a country defined by de jure racial segregation, liberals oriented toward the New Deal (nationally and globally) held no monopoly on the emerging conversation on race. What form American internationalism would take after the war, moreover, remained entirely undetermined. Here the Cold War proved decisive. Interventionism in the name of anticommunism put the "people's century" (along with Henry Wallace's political career) to the sword. It reanimated white supremacist associations of labor and civil rights struggles with Communist subversion, such as future Georgia governor (and later U.S. senator) Herman Talmadge's charge that the Congress of Industrial Organizations' union-organizing campaigns in his state were infiltrated by "Moscow-Harlem zoot-suiters."[29] And it enhanced the public profile of professional military men, such as Douglas MacArthur, whose careers were steeped in an expansionist lineage, from the last Indian wars to the Philippines adventure, the occupation of Japan, and coming wars in the Asian rimlands. The liberal anti-Communists who gathered under the banner of Americans for Democratic Action sought to distinguish the excesses of the growing "red scare" at home from a calibrated containment doctrine focused upon the European continent and the avoidance of atomic warfare. Global anticommunism, however, had a domestic twin, hostile to the New Deal and suspicious of racial liberalism. Rising hysteria over the "loss of China" at the end of 1949 added fuel to domestic political conflict. U.S. views of international affairs in turn darkened appreciably under the influence of a countersubversive paranoid style of politics that included adventurist, right-wing calls to roll back communism around the globe.

At the same time, a complex consensus about the meaning of domestic racial division for U.S. foreign policy began to emerge during this period. For a brief moment after World War II, the National Association for the Advancement of Colored People (NAACP) had considered the United Nations an appropriate forum for adjudicating racial grievances as a global, human rights concern. With the onset of the Cold War, distance from comparative, transnational approaches to racial and colonial questions came to define mainstream American civil rights advocacy.[30] Successfully agitating for the desegregation of the U.S. armed forces in 1948—arguably the most significant civil rights achievement of the period—A. Philip Randolph called racial segregation "the greatest single propaganda and political weapon in the hands of Russia and international communism today."[31] Republican senator Henry Cabot Lodge Jr., a leading internationalist, referred to racial discrimination as America's "Achilles heel before the world," while Dean Acheson, Truman's secretary of state, labeled it "a handicap in our relations with other countries."[32] A few years later, the Department of Justice amicus brief in *Brown v. Board of Education* (1954) emphasized the importance of desegregation as a foreign policy imperative: "the United States is trying to prove to the people of the world, of every nationality, race and color, that a free democracy is the most civilized and secure form of government devised by man."[33] Cold War civil rights, in Mary Dudziak's phrase, comprised a dense framework of affirmations and sanctions by which black demands for full citizenship and U.S. national security imperatives were gradually aligned with each other during the 1950s. At one end of the political

spectrum, cantankerous radicals, including old lions of the black freedom movement like Du Bois and Paul Robeson, were denied the right
to travel overseas, persecuted, and prosecuted for seditious speech.
At the other, conservative Republican president Dwight Eisenhower,
while publicly ruing his appointment of Earl Warren, the Supreme
Court justice who penned the *Brown* decision, deployed U.S. para-
troopers to enforce new civil rights laws at Little Rock, Arkansas, in
order to "restore the image of America . . . in the eyes of the world."[34]
With much the same goal in mind, the State Department sent a train
of black and white jazz musicians touring overseas.

Neither hard nor soft power, however, staunched the flow of negative
ink in newspapers at home and around the world each time a black
protester was bloodied by a Southern policeman's baton, or an African
or Asian diplomat was denied a hotel room in the nation's capital.
Nor could Cold War civil rights contain the older associations and
"strangely analogous" thinking by which U.S. blacks continued to link
racial and colonial conditions as they scrutinized and evaluated U.S.
policies toward the rest of the world. As much as official discourse and
moderate black leadership of organizations like the NAACP framed
the burgeoning civil rights movement of the 1950s as a patriotic, almost entirely domestic, affair, black struggles for justice retained a
wider ambit and longer view and yielded views of the world and claims
to truth that sharply clashed with the prevailing terms of Cold War
foreign policy. There was simply no way to compartmentalize civil
rights struggles at home from racially inflected decolonization struggles abroad. As early as 1959, on his first trip to India, King hailed "the
common cause of minority and colonial peoples in America, Africa and
Asia struggling to throw off racism and imperialism."[35] Not only were
black publics less easily persuaded by anticommunism, they largely
understood something that has only recently become generally ad-
missible within the historiography of U.S. foreign policy, namely, that
the Cold War was in significant measure "a continuation of European colonial interventions . . . and attempts at controlling Third World
peoples."[36] It pitted North against South as much as West against East.
This was visible as early as 1948 when the United States began providing fiscal and material support for French efforts to regain control

over what they called Indochina. The never answered (later classified) letters that Ho Chi Minh had sent to the Truman administration asking for U.S. support for Vietnamese independence on the basis of shared anticolonial principles exemplified by the U.S. Declaration of Independence are a haunting testimony to the abortive dream of a people's century. Particularly in the years of Allen Dulles's tenure at the CIA, covert action aimed at thwarting revolutionary and reformist democratic change in Asia, Africa, Latin America, and the Middle East that appeared to threaten either corporate interests or the resource requirements and security needs of the world's dominant capitalist states formed a major theme of U.S. policy in the decolonizing world.

As decolonization struggles gained momentum around the world in the 1960s, black activists and intellectuals turned more sharply against U.S. Cold War prerequisites. As news of the murder of Congolese president Patrice Lumumba filtered through the streets of Harlem in 1960, for example, a predominantly black crowd spontaneously gathered and marched through Times Square chanting a version of a slogan made popular by the Cuban Revolution: "Congo, yes! Yankee, no!"[37] To this day, there has been no full public accounting of the CIA's role (in collusion with Belgian colonialists) in orchestrating divisions within Africa's largest country and the assassination of a popular and inspiring anticolonial nationalist leader. Engaged black publics inside the United States followed these events closely and greeted official explanations with thoroughgoing skepticism. Malcolm X's incendiary provocation that "the chickens had come home to roost" with the assassination of President John F. Kennedy was a direct reference to Lumumba's murder, an early insinuation that the Cold War was engendering "blowback." Part of Malcolm's genius was his inversion of the logic of Cold War civil rights. American actions in the world, he insisted, provided abiding evidence of domestic racial animus. "When I speak of some action for the Congo," he declared, "that action also includes Congo, Mississippi."[38] One of the first anti–Vietnam War editorials to appear in a major black periodical, written by Jack O'Dell, former King adviser, made the similar point that "contempt bred by the familiarity of violating the civil and political rights of black people was the 'link that connects Selma and Saigon.'"[39]

This enduring sense of "linked fate" between African Americans, on the one hand, and colonized and formerly colonized people subject to U.S. military force, on the other, found its most dramatic expression in Martin Luther King Jr.'s declaration of opposition to the Vietnam War in 1967 at Riverside Church in Harlem.[40] Widely repudiated by previously supportive tribunes of Cold War civil rights liberalism from the *New York Times* to the NAACP, and hysterically denounced by his many adversaries, King's complex views were never accorded full public hearing, particularly once his life was cut short by an assassin's bullet, one year to the day from his controversial speech. In one sense, King couched his argument within the language of domestic reform, suggesting (prophetically) that continuing incorporation of the black poor into the tributaries of the affluent society and the welfare state could not be sustained alongside increasingly bloated military commitments around the world. In a deeper sense, peering through the lens of black experience, King offered one of the most profound critiques of the Cold War and U.S. foreign policy ever penned. "It is a sad fact," he wrote, "that, because of comfort, complacency, a morbid fear of Communism and our proneness to adjust to injustice, the Western nations that initiated so much of the revolutionary spirit of the modern world have now become the arch antirevolutionaries."[41] Opposition to communism, King argued, could not justify the disproportionate uses of force and violence or the prioritizing of U.S. state and corporate interests ahead of the democratic values Americans professed to uphold. Leavening these commitments to militarism and materialism, King suggested, was an enduring racism: the normalized sense that some human life was simply less valuable—an axiom reinforced with every bombing run, every burned village, and every tortured or mutilated body.

King's effort to deploy his significant moral capital to antimilitarist ends wound up with little to show for it. His antiwar views have subsequently been rigorously segregated in public memory from the "dream" of full citizenship for black Americans for which he is now justly remembered. Such an eventuality appears to vindicate the viewpoint of those who opposed King in the late 1960s, including respected activists like Bayard Rustin, who had long argued for the tactical necessity of papering over any discrepancy between black freedom imperatives and U.S. foreign policy positions. Yet it was this very separation between the domestic and the foreign that King challenged as inadequate to the fact of living in "a world house" in which growing proximity and interconnectedness of different peoples demanded a heightened ecumenism, a willingness to "go beyond national allegiances," and also, paradoxically, greater attentiveness to the festering fissures of race and poverty at home that, once again, risked dividing the country from within. Despite the charges of anti-Americanism and subversion leveled against him, the challenge that King posed during this period was the fullest amplification of the democratic promise of the American political tradition. Given what he called "the tragic evasions and defaults of several centuries," King was under no illusions that the American Century would deliver on this promise. Offered from behind the barrel of American guns, he warned, America's "amazing universalism" would quickly change shape and confound us, "adding cynicism to the process of death."[42]

Although publicly denounced at the time, King's critique of U.S. foreign policy did not represent a radical departure from the normative baseline of American political discussion. Rather, it expressed a century-long tradition of black citizen diplomacy, fusing antiracism and anti-imperialism, while recognizing the global significance of racial inequality and domination. During the 1970s and 1980s, these viewpoints were developed in programmatic directions by Jesse Jackson and Jack O'Dell through the offices of People United to Serve Humanity and later the Rainbow Coalition. Starting in the mid-1970s, Jackson's organizations launched a number of significant foreign policy initiatives, including a campaign to support Senate ratification of the treaty restoring Panamanian sovereignty over the Canal Zone, along with well-publicized fact-finding tours of South Africa and the Middle East. From these tours came some of the first calls for corporate divestment from the apartheid regime, the earliest public challenges within the United States to Israel's expanding settlements in the occupied West Bank, and criticism of U.S. refusal (on the grounds of terrorism) to negotiate directly with the Palestine Liberation Organization. O'Dell recalls visiting a Palestinian refugee camp outside of Beirut with Jackson and "seeing the open sewage" seeping up from the ground, "and Jesse turned to me and said, "Jack, you know, I know this place. I've been here. This is South Carolina where I grew up." At the 1988 Democratic Convention, delegates aligned with presidential candidate Jackson forced the first foreign policy debate by a major U.S. political party regarding the legitimacy of a two-state solution in Israel-Palestine.[43]

If this commitment further fractured black-Jewish relations that had been so central to civil rights coalition politics, it also marked the apogee of civil rights and peace movement influence on U.S. foreign policy discussions. Enabled by U.S. openings to China, the Watergate scandal, the ignominious U.S. evacuation of Saigon, U.S.-Soviet détente, and the signing of the SALT treaties, the 1970s augured significant reordering of Cold War presumptions, including new congressional strictures on executive authority and covert action. Although seldom straying too far from the status quo, the Carter administration's emphasis on human rights partially detached foreign policy from anti-Communist doxa and national interests narrowly conceived. Carter had appointed O'Dell's and Jackson's former associate in the Southern Christian Leadership Conference, Andrew Young, ambassador to the United Nations. In the summer of 1979, Young met with the Palestinian representative at the United Nations in contravention of the U.S. "no-talk" policy. Having already drawn public ire for criticizing white minority rule in South Africa and Rhodesia, along with expanding Israeli settlements, for his benign attitude toward Cuban intervention in Angola, and for supporting the normalization of relations between the United States and Vietnam, Young was widely attacked in the U.S. media and eventually forced to resign. Explaining his resignation, Young described himself as someone who came "from the ranks of those who have known and identified with some level of oppression in the world," and who therefore had tried "to interpret to our country some of the mood of the rest of the world."[44] Implicit in this statement was not only King's ecumenical, postnationalist sensibility but also an argument for the United States to abandon expectations of a world forever accommodating itself to America's exceptional demands and imperatives.

Yet any possibility of the 1970s seeing a substantial rethinking of U.S. foreign policy prerogatives and approaches was stillborn. It was undone by the enduring associations of the American Century that linked domestic prosperity and growth with both a preponderance of power and military action pursuant to political and economic objectives. Unfolding, in the single, fateful year 1979, revolutions in Nicaragua and Iran, the Soviet invasion of Afghanistan, the spectacle of impotent, blindfolded U.S. hostages in Tehran, and right-wing hysteria about the "loss" of the Panama Canal rekindled Cold War discourse, much to the benefit of the incoming Reagan administration. A "Vietnam syndrome" disposing the U.S. military against major offensives (as well as post-Vietnam congressional controls) arguably still constrained the Reaganites, who turned once again to tried-and-true formulas of nuclear brinksmanship in Europe and covert action elsewhere. In Central America and southern Africa, the United States launched new proxy wars. In the Middle East and Central Asia, it developed connections with a range of shadowy operatives, helping forge the links between "Islam and terror" that are at the root of contemporary U.S. nightmares.[45] With demands for higher U.S. military spending trumping concerns about the dangers that a military-industrial complex might pose to democratic governance, a "new American militarism" took root, forming part of a triumphalist narrative that attributed the crumbling of the Soviet Empire to renewed American assertiveness rather than to long-standing structural deficits of the Soviet regime and Eastern European people power. In 1991 the first Gulf War, following closely on the heels of the collapse of the Soviet Union, promoted a belief within some U.S. foreign policy circles that, in the words of George H. W. Bush, the United States had "kicked the Vietnam syndrome, once and for all." To the American Century's messianic claims and a sprawling Cold War infrastructure of more than seven hundred overseas military bases, a new element was added: unprecedented and dangerous dreams of "permanent global military superiority."[46]

The Reagan era, however, saw more than a return to Cold War prerequisites. Reagan's promise of "morning in America" represented the first intimation that there would be a doubling down on the idea of an

American Century. This time, however, the challenge was not to persuade a potentially isolationist and war-weary public to go along, but to reassert the signs and symbols of muscular U.S. globalism as first proof of an enduring national supremacy. Although covert action received a renewed impetus during this period, there was also a new emphasis on militarism as narrative and spectacle, including the popular rewriting of the Vietnam War as frontier myth in the *Rambo* trilogy. These developments coincided with the culmination of long-term, secular political realignments strongly linked to race and region. During the Cold War, the influence of an internationally oriented Eastern establishment republicanism had diminished, supplanted by centers of Republican influence in Western "Sunbelt" states, their growth heavily subsidized by Cold War military spending. Meanwhile, the dissolution of the Democratic Party's New Deal coalition under the pressure of black protest and civil rights reform resulted in the large-scale defection of Southern whites to the GOP.

The regionalization of the Republican Party into a predominantly Southern and Western party accentuated the national expansionist impulse that has haunted U.S. foreign policy making since World War II. With few very exceptions, most historians continue to view this as the subordinate tendency. Even Bruce Cumings, who valuably asserts the centrality of "westward expansion and Pacific imperialism" throughout the twentieth century, concedes the dominance of Atlanticism in the post-1945 period, differentiating Kennedy's and Johnson's pursuit of a "new frontier" in Vietnam, Reagan's actions in Central America, and even George W. Bush's Iraq adventure as "occasional departures into unilateralism" that elicited decidedly sharp swings back to the status quo of restrained ethical realism and first-among-equals multi-lateralism.[47] In many ways, however, Cold War foreign policy unfolded in continuity with a longer tradition that Theodore Roosevelt famously defined as the exercise of international police power—a kind of open-ended, global counterinsurgency directed primarily at people deemed either incapable or untrustworthy of governing themselves.[48] During the Cold War, the explicit racial criteria once employed to justify this policing were normatively discredited and replaced with litmus tests defined by political ideology. Yet racialism repressed consistently returned as culturalism, for example, in stereotypical judgments by a William Westmoreland, Richard Nixon, Samuel Huntington, or Martin Peretz about how Asians, Africans, or Arabs simply do not value human life the way "we" do.

The profound racial divisions and conflicts that have defined the national political development of the United States while shaping U.S. views of the world and security policies have reverberated powerfully in what is now disturbingly referred to as the "homeland." One of the starkest developments of the Reagan period, for example, was the sharp escalation the devastating "war on drugs" begun by Richard Nixon. Characterized by a militarization of policing strategies and the targeting of black urban areas, this "war" produced an alarming growth of a prison complex to match the military complex, with several million people, the majority African American and Latino, now under lock and key or some form of criminal state supervision. Under Bill Clinton, statutory provisions for the "rendition" of foreign drug traffickers and for the suspension of ancient strictures against the use of military resources and personnel within U.S. territorial borders dissolved the moral and conceptual boundaries between inwardly focused practices of policing and public safety and externally directed military actions, adversely affecting both sides of the equation. Robert Kaplan (reputedly Clinton's favorite public intellectual) captured the zeitgeist in his widely read essay "The Coming Anarchy." Written in the wake of the Los Angeles riots of 1992, Kaplan diagnosed a fundamental mutation in the organization of the U.S. nation-state as an engine of homogenization and conflict stabilization, ascribing both to the pathologies of black urban dwellers who, unlike the Jews and Irish before them, preferred the hostilities and illusory gratifications of "negritude" to the virtuous trials of assimilation. Kaplan went further, warning that rising dangers of demographic fragmentation of the nation space, magnified by a global contagion of state failure, particularly in "Africa" (where else?), would inflame conflicts along racial and civilizational lines. In this context, he suggested, fighting crime and waging war were becoming indistinguishable and "national defense" was no longer defined by unitary territorial logic but, rather, by multi-scalar tactics and strategies of pacification and control.[49] Doctrines of counterinsurgency, in other words, have been repatriated, finding application at home as well as abroad.

Although the recent Iraq War (not to mention Afghanistan) has come to be widely viewed as a misguided misadventure, neither in the national interest nor fiscally sustainable, it has left a too-little-noticed legacy: a once latent narrative about permanent war as the raison d'être of U.S. global power has become frighteningly prominent. While public and scholarly discourse tends to endorse U.S. global commitments as conducive to collective security, producing since the 1940s a string of foreign policy achievements that includes the triumph over European fascism, the development of robust international institutions, and the defeat of Soviet totalitarianism, another story is also gaining traction. Without the mildest ethical shudder, pundits like Kaplan and Max Boot recall with favor the extremely violent Philippine counterinsurgency and Phoenix assassination program, citing them as important precedents for U.S. policy today. Walter Russell Mead affirms the centrality of "Jacksonianism" (an earlier instance of Southern/ Western regional political alignment) to America's "special providence" in the world—a foreign policy vernacular rooted in reflexively nationalist, eye-for-an-eye, friend-enemy politics. For his part, John Lewis Gaddis finds historical precedent for Bush-era doctrines of preventive war and open-ended counterinsurgency, citing the challenges of policing an insecure frontier against "non-state actors . . . native Americans, pirates, marauders, and other free agents."[50] Once continental in scope, that frontier has apparently gone global.

Such a permanent disposition toward war, if not permanent war itself, erases any meaningful distinctions between the American realm of action throughout the world and at home. The resulting viewpoint is less empirical than ideological. It renders uncontroversial something that is (and should be) fundamentally contested and in question. That it does so by once again evoking a history of continental conquest and indeed *race war* recalls Patrick Wolfe's observation that "settler-colonialism is a structure not an event."[51] Complicating the picture, of course, are the various postracial, historical disclaimers that now preface such claims. Mead, for example, points out the high levels of African American inclusion in the military and black martial prowess as evidence that Jacksonianism has outgrown its white supremacist origins. For his part, Gaddis dismisses squeamishness about settler-colonial ethics and practices, quipping that no one wants to give it all back to the Indians. The issue is not the litigation of the past, however, but the ways in which a violently racialized national history continues to distort and undermine the development of an ethical relationship to the wider world. Evidence that the haunting, even if categorically disavowed, presence of racialized warfare continues to reside at the very center of U.S. war-making and scholarly discourse alike abounds. Consider only the following: in 2003, U.S. officials hired Lane McCotter, the former head of the notoriously brutal Texas prison system, to run Abu Ghraib; several of the more infamous torturers in recent years started their careers as domestic prison guards; in Afghanistan, the United States employs "killer teams" akin to the Vietnam era death squads such as Tiger Force; and the SEALs sent into Pakistan to kill Osama bin Laden used the code name "Geronimo" to describe their prey.

Recalling the unfinished dialectic of color and democracy that shadowed the Short American Century, Obama's call during the 2008 presidential campaign to "choose our better history" might be read productively in this light as a commentary about the future of the United States in the world. The very idea of "our better history" constituted a rejoinder to Senator John McCain's preferred formulation: "We face no enemy, no matter how cruel; and no challenge, no matter how daunting, greater than the courage, patriotism and determination of Americans. We are the makers of history, not its victims."[52] Although McCain strongly eschewed the direct (and at times murderous) racist appeals of some of his supporters, he nonetheless tapped into the exclusivist, supremacist kernel of the American political tradition—the racial nationalism often invisibly braided with civic American universalism. History for McCain—as for many other Americans—is a domain of friends and enemies. Make history (my friends), he seemed to say, or *become its victims.* How to know the difference? Americans (hailed in this idiom) understand that making history often requires turning another people into victims. The idea of "our better history," by contrast, expressly adopts what Frederick Douglass called "the standpoint of the victims of American history."[53] This standpoint, however, is no end point, for it is through the aspirational struggles of the trammeled and dispossessed—slaves, women, workers, the segregated, all those who are disfranchised, stigmatized, and colonized—that "our better history" has presumably been realized. In other words, even as Obama evokes timeless values and solid foundations, his conception of history remains explicitly revisionist and *revisionary* in this sense: it is possible to choose a different way forward.

The contrast between Henry Luce's "American Century" and Henry Wallace's "People's Century" reveals the contradictory strands within U.S. political culture that have shaped and continue to shape underlying dispositions and orientations toward the wider world. Especially in the domains of national security and so-called foreign policy, powerful, centralizing state institutions, structured by a "bipartisan" agreement, have sadly retained in equal measure the moral absolutism, easy resort to blunt force, and casual racism characteristic of Luce's vision. But we must ask: In what ethical universe can the eminently foreseeable destruction of civilian noncombatants, who must be bombed in order to be saved, or tortured in order for us to be safe, be justified? Is this "realism"? Or is it a philosophical standpoint according to which some human lives are simply less valuable and therefore become expendable? It seems likely that the Barack Obama—of Honolulu, Jakarta, Nairobi, and Chicago's South Side—who seemingly promised a return to multilateralism and a soft landing for an empire in terminal crisis would reject such a standpoint. Yet the Barack Obama who became president of the United States—the one who aborted his campaign promise to close the Guantánamo Bay prison camp, escalated war in Afghanistan, acceded to yet a new war in Libya, and spares an already bloated military from the severest exigencies of fiscal austerity—has become "part of the mechanism that recommends it."

Being part of "the mechanism that recommends it" is how Robert McNamara, former secretary of defense, described his own dire contribution to the contemporary history of U.S. war-making in Vietnam, which before Afghanistan was America's longest war. In doing so, McNamara belatedly acknowledged a deeply criminal complicity. Yet, somehow, the belief that our killing is not murder, and that the United States can use force with thoughtful, prophylactic discretion, refuses to die. Couched in an increasingly threadbare rhetoric of freedom and democracy, the ethical and fiscal unsustainability of America's global imperial presence confronts us—hidden in plain sight—propped up by the hollow promise that it will save us from the Third World that is always just around the corner. The fact is that clear and certain lines of nation and geography, time and syntax no longer (and perhaps never did) separate the victims from the makers of history. In this context, all efforts to perpetuate the American Century make little sense and only mislead us from the necessary challenge of common living among diverse peoples in an ever more austere, beleaguered, and dangerous world.

CHAPTER 5

Pragmatic Realism versus the American Century

T. J. Jackson Lears

The dream of an American Century depended on a teleology of empire. This worldview animated U.S. foreign policy for several decades before Henry Luce articulated it in 1941. The American Century did not spring fully formed from Luce's brow. Like the journalistic genius that he was, the editor in chief of *Time-Life* was merely repackaging sentiments already in wide circulation.

The assumptions underlying expectations of an American Century were implicit but pervasive: history is on our side; everybody wants to be like us. In the rhetoric of empire, providential destiny blended with economic necessity: progress was inevitable, but American global leadership could hasten its advance. The imperative was to look ahead. Arguments for war emphasized what would be or what might be rather than what actually was. Pretending to deal with the facts on the ground, interventionists floated in a haze of futurist and determinist abstraction.[1]

Critics rejected the teleology of empire, grounding their critique in lived experience rather than absolutist vacuities. Their anti-imperial vision arose from deep-rooted American traditions: republican distrust of executive aggrandizement, a realist refusal of global hubris, and pragmatic concern for the consequences of ideas in the everyday conduct of life. Yet however plausible their arguments, these dissenters could not sustain a successful alternative to the American Century.

Their roads not taken often ended in marginality or irrelevance—or else they circled back around to the main highway of interventionism. The failure of dissent reflected in part the power of economic and bureaucratic interests invested in globalism. These interests possessed a formidable capacity to patrol the boundaries of "responsible debate." Yet the difficulties of dissent arose as well from certain ambiguities in the dissenters' own thought: the murkiness of the appeal to experience and the ease with which pragmatism and realism could be recast to justify foreign military adventures.

Subtler difficulties also beset the dissenters. They were educated men of ideas in a culture that equated manhood with action. Not wanting to be consigned to the realm of ineffectual abstraction, they shared a common temperamental tendency that had afflicted male American intellectuals since the days of the early Republic—a fear of sterility and impotence and a secret self-mistrust. In "The American Scholar" (1837) Ralph Waldo Emerson captured this mood in words that resonated for generations to come:

> There goes in the world a notion, that the scholar should be a recluse, a valetudinarian,—as unfit for any handiwork or public labor, as a penknife for an axe. The so-called "practical men" sneer at speculative men, as if, because they speculate or *see,* they could do nothing. I have heard it said that the clergy,—who are always, more universally than any other class, the scholars of their day,—are addressed as women; that the rough, spontaneous conversation of men they do not hear, but only a mincing and diluted speech. They are often virtually disfranchised; and, indeed, there are advocates for their celibacy. As far as this is true of the studious classes, it is not just and wise. Action is with the scholar subordinate, but it is essential. Without it, he is not yet man.[2]

The passage articulated anxieties that have troubled intellectuals down to our own time—the fears of isolation and emasculation along with longings to join "the rough, spontaneous conversation of men" and embrace the strife of the world. These anxieties existed on both sides of the Atlantic, but they resonated with special force in the United States, where practical action lay at the core of the national identity.

The recoil from effete intellectualism gave rise to the pragmatic strain in American social thought and endowed the critique of empire with its weakness as well as its strength.[3]

The gender dimensions of intellectual activism are inescapable. For much of American history, and for decades after women won the right to vote, public life remained an overwhelmingly male realm. Indeed, it became more self-consciously and narrowly masculine over time. Emerson, like his republican forebears, fretted about the perils of effeminacy—the "mincing and diluted speech" of the speculative man. Still, for most of the nineteenth century, the achievement of manhood required acceptance of larger public responsibilities and commitments to family and community. Only toward the end of the century, as members of the post–Civil War generation came of age in the shadow of their heroic predecessors, was manhood recast in the language of physical toughness and military violence.[4]

During the 1890s and throughout the century that followed, many educated men embraced this militarized definition of manliness. The consequences for foreign policy debate were far-reaching. Imperial interventions abroad were defined in heroic military terms; opposition was cast as effete withdrawal from manly duty. In the rhetoric of empire, there were few (usually no) alternatives between heroism and cowardice. As manliness and militarism merged, few contributors to foreign policy debate had the temerity to suggest that heroism might come in many forms—some of them having nothing to do with military adventure. If women participated in this public conversation, they tended to be pacifist outliers who could be dismissed as hopeless idealists (Jane Addams) or—later in the century—those who in striking a militaristic posture (Jeane Kirkpatrick and Madeleine Albright) thereby became more royalist than the king.

Gender preoccupations shaped foreign policy discourse throughout the twentieth century, encouraging the confusion of physical courage with moral courage and promoting the personification of the nation as a (male) individual who could "stand and fight" or "cut and run." To the detriment of serious debate, gendered dualism reigned. Anti-imperialists strained to distance themselves from feminizing epithets to show that they were neither "mollycoddles" (Theodore Roosevelt's term for timid men) nor "nervous Nellies" (the preferred phrase of Lyndon Johnson and George W. Bush). Like the imperialists they criticized, opponents of empire yearned to demonstrate their manliness by plunging into the maelstrom of "real life."[5]

In most foreign policy debates, both sides shared an activist frame of mind. Consider the controversy over empire at the dawn of the twentieth century. William James hated Theodore Roosevelt's bullying moralism and its catastrophic consequences in the Philippines; the philosopher was in every way a more humane and thoughtful man than the bellicose president. Yet in their common commitment to activism, the two men were brothers under the skin. The epigraph to Roosevelt's *The Strenuous Life* (1899), from Tennyson's *Ulysses,* suited James's sensibility as well:

> How dull it is, to pause, to make an end,
> To rust unburnish'd, not to shine in use!

Like Roosevelt, James believed that life "*feels* like a real fight"; in fact, he needed to sustain that feeling to make life worth living. He craved the sense of vitality that could only arise, for him and many of his male contemporaries, through strenuous engagement with the world. He defended religious faith on the pragmatic grounds of its revitalizing consequences; it gave believers the psychic wherewithal for lives of heroic struggle. A man who abhorred war but admired the martial virtues, James sought "a moral equivalent to war"—courage without killing. He recognized that heroism did not require violence, and that manliness did not require militarism.[6]

James's capacious vision allowed him to resist imperial delusions. It also inspired his closest follower in matters of foreign policy, Randolph Bourne. The careers of James and Bourne demonstrated that pragmatism could be more than a capitulation to the logic of events. By moving beyond the demented either/or of military activism and absolute passivity, they created cogent alternatives to empire.[7]

But for other intellectuals, who also considered themselves pragmatic realists, an activist predisposition undermined skepticism toward military interventions abroad. Long after the swaggering idiom of strenuousity fell from favor, they continued to embrace action for its own sake, to fear softness and to cultivate what came to be known as "tough-minded realism." Walter Lippmann, an early advocate of U.S. intervention in World War I, nurtured a longtime fascination with personal vitality, embodied by TR. Reinhold Niebuhr's realist apologetics for the Cold War reflected his own dread of stasis. Like other American thinkers in the Emersonian tradition, he feared being exiled from the rush of events and becoming an ineffectual bystander. A restless, mobile member of the mid-century intelligentsia, Niebuhr kept his suitcase packed by his podium at Union Theological Seminary, ready to fly off to the next lecture, the next conference, or the next meeting with influential men. Yet frenetic activism of this sort could lead to de facto acquiescence in established power.[8]

Still, even the most acquiescent critics could learn from their mistakes and rethink their positions. Compromising with conventional wisdom prevented their consignment to disrepute—the fate of such consistent anti-interventionists as Charles Beard or Robert Taft. Niebuhr came to question the Manichean nuclear policies of John Foster Dulles and as early as 1965 he opposed the Vietnam War. Lippmann, like George Kennan and William Fulbright, lived long enough to repudiate interventionist dogma altogether. Lippmann thereby risked being labeled an "isolationist," the word itself testifying to the persistent power of dualism: to oppose a foreign war was to invite the charge of wanting to retreat from the world altogether. (What could be less manly?) Yet some critics of empire did manage to avoid the isolationists' fate—the disgrace of guilt by association with men later generations dismissed as cowards and traitors.

What follows is an effort to tour the tangled history of the antiimperial tradition during the decades encompassing the rise and decline of the American Century. The aim is to explore the difficulties of locating alternatives to the dualist consensus and to show how some dissenters managed to do so despite those difficulties. Throughout I focus on the political class of policy makers and public intellectuals rather than on ordinary Americans—the vast majority of whom remained resistant to foreign military adventures. And I will be primarily engaged with the tradition I call pragmatic realism, since (unlike pacifism) its adherents sustained some legitimacy in public debate. Yet the price of legitimacy was sometimes a loss of independent perspective.

Pragmatic realists preserved their critical edge when they transcended the mindless cult of national vitality that underwrote military adventures abroad. The anti-imperial tradition prospered when it hewed to the pragmatic spirit of William James and Randolph Bourne: grounded in the actualities of experience, distrustful of abstraction masquerading as realism, and radically empirical in its willingness to take seriously all forms of evidence. The pragmatism of James and Bourne depended on a bedrock commitment to a pluralistic universe—an openness to multiple perspectives on reality, including those of foreigners whose values might seem strange or threatening. This formed a crucial and neglected dimension of the anti-imperial tradition, so often falsely accused of xenophobic isolationism. This pluralism linked James and Bourne with later anti-interventionists, from Beard and Taft to Kennan and Fulbright. The grounded critique of empire coexisted with a cosmopolitan spirit. The real provincials were not those who opposed empire but those who coveted it.

Yet the pragmatic concern for consequences complicated the picture. Futurist arguments for military intervention could seem superficially pragmatic and realistic in their warning that inaction would invite disaster. Such claims were not easy to evaluate and carried more weight on some occasions than on others. But a more consistent pragmatic realist, or at least one truer to the Jamesian tradition, might well observe that war is the least predictable of human enterprises and the least subject to management and control. Regarding war, one thing alone is certain: when it ends, there will be a lot of dead and maimed bodies lying around. Lives will be lost, damaged, and wasted. This was why the pragmatic realist tradition, at its best, counseled war only as the last resort—the least desirable alternative in the policy maker's arsenal.

James, Bourne, and War:
The Ambiguities of Pragmatic Realism

As James and his contemporaries knew, the framers of the U.S. Constitution were the original pragmatic realists. They had created a republic based on assumptions that human nature is flawed, power corrupting, and hubris a constant temptation. Hence the imperative of decentralizing power to keep the Republic from turning into an empire. This perspective rejected linear notions of progress and in fact reflected a cyclical view of history. The only way to break the endless cycle of imperial corruption was to devise institutional restraints on power—the functional separation of powers among executive, legislative, and judicial branches of government and the protections of personal liberty in the Bill of Rights.

None of these constitutional constraints prevented the spread of a settlers' empire westward across the North American continent and the near extermination of the aboriginal population. But the constitutional tradition did institutionalize a distrust of concentrated executive power and a reluctance to become involved in foreign quarrels. In the words of Thomas Jefferson's Inaugural Address of 1801 (reiterating themes found in George Washington's Farewell Address of 1796), the United States would seek "peace, commerce, and honest friendship with all nations; entangling alliances with none." Twenty years later, John Quincy Adams affirmed this commitment, announcing that America's sympathy for foreign struggles against tyranny did not extend to military intervention. "Wherever the standard of freedom and independence has been or shall be unfurled, there will her heart, her benedictions and her prayers be," said Adams. "But she goes not abroad, in search of monsters to destroy."[9] It was a familiar rhetorical device, this feminine personification of the nation, and it survived in such sacred texts of the American civil religion as Irving Berlin's song "God Bless America" (1938).

By the end of the nineteenth century, however, the nation had (rhetorically) become a man. As Roosevelt said in support of American empire in 1900, "A man goes out to do man's work, to confront the difficulties and overcome them, and to train up his children to do likewise. So it is with the nation." This kind of portentous mystification, equating war-making with character-building, was characteristic of Roosevelt, Henry Cabot Lodge, and other imperialists. They were inspired by dreams of physical and moral regeneration as well as Christian righteousness—along with less exalted desires for foreign markets, resources, and investment opportunities. Their arguments for empire were rife with bogus analogies between nations and plants (grow or die). Even their economic claims rested on fantastic projections, like the one about the China market—400 million eager consumers!—which failed to materialize. They allowed neither constitutional constraints nor inconvenient facts to clutter the case for empire.[10]

In the wake of the Spanish-American War, the Filipino nationalist leader Emilio Aguinaldo expected American support for Philippine independence. When the U.S. occupiers refused to leave, the Filipinos fought back. The resulting military campaign to pacify the Philippines lasted years. The American approach to counterinsurgency featured torture, the killing of suspects (anyone over ten years old was a potential target), laying waste to the Filipinos' fields and villages, and, in general, deploying atrocities as a legitimate military tactic. Though the Indian wars of the 1870s and 1880s had provided a dress rehearsal of sorts, this Philippine Insurrection, as Washington called it, was the first American experiment in occupying a distant country with an alien culture while trying to quell a determined insurgency. The result was a bloody mess of a war.[11]

James, for one, was outraged: "God Damn the United States for its vile conduct in the Philippine Islands," he wrote a friend. This was more than a mere emotional outburst; it was an expression of James's mature worldview. "Let me repeat once more that a man's vision is the great fact about him," said James, in *A Pluralistic Universe* (1909). The emotional core of James's vision was his recognition that all of us—psychologists like himself included—suffered from "a certain blindness" toward the feelings of others, especially "the feelings of creatures and people different from ourselves." James cited Robert Louis Stevenson's story of how during the first long nights of the fall, Stevenson and his schoolmates would "sally forth . . . each equipped with a tin bull's eye lantern." They kept the lanterns tied to their belts, concealed under their coats, as their common secret, only fitfully revealed to one another in rituals of camaraderie. "To one who has not the secret of the lanterns," James wrote, the boys' rituals would seem silly or meaningless. But to the boys, the lanterns were the spark at the center of their being. James knew he could never fully know the spark at the center of anyone else's being, could never really know the inner lives of others. Still, he never stopped trying, always remembering that his effort would remain unfinished. This combination of humility, curiosity, and empathy was the ethical corollary of James's rejection of absolutism, the core of his conviction that we inhabit a pluralistic universe.[12]

Pluralism, in turn, provided the foundation for James's anti-imperial thought. As Robert Richardson writes, James's opposition to empire "grew naturally from his advocacy of pluralism and individual self-determination and from his conviction that we are mostly blind to the vital centers of the lives of others—to the lives, for example, of Filipinos."[13] Imperialism was nothing if not an expression of blindness to others' aspirations—a failure to consider the possibility of multiple perspectives on the world. Arguments for empire discounted the Filipino desire for independence and instead celebrated the uplifting mission of the American invaders. A pluralistic foreign policy, in contrast, would sanction multiple vital centers, granting legitimacy to local desires even among "backward" peoples—as James and his anti-imperial contemporaries granted legitimacy to the Filipino yearning for independence. Imperial foreign policy denied those aspirations in the name of progress, a teleological creed that demanded the replacement of idiosyncratic traditions with universal modernity. Imperialists suppressed Filipino longings for self-determination, while braying at home about its fulfillment. The pluralist alternative to this hypocrisy was an outlook, as James wrote, that

> forbids us to be forward in pronouncing on the meaninglessness of forms of existence other than our own; . . . [that] commands us to tolerate, respect, and indulge those whom we see harmlessly interested and happy in their own ways, however unintelligible these may be to us. Hands off: neither the whole of truth nor the whole of good is revealed to any single observer, although each observer gains a partial superiority of insight from the peculiar position in which he stands. . . . It is enough to ask of each of us that he should be faithful to his own opportunities and make the most of his own blessings, without presuming to regulate the rest of the vast field.[14]

Like Roosevelt, James linked individual and national conduct, but to a radically different purpose: nations, like individuals, must resist the impulse to remake the other in their own image. Hands off. Pluralism underwrote skepticism toward uplifting crusades. It animated Mark Twain's polemics, which exposed the violence behind missionary virtue and urged the "Blessings of Civilization Trust" to leave "The People Who Sit in Darkness" alone. And it survived long enough to prompt resistance to Henry Luce's American Century.[15]

Yet pluralism alone did not suffice to counter imperialist claims. It formed part of a broader pragmatic outlook that rejected absolutes and evaluated ideas with respect to their impact on human conduct. For a Jamesian pragmatist, pluralism could promote neither absolute pacifism nor absolute tolerance; circumstances might arise when either could be mistaken. The counterinsurgency war in the Philippines was a flagrant attempt to crush native aspirations. The facts in the case plainly demanded that the United States keep its hands off. Yet "hands off" could not be an absolute.

The problem here was not simply a need for philosophical consistency, which was never James's overriding concern; nor was it his activist temperament, which found expression in seeking a moral equivalent of war. The chief difficulties with absolute tolerance were empirical. What if the foreign "forms of existence" that James judged harmless actually threatened our own interests, indeed, our very way of life? Or what if the foreigners were not "happy in their own ways" but instead desperately sought deliverance from oppression? To allow such questions was to create opportunities for interventionists to adapt pragmatism to their own ends. Military intervention intended to preempt an enemy attack or prevent the slaughter of innocent civilians could find justification on pragmatic grounds as a lesser evil. Yet such justifications for war did not necessarily void a pragmatic critique. After all, claims of military or humanitarian necessity could camouflage less compelling or exalted agendas. Given war's inherent unpredictability, the resort to violence can and often does produce consequences more horrific than the conditions it set out to remedy. From a pragmatic perspective, the burden of proof—or at least of persuasion—must rest upon the war-makers. In the event, most advocates for war prefer to circumvent reasoned argument altogether by creating an atmosphere of emergency, insisting that the need for war is urgent and immediate, with no time available to weigh alternatives. Yet this amounts to a betrayal of pragmatism.

So Randolph Bourne concluded. He found his own pragmatic convictions strained by the debate over American entry into World War I. As a scholarship student at Columbia University in the early 1910s, he had first encountered pragmatism through the prism of John Dewey, whose notion of "education for living" seemed a vital alternative to the stale indoctrination Bourne had received in the public schools of Bloomfield, New Jersey. Like other intellectuals (especially male intellectuals) of his time and since, he craved immersion in the "real life" of unmediated experience. He was also, from the outset, an instinctively Jamesian pluralist.

The outbreak of war in Europe intensified Bourne's pluralistic convictions. Writing in 1916, he worried that the virus of intolerant nationalism was spreading to American shores, accelerating efforts to "Americanize" immigrants into conformity with an Anglo-Saxon standard. In what he called the "distinctly American spirit" of Whitman and Emerson and James, he urged "a new and more adventurous ideal" than uniform Americanization—"something utterly different from the nationalisms of twentieth century Europe." Already it was clear that immigrant groups were "no longer masses of aliens, waiting to be 'assimilated,' waiting to be melted down into the indistinguishable dough of Anglo-Saxonism. They are rather threads of living and potent cultures, blindly striving to weave themselves into a novel international nation, the first the world has seen." This "Trans-national America," as Bourne called it, would not "remain aloof and irresponsible" during the world crisis but would instead provide a vision of what nationality could be: a pluralistic and pragmatic alternative to the absolutist ideologies that had led to war in the first place. "Is it a wild hope that the opposition to metaphysics in international relations, opposition to militarism, is less a cowardly provincialism than a groping for this higher cosmopolitan ideal?" Bourne asked. In the end, of course, it was indeed a "wild hope." Yet even today, nearly a century later, it still commands respect.[16]

Bourne knew that for the United States time was running out, that the pressures for "preparedness" were building inexorably toward military intervention. "We suddenly realize that if we are to defeat the militaristic trend which we loathe we shall have to offer some kind of action more stirring and creative," he wrote in 1916. "There looms up as a crucial need that 'moral equivalent of war' with which William James first aroused our imaginations. It no longer seems so academic a proposal. Confronted with the crisis, we see that he analyzed the situation with consummate accuracy." Still, Bourne wanted to expand James's vision of alternative service beyond the strenuous tasks of late Victorian manhood. His "A Moral Equivalent for Universal Military Service" included necessary work of all kinds, done by girls as well as boys—caring for the old and sick, repairing roads, building playgrounds, cultivating gardens, destroying insect pests, inspecting food and factories. To those who might protest that this will not promote the stern heroism only war can bring out, Bourne replied, "We want to turn the energies of our youth away from their squandering in mere defense or mere drudgery. Our need is to learn how to live rather than die; to be teachers and creators, not engines of destruction; to be inventors and pioneers, not mere defenders." This vision of service to the commonweal turned out to be a wild hope too.[17]

That became apparent in April 1917, when Congress declared war. Woodrow Wilson's war aims were breathtaking: not only would the war make the world "safe for democracy," it would also create an international organization that would make war obsolete. This would be a war to end war.

U.S. entry into the war left Bourne deeply embittered, especially toward his fellow intellectuals. The catalog of their missed opportunities was stunning. They had failed to provide any policy alternatives to the relentless buildup toward war. "Was the terrific bargaining power of a great neutral ever really used?" Bourne asked. Nor had they challenged the provincial Anglo-Saxonism that fed war fever. "Our intellectual class might have been occupied . . . in discovering a true Americanism which would not have been merely nebulous but might have federated the different ethnic groups and traditions," Bourne wrote. "America might have been made a meeting ground for the different national attitudes." Instead it became just another breeding ground of jingoism and xenophobia. Even the proposed League of Nations served to reaffirm existing imperial hierarchies. Its program, Bourne observed, "contains no provision for dynamic national growth or for international justice." Wilson's agenda was bound to end in disillusionment.[18]

So why had intellectuals embraced that agenda? Bourne's explanation caught the ironies at the core of military interventionism. American intellectuals, true to the tradition of Emersonian masculinity, did not want to be on the sidelines; they felt "the itch to be in the great experience which the rest of the world was having." Humanitarian sentiment, supposedly central to the prowar cause, turned out to be curiously selective. "Numbers of intelligent people who had never been stirred by the horrors of capitalistic peace at home were shaken out of their slumber by the horrors of war in Belgium," Bourne observed. "Hearts that had felt only ugly contempt for democratic strivings at home beat in tune with the struggle for freedom abroad." The "primitive idea" of war for democracy, he concluded, was in the end little more than "a craving for action."[19] Yet it was action in remote locales that intellectuals craved rather than in places that were local, familiar, and, in their eyes, banal. The parallel with contemporary events could not be more apparent: too often, advocates of military intervention abroad seek support by shedding crocodile tears over the pain of Iraqis and Afghans while ignoring the travails of those living in Camden and Detroit. Bourne's critique reminds us that we have been here before.

In the prowar rhetoric of his time, as of ours, unthinking activism translated into a pseudo-realism. "The pacifist is roundly scolded for refusing to face the facts, and retiring into his own world of sentimental desire," Bourne wrote. "But is the realist, who refuses to challenge or criticize facts, entitled to any more credit than that which comes from following the line of least resistance?" For intellectuals seeking to be "relevant," realism became a rationale for acquiescing in the plans of the powerful. "If we responsibly approve," the argument went, "we then retain our power for guiding. We will be listened to as responsible thinkers, while those who obstructed the coming of war have committed intellectual suicide and shall be cast into outer darkness."[20] Bourne anticipated the pattern of foreign policy debate down to our own time—a time when those who advocated the invasion of Iraq (however mistakenly) preserve their status as "responsible thinkers," while those who opposed the war (however presciently) remain in "outer darkness." *Plus ça change, plus c'est la même chose.*

What especially distressed Bourne was the failure of Dewey's version of pragmatism to provide any basis for a critical perspective on the war. "If William James were alive would he be accepting the war-situation so easily and completely?" Bourne wondered. Dewey had turned his philosophy into little more than a rationale for adjustment to the logic of events. As Bourne saw it, Dewey did not grasp "the sinister forces of war," its power to unleash fanatic intolerance; his mentor's belief in the pragmatist's power to control war, to mold it to his own liberal ends, overlooked "the mob-fanaticisms, the injustices and hatreds" that inevitably accompanied the mass mobilization of "the war-technique." War ended pragmatic hopes for intellectual progress through open-minded experiment. No "passion for growth, for creative mastery," Bourne argued, could "flourish among the host of militaristic values and new tastes for power that are springing up like poisonous mushrooms on every hand." Deweyan pragmatism was a philosophy for the schoolroom, not the high-stakes arena of wartime debate.[21]

Dewey himself was a decent man with humane aspirations, but his followers had taken his instrumentalist attitude toward life too literally: they had "no clear philosophy of life except intelligent service, the admirable adaptation of means to ends." To Bourne, who had embraced Dewey's pragmatism as a revitalizing moral force, "it never occurred that values could be subordinated to technique." But that is what the prowar pragmatists—including Dewey himself—had done. Transcending the "war-technique" required a return to the restless spirit of William James. As Bourne concluded:

> Malcontentedness may be the beginning of promise. That is why I evoked the spirit of William James, with its gay passion for ideas, and its freedom of speculation, when I felt the slightly pedestrian

gait into which the war had brought pragmatism. It is the creative
desire more than the creative intelligence that we shall need if we
are ever to fly.[22]

This was a pragmatic critique of pragmatism, as the historian Robert Westbrook has observed.[23] Bourne evaluated the consequences of interventionist beliefs and found them wanting. Dewey and other liberal interventionists expected American entry into the war to create opportunities for implementing progressive agendas: regulation of business in the public interest at home and a League of Nations to promote peace and democracy throughout the world. Bourne challenged these benign expectations, arguing that American participation in the war would unleash intolerance at home and—by assisting the triumph of the Allies—perpetuate imperial hierarchies and nationalist rivalries abroad. He was right on all counts. War was unmanageable and unavoidably brutal. Its inherent chaos resisted predictable outcomes. To adjust uncritically to its reality, to accept its inevitability, Bourne argued, was to jeopardize any hope of transcending the hatreds it aroused.

Bourne lost the argument. His vision of pragmatic realism acquired legitimacy only after he died, in the flu epidemic of 1918—and after the failure of Wilson's crusade had become apparent. In the run-up to American intervention, as Bourne observed, young men like himself—men who considered themselves pragmatic realists—could scarcely contain their enthusiasm for the possibilities that war created—career possibilities not least of all. Foremost among them was Walter Lippmann, whose foreign policy outlook combined with Reinhold Niebuhr's to redefine pragmatic realism in the decades after World War I. By the outbreak of World War II, it had become policy intellectuals' dominant rationale for military intervention.

Interventionist Realism: Lippmann and Niebuhr between the Wars

As early as the 1910s, imperial rhetoric shifted from the moralistic bluster of Theodore Roosevelt and his ilk to the lower-keyed idiom spoken by young men seeking influence with the Wilson administration. Lippmann was a key figure in that group, though he was not a Democratic Party loyalist. Indeed, at age eight, he was already thrilling to the performances of TR, who had stopped by Saratoga Springs (where the Lippmanns were summering) during the campaign of 1904. Lippmann never got over the excitement evoked by the Rough Rider's energy. He studied at Harvard with William James, a man devoted to a strenuous life that was subtler than Roosevelt's but just as dedicated to the pursuit of vitality.[24]

From these sources, as well as the more diffuse atmosphere of upper-class male revitalization in the early twentieth century, Lippmann developed an early preoccupation with personal energy as the key to private and public success. Whether the energy in question was psychic or physical, Lippmann was obsessed with harnessing it to his own ambitions. Like TR, he kept up a regime of weight lifting throughout his life, and until his views matured, he believed that doing something was nearly always better than doing nothing. But after the catastrophe of World War I, he was never as certain as TR that activism necessarily implied the use of armed force.

Soon after his graduation, Lippmann joined Walter Weyl and Herbert Croly in founding *The New Republic*. All three were young men fired by a fascination with action, especially as the United States drifted toward entry into World War I. After the declaration of war, Lippmann was filled with patriotic ardor and desire for engagement. Ardor did not translate into a desire to serve in the trenches, however. "What I want to do is to devote all my time to studying and speculating on the approaches to peace," he wrote to Secretary of War Newton Baker. "Do you think you can get me an exemption on such highfalutin grounds?" Lippmann's attitude fit a familiar twentieth-century pattern: war intellectuals prefer to hatch their grandiose dreams far from the scene of battle. In fact, Baker did get Lippmann an exemption on "highfalutin grounds." The young intellectual, barely out of college, secured a job with The Inquiry, Woodrow Wilson's forerunner to the National Security Council.[25]

Lippmann and the other interventionists spoke a language pruned of hypermasculine excess, rhetorically pragmatic and tough-minded

but as wedded to lofty purpose as ever. Like Dewey, a frequent contributor to the magazine, the editors of *The New Republic* urged pragmatic adjustment to the realities of U.S. intervention as a way to ac-
complish Wilson's larger, noble goal: the remaking of the entire world
on the U.S. model. The pattern of realistic rhetoric and unrealistic aims
continued to characterize arguments for military intervention for decades to come, down to our own time.

Soon after the armistice, the apologists for intervention found themselves eating their words. The Treaty of Versailles conspicuously failed
to embody Wilsonian ideals; Lippmann himself, bitterly disillusioned,
denounced it. Eventually he retreated to a tower office at the *New York
World,* from which he commented on the course of empire in the
1920s. "We continue to think of ourselves, as a kind of great, peace-
able Switzerland, whereas we are in fact a great, expanding world
power," he complained in 1926. "Our imperialism is more or less un-
conscious."[26] This was a common complaint among the interventionists of Lippmann's generation. From their view, the United States was
a big-hearted kid who didn't yet know his own strength and couldn't
see through the stratagems of his crafty European elders. The boy-
nation needed to lose his innocence and face up to his global responsibilities. In fact, of course, the big kid was far from innocent—he just
protested his innocence more loudly than the Europeans, while stick-
ing his fingers in every pie from Port-au-Prince to Peking.

Meanwhile, down on the street, disillusionment with great crusades ran rampant. Among the educated classes, pacifism became a
respectable intellectual position, especially in liberal Protestant churches.
The crash of 1929 and the coming of the Great Depression turned
churches to the left on social issues, even as they clung to ideals of
nonviolence. Reinhold Niebuhr, a German Evangelical pastor in Detroit, before joining the faculty of the Union Theological Seminary in
1928, found himself increasingly frustrated by what he saw as the
sentimental evasions of his fellow Christians. They wanted social justice but seemed afraid to fight for it, falling back instead into the familiar rhetoric of individual morality. Pacifism, he decided, sometimes posed an obstacle in the struggle for class equality. Eager to

press religion into the service of social action, Niebuhr struggled to combine his Christian belief with his growing attraction to Marxian socialism. Capitalism was in collapse and the Soviet alternative had not yet descended into Stalinist terror. Niebuhr believed that social conflict, between classes and between nations, was inevitable, given man's fallen state and the capitalist drive to maximize surplus value. Niebuhr's Augustinian Christianity, his sense of inherent human imperfection (call it original sin), led him to distrust all utopian schemes that disavowed the use of force. So did his Marxism.

This was the outlook that animated *Moral Man and Immoral Society* (1932). The book's title expressed its thesis. As Niebuhr wrote,

> the nation is a corporate entity, held together much more by force and emotion, than by mind. Since there can be no ethical action without self criticism, and no self criticism without the rational capacity of self-transcendence, it is natural that national attitudes can hardly approximate the ethical.

Nations will always be vain, proud, complacent, and hypocritical— they cannot be held to the same standards as individuals. The elimination of violence between nations or social groups was therefore a futile goal. Violence, moreover, was not inherently unethical, if deployed in the service of "equal justice," which was, according to Niebuhr,

> the most rational ultimate aim for society.... A societal conflict which aims at greater equality has a moral justification which must be denied to efforts which aim at the perpetuation of privilege. A war for the emancipation of a nation, a race or a class is thus placed in a different moral category from the use of power for imperial rule or class dominance.[27]

By this point in the book the strains in Niebuhr's argument were beginning to show. He had already devoted several scathing pages to the hypocrisy of the Spanish-American War, dismissing its advocates' claims of benign intent. If nations were always hypocritical, would they not invariably cloak sordid aims in professions of righteousness? There was another problem as well: Niebuhr did not acknowledge that militarists as well as pacifists could confuse national interest with individual morality. Both made the same category mistake, but with opposite consequences: if pacifists wanted the nation to embrace the moral courage of the believer, militarists wanted it to embrace the physical courage of the fighter. Given Niebuhr's desire to distinguish between "moral man and immoral society," he could have questioned the personification of the nation—as tough or soft, heroic or cowardly—that pervaded militarist rhetoric since the days of Theodore Roosevelt. But he was more eager to demystify pacifism than to challenge militarism.

During the 1930s and early 1940s, Niebuhr gradually turned away from Marxism while his version of Christianity provided a bracing counterpoint to the reigning tenets of liberal theology. The key elements of his critique were his resurrection of original sin, his recognition that unresolved conflict was at the heart of human existence, and, above all, his celebration of what he called "the spiritual discipline against resentment." This was the ability to discriminate between the evils of a social system and the individuals involved in it, to recognize that "the evil in the foe is also in the self"—for Martin Luther King, decades later, this became the core of Niebuhr's message.[28] Niebuhr remains a towering figure in American religious history. His role in foreign policy history, though, was a bit more problematic. In that realm, he often failed to recognize that the evil in the foe is also in the self—easy enough to do in the 1930s and 1940s.

For a long time, historians assigned Niebuhr a central role in a story they liked to tell about the middle third of the twentieth century: a small band of liberal realists saves the country from pacifists and isolationists in the 1930s and from hysterical cold warriors in the 1940s and 1950s. Steering a sober middle course, they provide a pragmatic, empirical alternative to hazy abstractions and ideologies on both the Left and the Right. This centrist fairy tale contains some truth but leaves much out, discounting the grounded, pragmatic critique of imperialism inherent in the isolationist position and failing to recognize how easily interventionist realism could legitimate an imperial ethos.

Isolationism and the Chastening of Realism

Judged guilty by association with the anti-Semites and crypto-fascists who had no problem with Hitler, Americans who opposed intervention in World War II have not fared well historically. In fact, however, the polemical label "isolationist" covered a wide variety of perspectives, many of them thoughtful and reminiscent of Jamesian habits of mind. Senator Robert Taft of Ohio, for one, presented what amounted to a pluralist critique of the American Century. Luce and his interventionist allies, Taft wrote, "seem to contemplate an Anglo-American alliance perpetually ruling the word. Frankly, the American people don't want to rule the world, and we are not equipped to do it. Such imperialism is wholly foreign to our ideals of democracy and freedom. . . . We may think we are better than other peoples, more equipped to rule, but will they think so?" These were republican ideals, rooted in realistic suspicions of power—of executive tyranny, secrecy, and deceit.[29]

There was ample justification for such suspicions by the fall of 1941, when Franklin Roosevelt claimed that German U-boats torpedoed the USS *Kearny* without provocation. Even as Roosevelt railed against German aggression, Taft remained skeptical: FDR, he said, was seeking excuses "to prowl the ocean in quest of offensive warfare." In fact (as historians have since demonstrated), Taft had reason to be wary: the destroyer *Kearny* was convoying British merchant ships and had already dropped depth charges on the German U-boats.[30] The *Kearny* incident eerily anticipated the Gulf of Tonkin affair: a president intent on going to war fabricates a phony event to justify it, then gets away with the lie. The war against Hitler was far more justifiable than the war against Ho Chi Minh, but the deceit was equally deliberate in both cases. Concealing or excusing such chicanery makes a mockery of democracy.

Charles Beard, perhaps the preeminent historian of his time, was one of those who exposed FDR's deceit—and in the process sentenced himself to permanent professional exile. In fact, Beard's work offers a fine example of the grounded, pragmatic critique of empire. Beard believed in honesty to the evidence, and he deployed it against imperial bombast with devastating results. His skeptical portraits of TR and Alfred Thayer Mahan are among the most incisive ever penned, as he punctured the flatulent pieties of their arguments for expansion. Of Mahan's insistence that the nation must expand or die, advancing its claims by violence if necessary, Beard wrote: "Perhaps in the whole history of the country there had never been a more cold-blooded resolve to 'put over on the people' such a 'grand' policy, in spite of their recalcitrance, ignorance and provincialism." Beard saw FDR as the legitimate heir of TR and Mahan. The later Roosevelt shared his predecessors' disdain for popular mistrust of foreign wars, and he resurrected their interventionist policies—distracting public attention from domestic problems by engaging in foreign quarrels, sustaining imperial rivalries in Asia, and seeking surreptitiously (as in the *Kearny* incident) to enter war in Europe.[31]

Beard's alternative to interventionism was "Continental Americanism"—resistance to foreign intrusions over here, avoidance of foreign entanglements over there. One could object to this formulation with respect to specific circumstances or propose foreign commitments less entangling than war. Although Roosevelt seemingly took the latter course with Lend-Lease aid to Great Britain, he and other interventionists remained eager for military engagement as well. This proved harder to justify on empirical grounds. The overarching interventionist arguments floated in the rarefied atmosphere of Luce's American Century, deploying the vaporous teleology of empire. The United States, interventionists argued, must take up the "burden of world leadership" whether it wanted to or not; modern transportation and communication technology had created one world, leaving Americans with no realistic alternative. Anything less than a full embrace of "global leadership" signified a retreat into the false comforts of isolation. In fact, Beard's "Continental Americanism" was far more empirically grounded and pragmatically flexible than the dualisms and determinisms of the interventionists. It had the added advantage of being rooted in the republican tradition, with its suspicions of imperial power at home and abroad.[32]

Beard foresaw the continuity of interventionist foreign policy from World War II through the Cold War, especially the continuing globalization of national interest. By 1947, when Harry Truman announced what became known as the Truman Doctrine, the refusal to accept limits had become clear. Transforming an internal Greek conflict between Left and Right into a Manichean struggle between freedom and slavery, Truman asserted an open-ended commitment "to support free peoples who are resisting subjugation by armed minorities or outside pressures."

Beard was struck by Truman's political motives, his determination to appear tougher than the rabid Republicans who were calling for a "rollback" of communism in Eastern Europe. "The Democrats are playing the old game of crisis," Beard said, "and trying to wring one more victory out of the bloody shirt!" It formed part of their larger agenda: "perpetual war for perpetual peace." The domestic consequences were clear, Beard thought: the United States would become an "armed camp for defense," with "a conscript army, multiplied annual outlays for armaments, a huge national debt and grinding taxes," and "cessation of beneficial reforms at home." Apart from the disappearance of the draft, one could hardly ask for a more accurate prediction of our contemporary plight. Here was an example of ostensibly naïve isolationists proving to be more realistic than the self-described "tough-minded realists."[33]

Yet some "tough-minded realists," at least, did reveal a capacity for growth, as the subsequent careers of Niebuhr, Lippmann, George Kennan, and William Fulbright demonstrate. This flexibility, this willingness to change their minds, stemmed from their preference—however fitful or belated—for grounded argument over theoretical models and abstract principles. Whether consciously or not, they were returning to the pragmatic realism of James and Bourne.

Niebuhr was "a radical empiricist if ever there was one," the *Christian Century* observed in 1944, an outlook evident in Niebuhr's willingness to take all sorts of experience seriously as sources of knowledge, even knowledge not scientifically verifiable. He was likewise a Jamesian pragmatist in his concern for the consequences of beliefs in the conduct of everyday life. When combined with his awareness of evil, Niebuhr's pragmatism promoted his sensitivity to Nazi horror. In May 1941, arguing the urgency of military intervention, he reported that a German publisher had offered a friend of his a book contract, which contained a clause stating that no Jew shall have anything to do with the book's manufacture or publication. That is "the kind of world we will have to live in," Niebuhr said, if the United States failed to stop Hitler. This was a rare instance when interventionism and imperialism were separable. The Jamesian tradition might be anti-imperial but not necessarily anti-interventionist—if the interventionist argument was grounded in a convincing assessment of consequences.[34]

The problem, of course, was that consequences were ambiguous, difficult to forecast, and subject to shifts in historical circumstance. The debate over intervention ended on December 7, 1941, with the Japanese attack on Pearl Harbor and Hitler's declaration of war on the United States two days later. But in May 1941 the events that thrust Americans into simultaneous wars against both Germany and Japan were not self-evidently waiting just over the horizon. The future was shrouded in uncertainty. Much the same can be said regarding the fate that awaited European Jews. Even if American policy makers had shared Niebuhr's sensitivity to their plight, it was by no means clear in the spring of 1941 that immediate U.S. military action offered the best way to protect them from extermination. Not even Niebuhr suspected the enormity of the Holocaust to come. Furthermore, the course of events in the spring of 1941 was actually reducing the urgency of U.S. intervention. In May Great Britain stood "alone" against the Nazis; within a month Hitler's invasion of the Soviet Union had transformed the war and raised the possibility that the two tyrannies might fight to a stalemate. Meanwhile nonmilitary aid was working: thanks in part to Lend-Lease, the British had withstood Nazi bombings and Hitler had apparently shelved any plans for a cross-Channel invasion. As always, the only sure consequence of the military action proposed by interventionists like Luce was mass violence, afflicting just and unjust alike.

For all his subtlety, Niebuhr contributed to the dualistic assumption that only two choices existed: military intervention or pacifist isolation. *Moral Man and Immoral Society* had issued a blank check for violence in the name of "equal justice"—a check underwritten by Niebuhr's own apocalyptic expectations from 1933 on. With the rise of fascism, he believed the world was hurtling toward Armageddon.

Niebuhr's dark, messianic vision was linked to his own restless personal style: "He was afraid of keeping still," writes Richard Fox, his biographer, "pondering endlessly; he thought he would dry up, lose the vitality that he never ceased to claim as the crucial human attribute." Like the young Lippmann and other realist intellectuals, Niebuhr believed that doing something—and usually something military—was always better than doing nothing. (His brother, the theologian Richard Niebuhr, had meanwhile championed "the grace of doing nothing" in the face of Japanese aggression in Manchuria.) Still, Niebuhr criticized Luce's "American Century" for proposing a "new white man's burden." Luce did not know, Niebuhr observed, that "our salvation must be worked out in fear and trembling." He urged Americans to recognize that their own pretensions of virtue threatened the United States as much as did the evil actions of others.[35]

The question remains: How exactly should a Niebuhrian awareness of America's own capacity for evil affect the conduct of foreign policy? On this score, Niebuhr himself appeared ambivalent. Although he signed a Federal Council of Churches protest against the dropping of atomic bombs on Hiroshima and Nagasaki, he privately regretted doing so. James Conant—president of Harvard, a member of the National Defense Research Committee, and a key promoter of the Manhattan Project—complained to Niebuhr about his protest. The theologian apologized, saying the bombs were a quintessential example of "how much evil we must do in order to do good."[36] This troubling formulation justified the unbridled use of military power in the name of "doing good." In addition, it tacitly endorsed the Allied demand for unconditional surrender, which seemingly reduced the choices available to President Truman in the summer of 1945 to two: either using the bomb or launching a full-scale invasion of mainland Japan. Interventionist realism, selectively applied, allowed certain absolutist assumptions to remain unchallenged.

During the postwar years, as during the 1930s, Niebuhr sometimes allowed his horror of evil abroad to engulf his belief that "the evil in the foe is also in the self." Throughout the early Cold War, he was haunted by a monochromatic vision of communism—"faceless men who are immune to every form of moral and political suasion." He was not alone in this fear, which gripped liberals as well as reactionaries. Like Arthur Schlesinger Jr. and other interventionists, Niebuhr allowed anti-Communist paranoia to undermine his restraint. In 1946 he equated Stalin with Hitler—both bent on world domination, and both employing brute force to extract concessions intended to pave their path to ultimate power. He came to believe, as Fox writes, that "the way to avoid war was not to fear it too much." Luce, his former bête noire, loved this sort of mystification and published it in *Life* under the title "A distinguished theologian declares America must prevent the conquest of Germany and Western Europe by unscrupulous Soviet tyranny." Embarrassed, Niebuhr backpedaled, saying that the United States must leave Eastern Europe to the Soviet Union on the grounds that the Soviets had historical reasons for wanting a cordon sanitaire against invasion from the West.[37]

As the hysteria of the early 1950s subsided, Niebuhr's realist tendencies reasserted themselves. In 1950 he had refused to rule out the possibility of "first use" of nuclear weapons against the Soviet tanks that U.S. policy makers imagined were poised to invade Western Europe; in 1961 he wrote: "The first use of nuclear weapons is morally abhorrent and must be resisted." He opposed the hard line against Cuba taken by both Eisenhower and Kennedy, the economic embargo as well as the Bay of Pigs invasion. In general he increasingly emphasized what Fox calls "the futility of military responses, the inanity of American ideology, the primacy of economic aid" in creating alternatives to Soviet domination. By 1965 he was a sharp critic of the Vietnam War.[38]

In contrast, Lippmann's growth toward a mature anti-imperial stance was more straightforward than Niebuhr's, albeit with some initial zigs and zags. After flirting with "effective pacifism" (based on military strength) in the early 1930s, he called for regenerative war in June 1940, hoping it would transform American "soft vices" into "stern virtues."[39] Traces of Rooseveltian masculinity still lingered in his thought. He endorsed FDR's economic sanctions against Japan in the summer of 1941, knowing that demands for an Open Door in Asia would exacerbate imperial rivalries in the region. A pragmatic realist might have seen the double standard involved in pressing for an Open

Door in Asia while demanding respect for the Monroe Doctrine in the Western Hemisphere; Lippmann did not. But he was more consistent in *United States Foreign Policy: Shield of the Republic* (1943). This was Lippmann's attempt to steer between sentimental one-worldism, missionary imperialism, and Fortress America. Keep the wartime alliance of Great Britain, the United States, and the Soviet Union alive after the war was over, he argued, and ensure that the Atlantic highway stays open. On the idea of reviving a "world society" like the League of Nations, Lippmann wrote: "The construction of the world society should not be based on the idea that everything is everybody's business. We must not write into the construction of the world society a license to universal intervention. For if we license it, we shall invite it. And if we invite it, we shall get it." Lippmann rejected open-ended ideological aims—the promotion of freedom and democracy, for example—and recoiled from the use of force to promote them. It was an insult to soldiers, he wrote, to measure their accomplishments by how well they achieved "some abstract principle from the Atlantic Charter." These outbursts were harbingers of a more chastened perspective, which served to sharpen Lippmann's critique of foreign policy throughout the Cold War. With the passage of time came an ever-growing tendency to counsel restraint.[40]

The Return of Pragmatic Realism

Through the 1950s and early 1960s Lippmann refurbished and revived the pragmatic realism of James and Bourne. He criticized the militarization of George Kennan's containment policy toward the Soviet Union as a recipe for overextension and dependence on client states and assailed the creation of the North Atlantic Treaty Organization as a carte blanche commitment to fight other nations' wars without congressional approval. In the early days of the Cuban Missile Crisis, he asked: Why a public ultimatum rather than private diplomacy? And why not swap U.S. missiles in Turkey for Russian missiles in Cuba? And, like Niebuhr, Lippmann was especially probing and prescient with respect to the growing American involvement in Vietnam.

George Kennan, Lippmann's contemporary, revealed a comparable journey toward pragmatic realism. Kennan began as a militant Cold Warrior, in the guise of a realist. In 1947 he made his career and much of his subsequent reputation with the publication of a single essay "The Sources of Soviet Conduct." Yet what impresses anyone reading his essay today is not its carefully reasoned argument but its shrill tone. Like Niebuhr and Schlesinger, Kennan at this stage repeatedly emphasized the implacable fanaticism bred by Communist ideology, especially its commitment to inevitable triumph over capitalism. Do not be misled by conciliatory gestures, he warned his readers. "Basically the antagonism remains. It is postulated." Ideological postulates rather than facts on the ground dictated "a firm policy of containment, designed to confront the Russians with unalterable counterforce at every point where they show signs of encroaching upon the limits of a peaceful and stable world." Concluding with a flourish, Kennan expressed "a certain gratitude to a Providence which, by providing the American people with this implacable challenge, has made their entire security as a nation dependent on their pulling themselves together and accepting the responsibility of moral and political leadership that history plainly intended them to bear." Neither Luce nor any other exponent of upper-class male moralism in the American Century could have said it better.[41]

Kennan came to regret the doctrine that he conceived. As Lippmann predicted, containment did become a prescription for overextended global commitments and rickety alliances with dictators. Kennan insisted he had never advocated military containment, only political containment. Still, the militarization of U.S. policy under the rubric of containment proceeded apace. The Truman Doctrine gave an inkling of what was to come. In retrospect, Kennan attributed the tendency to trace all leftist insurgencies to a Soviet source to

a curious American tendency to search, at all times, for a single external center of evil, to which all American troubles can be attributed, rather than to recognize that there might be multiple sources of resistance to our purposes and undertakings, and that these sources might be relatively independent of each other.[42]

The words recall the pluralism of James and Bourne; they also re-verberate down to our own time, presaging the ideological blinders of the "war on terror" with its "axis of evil" and elevation of Osama bin Laden and Saddam Hussein to the status of Adolf Hitler.

Recoiling against Manichaean dualism, Kennan became a prophet of discriminating restraint. To "bear in mind the limits of our national capabilities," he said, was not to succumb to isolation but to practice calculated reserve.[43] Like other pragmatic realists, he tended to see U.S. foreign policy as a product of overweening pride and perverse idealism. Like them (and unlike Beard or the historian William Appleman Williams, who began to challenge the Cold War consensus in the late 1950s), Kennan overlooked the role of economic interests—above all, the continuing search by capital for foreign markets, re-sources, and investment opportunities. This was a major flaw in Kennan's thinking, arising partly from his pronounced Eurocentrism. It was easier to talk about idealistic overreaching if one averted one's eyes from Latin America or the Persian Gulf, where imperial interests most clearly dictated U.S. policy.

But Kennan's emphasis on *discrimination,* especially with respect to weapons, made him a powerful critic of the nuclear arms race and of relying on nuclear weapons as an instrument of foreign policy. Here was the portfolio Kennan claimed in the twilight of his career. He understood that the language of nuclear policy was the opposite of republican plain speech: quantitative, denatured technobabble, al-together detached from the actual experience of war. The reliance on nuclear weapons offered a perfect expression, Kennan thought, of the absolutist tendency to embrace wars of annihilation and doctrines of unconditional surrender. Like James, he recognized the menace of the absolute.

Though he did not share Niebuhr's belief in original sin, Kennan did acknowledge the tragic limitations on all human striving. Man, he wrote in his last book, *Around the Cragged Hill* (1993), was a "cracked vessel," whose imperfections would always curtail and confound his aspirations. So the mature Kennan rejected "all messianic concepts of America's role in the world . . . [all] prattle about Manifest Destiny and the American Century." The teleology of empire was unsupported by evidence: "I know of no reason to suppose," Kennan wrote, "that 'democracy' along western European or American lines is necessarily, or even probably, the ultimate fate of all humanity." He noted the im-probability of achieving noble ends by employing ignoble means. He questioned open-ended commitments to vague abstractions like "human rights." He distrusted the ideology of progress, which sanc-tions all sorts of mischief in the name of human betterment. Unlike Barry Goldwater or Ronald Reagan, he could genuinely claim allegiance to conservative tradition.[44]

Kennan deplored the secrecy and deceit of the national security state, regretfully acknowledging his own role in creating those poli-cies. He knew all too well (as he said) that "there is, as Reinhold Niebuhr so brilliantly and persuasively argued, no power, individual or collec-tive, without some associated guilt."[45] By the time he wrote those words, in his nineties, George Kennan had moved a long way from the providentialist assumptions of his younger days. Yet secular provi-dentialism remains a keystone of the American civil religion. Its cor-ollary assumption is that (contrary to Niebuhr) power and virtue are twinned.

This hubris animated the overreaching of the Cold War, which collapsed in the catastrophe of the American counterinsurgency in Vietnam. The enormity of U.S. failure in Southeast Asia encouraged a revival of grounded alternatives. In the 1960s William Appleman Williams's books became required reading on college campuses, and his PhD students produced a historically informed critique of Ameri-can empire. George McGovern's ill-fated campaign theme of 1972— "Come Home, America"—captured the core of the anti-interventionist critique, even as the election's outcome demonstrated how difficult it was for that critique to win legitimacy. But what really got a boost from the war was pragmatic realism, articulated most forcefully by Lippmann and Fulbright.

U.S. involvement in Southeast Asia provided Lippmann with the opportunity for a brilliant final act to an illustrious career. The Com-munist uprising in Vietnam, he argued, was an anticolonial insurgency, far from our legitimate sphere of influence. He disdained the accusa-tions of "appeasement" against those reluctant to commit troops to

Cuba, Laos, or Vietnam. As early as 1961, he warned that war was too serious a business for talk of masculine regeneration through bloodshed. Lippmann had learned a lot since his days as a young war intellectual. The notion that we should "shed a little blood to prove we're virile men" was utter nonsense. "I don't think old men ought to promote wars for young men to fight," he said, in words that retain their resonance to the present day.[46]

The Vietnam War was part of an overreaching pattern, Lippmann charged, that had characterized U.S. foreign policy since World War II. A realistic appreciation of limits implied an obligation to pull back from overextended commitments. "If it is said that this is isolationism," Lippmann wrote in 1964, "I would say yes. It is isolationism if the limitation of our power is isolationism. It is isolationism as compared to the globalism which became fashionable after the Second World War." Embracing the epithet that had been used against anti-interventionists for decades, Lippmann ended his career by asserting a pragmatic, grounded realism that he was not ashamed to call "neo-isolationism" when critics raised that charge. "Neo-isolationism is the direct product of foolish globalism," he said in a 1971 interview. "Compared to people who thought they could run the universe, or at least the globe, I *am* a neo-isolationist and proud of it." Seldom has a respected American intellectual revealed a greater willingness to touch the third rail of foreign policy discourse.[47]

As the Vietnam War unfolded, any realist worth the name had to challenge the hubris at the heart of the enterprise. This William Fulbright did in *The Arrogance of Power* (1966). "America is the most fortunate of nations," he wrote, implying that our preeminent position in the world was a product of luck rather than divine will. Yet America was losing its perspective on what was within its capability to control and what lay beyond it. Providential ideas reinforced illusions of omnipotence and infallibility. As Fulbright observed, in words that should be embossed in gold over the door to the Oval Office, "power tends to confuse itself with virtue and a great nation is peculiarly susceptible to the idea that its power is a sign of God's favor, conferring upon it a special responsibility for other nations, to make them richer and happier and wiser, to remake them, that is, in its own shining image."[48]

Fulbright knew that this God-intoxicated mentality had been a staple of colonialism for centuries, its American version justifying overseas intervention since at least the Spanish-American War. He detested the bullying sanctimony of this tradition and found alternatives to it in the American past.

There were, he believed, two main American traditions of thinking about the national destiny, derived from two fundamentally different sensibilities. The tradition of arrogance was embodied in the Roosevelt Corollary to the Monroe Doctrine, which anointed the United States the moral policeman of the Western Hemisphere. The other, more humane tradition animated Lincoln's second inaugural address, which magnanimously interpreted the Civil War as a national expiation for the sin of slavery rather than a triumph of Northern virtue over Southern perfidy. In Fulbright's view the architects of American foreign policy in the 1960s clung stubbornly to the self-righteous tradition of the Roosevelt Corollary; they badly needed to reconnect with the more generous and self-critical approach personified by Lincoln. Virtue unleashed was at best an annoyance, at worst a holy terror. "I am not prepared to argue that mankind is suffering from an excess of virtue but I think the world has endured all it can of the crusades of high-minded men bent on the regeneration of the human race," Fulbright said. For starters, not everyone shared the same notion of regeneration: American emissaries of virtue all too often found themselves in the position of the Boy Scouts who, when asked by their scoutmaster why it took three of them to help an old lady across the street, explained that "she didn't want to go."[49]

Instead of this intrusive moralism, Fulbright proposed what he identified as a "*conservative* policy" inspired by Burke, Castlereagh, and Metternich: "They believed in the preservation of indissoluble links between the past and the future, because they profoundly mistrusted abstract ideas, and because they did not think themselves or any other men qualified to play God." Fulbright shared the European conservatives' historicism—which was not a simpleminded belief that one could extract discrete "lessons" from history but a recognition that the power of the past pressed inescapably into the future, shaping policy decisions in ways that messianic utopians could only dimly understand. A sober appreciation for history tempered grandiose delusions.[50]

Like his predecessors in the foreign policy debate, Fulbright equated great nations with great individuals. Both, he insisted, acknowledged their own fallibility. They adjusted pragmatically to the discovery that certain strategies were not working; they took criticism seriously, and if they found it persuasive, they changed course. This became a crucial issue for Fulbright as he watched the American presence increase in Vietnam and heard critics of the war accused of giving "aid and comfort to the enemies of the United States." On the contrary, wrote Fulbright, criticism was "an act of patriotism."[51] Refusal to acquiesce in mistaken military adventures was neither a failure to "support our troops" nor a symptom of national weakness. It was a sign of national maturity—a recognition that our own powers were not limitless, and that the aspirations of other nations demanded serious consideration, even if they challenged our own.

This pluralist outlook underwrote magnanimity toward others' claims. For Fulbright, magnanimity was the key criterion of genuine national greatness. He summoned Lippmann, Kennan, Winston Churchill, and Charles de Gaulle to testify that great power was often most effectively exercised through renunciation rather than assertion. And perhaps the most effective renunciation was the open acknowledgment of error. As Kennan, another early critic of the Vietnam War, testified at Fulbright's Senate hearings on the war in 1966, "there is more respect to be won . . . by a resolute and courageous liquidation of unsound positions than in the most stubborn pursuit of extravagant or unsound objectives."[52] Fulbright joined Kennan in arguing that the possession of vast power demanded the cultivation of unprecedented restraint.

Fulbright's views acquired momentary legitimacy, largely through the press of circumstance. By 1968, when polls indicated that a (bare) majority of Americans had turned against the war, more than a few wondered how U.S. involvement had come about. The idea that the United States had been mistakenly fighting indigenous nationalism (which happened to be Communist) provided a powerful explanation for the failure of the interventionist enterprise in Vietnam. It also had the merit of being true. In universities, in the mainstream press, and even in some of the corridors of government power, Fulbright became celebrated as a seer. His skeptical outlook spread during the early 1970s as revelations of government mendacity multiplied and provoked a broader reevaluation of imperial hubris. Eventually the waste of life in Vietnam led many Americans of all ages and social backgrounds, even many members of Congress, to question the equation of power and virtue that had sustained a foreign policy of global intervention since World War II.

But that sort of self-questioning did not survive for long. Almost as soon as the last helicopter left the roof of the American embassy in Saigon, the American Right began to construct a revanchist narrative of American defeat. Like the tale concocted by German rightists in 1919, this was a story of a stab in the back. According to this fantastic account, the war effort foundered not on the battlefield but on the home front, undermined by the antiwar movement and the "liberal media." A lack of "political will" had deprived U.S. troops of victory they had all but won, producing instead ignominious and utterly unnecessary defeat. Fainthearted liberals had fatally undermined what Ronald Reagan retrospectively labeled a "noble cause."[53]

During the 1980s, a resurgent American Right revived Cold War anxieties at every opportunity. Characterizing the Soviet Union as an "evil empire" bent on world domination, Reagan sponsored rightwing insurgents' efforts to overthrow the democratically elected Sandinista government of Nicaragua, the Sandinistas portrayed as agents of world communism. Mercenary "death squads" dedicated to political assassinations, illegal funding for "Contra" fighters channeled from secret arms sales to Iran—nothing was out of bounds in the war against the evil empire. Jeane Kirkpatrick and her colleagues in the Committee on the Present Danger did their best to sustain the myth of the Soviet menace, inventing evidence of an arms buildup when government intelligence reports failed to satisfy their ideological needs. Popular culture, in movies such as *Rambo* and *Top Gun*, promoted the fantasies of revived masculinity that underwrote a resurgence of militarism. Despite the questions raised by the U.S. failure in Vietnam (or perhaps due to the threat those questions posed to entrenched power), the rationale for military intervention was quickly rebuilt. When the Soviet Union collapsed and the Cold War ended, militarist impulses required a new target. Saddam Hussein soon supplied one by invading Kuwait. The American military response was swift and spectacularly successful but ultimately disappointing to the hard Right— especially Republican Party operatives and policy intellectuals who took to calling themselves neoconservatives and (a smaller group) Vulcans. They had hoped to capitalize on the U.S. victory by marching on Baghdad and deposing Saddam Hussein. Frustrated by the quick withdrawal of U.S. ground forces, they seethed and plotted, agitating for new opportunities to invade Iraq and unseat Saddam Hussein.[54]

Vietnam haunted and obsessed the Vulcans. Led by Dick Cheney and Donald Rumsfeld, former Nixon and Ford administration officials who had endured the humiliating spectacle of the last Americans leaving Saigon, they made common cause with William Kristol, Robert Kagan, and other ideologues associated with the aptly named Project for a New American Century. The members of this motley group differed in their definition of the American Century, but all saw "regime change" in Iraq as essential to its revival. Overthrowing Saddam Hussein, they believed, would erase the memory of defeat in Vietnam by reasserting a brash muscularity in U.S. foreign policy. The yearning to revitalize national manhood returned to the foreign policy agenda—no longer as explicit as in the days of Theodore Roosevelt but still a powerful impetus for military intervention abroad.

The 9/11 attacks created the opportunity the Vulcans had been waiting for. With George W. Bush's declaration of a "global war on terror," policy intellectuals resurrected the Cold War narrative, justifying a new round of military intervention as a combination of self-defense and sanctified mission: imperialism as idealism. The very notion of an open-ended "war" against an enemy as abstract and elusive as "terror" displayed the militarist mentality at its most vacuous— with self-described realists now completely untethered from reality.

Yet once again, as during World War I, intellectuals, including self-proclaimed liberals, played an important supporting role in legitimating the militarist agenda. Less than a month after the attacks on the World Trade Center, the prominent journalist George Packer praised Americans—and fellow liberals in particular—for "recapturing the flag" and thereby refusing any longer to leave patriotism solely to working-class folk. On closer examination, however, what Packer called patriotism turned out to be something more akin to militarism. Although quick to deny that he was celebrating war, Packer left no doubt about its tonic effects. "I don't desire war," he wrote, "but I know that patriotic feeling makes individuals exceed themselves as the bland comforts of peace cannot. . . . I've lived through this state, and I like it." Like the activist intellectuals who preceded him, Packer allowed his desire for vitality to obscure the actual devastations of war. It was easy to prefer the excitement of war fever over "the bland comforts of peace" when seated comfortably at one's keyboard.[55]

As Bush's "war on terror" unfolded, political success required systematic lying about the present (Saddam's supposed possession of weapons of mass destruction; his alleged links to Al Quaeda) and about the past. Revisionist historians emerged, insisting that in Vietnam the counterinsurgency strategy had been poised to carry the day just when the nation lost its nerve. Apologists for Bush's wars warned that another failure to "support our troops" could signal a similar flagging of national resolve. The best way to show resolve, Bush said, was for citizens to give him a free hand to make war when and where he wished while they preoccupied themselves with shopping.[56]

This trivialization of war in the present combines with systematic forgetting of war in the past. Official definitions of patriotism forbid the remembrance of failure in Vietnam and forbid any acknowledgment that planning to remake an entire region through military force signifies a revival of deeply rooted American delusions. The itch to revive masculinity reappears as farce, in Bush's swaggering (and premature) claim: "Mission Accomplished." The architects of contemporary foreign policy remain trapped in messianic dreams of their predecessors, imprisoned by the same arrogance that trapped the United States in Vietnam forty years ago and expressing contempt for the respect for restraint that resurfaced ever so briefly during that war. The vision of an American Century persists, even as its economic basis crumbles.

Conclusion

How can Americans best challenge this destructive fantasy? Unfortunately any serious challenge will require more than mustering persuasive arguments. The impulse toward military intervention is deeply embedded in powerful institutions, perhaps even more deeply embedded today than it was during the Cold War. As William Pfaff has observed, since the Clinton years (and especially since 9/11) the Pentagon has vastly expanded its role and seized new territory, both bureaucratic and geographic. An expanded system of regional commands has created "U.S. military proconsuls" who act as political representatives of the United States in their areas of responsibility. As the State Department has receded in influence, men like David Petraeus have became more important than ambassadors, with foreign policy increasingly militarized. The global military base system has expanded as well, fueled by voracious private contractors and blank checks from the U.S. government. As Pfaff writes, "it is a system intended to deter war, but from the start, it has provided the means, the opportunity, and an incentive for U.S. military interventions in foreign countries." Any effort to create an alternative to military interventionism will have to come to terms with the formidable power of entrenched bureaucratic and commercial interests. It will also require some effort to spell out in concrete terms what an alternative, noninterventionist foreign policy would look like. Pfaff has taken us some distance toward that goal:

> Within its borders, the United States is invulnerable to conventional military defeat; that cannot be said of its forces deployed elsewhere. U.S. security is far more likely to be found in a noninterventionist foreign policy designed to produce a negotiated military withdrawal from both Afghanistan and Iraq, without leaving bases behind, and a general disengagement from military interference in the affairs of other societies, leaving them to search for their own solutions to their own problems. So drastic a reversal of U.S. policy will not be possible without heavy political costs, both domestic and foreign. Nevertheless, the time has come for U.S. policymakers to begin considering reversing course.[57]

Jettisoning illusions of an American Century will entail dramatic changes in how Americans think. One prerequisite will be to restore pragmatic realism to public debate. Yet doing so will not be without pitfalls, as the problematic history of pragmatic realism reveals. Just as citing "the national interest" can provide a basis for avoiding ideological crusades, that phrase itself can be—and has been—used to justify a multitude of misadventures. The covert subversion of democratically elected governments in Latin America and the carpet bombing of North Vietnam by an ostensibly hardheaded exponent of realism such as Henry Kissinger offer just two examples. A definition of national interest informed by pragmatic realism requires a sense of proportionality between means and ends, as well as a careful consideration of consequences—above all, the certain, bloody consequences of war. Pragmatic realism will never sanction destroying a village (let alone a country) in order to save it.

A pragmatic realist will also reject the dualistic assumption that restricts policy alternatives to either military engagement or pacifist isolation while cultivating instead an active restraint that seeks bold, imaginative ways to protect the American people without resorting to force. This would involve, among other things, a revitalization of diplomacy as the art of conflict resolution and a redefinition of national security that emphasizes strengthening domestic capacity—rebuilding infrastructure, reviving public education, sustaining an informed citizenry committed to a vigorous commonwealth—rather than pursuing vague, far-flung commitments that squander wealth, provoke antagonism, and ensure endless war. No doubt the military must remain an essential component of national security, but only in its properly limited role as a national defense force, not as an instrument for providing "government in a box" in remote countries that remain fundamentally alien to the nation builders themselves (mostly young soldiers unfamiliar with native language or culture).[58] Real security implies nation-building at home. The old idea that the United States can be a beacon of hope to others remains valid, but only if Washington abandons its efforts to impose the American way of life by force in distant lands and instead seeks to lead by example. This vision of leadership returns us to the pragmatic realist sensibility of James and Bourne.

Pragmatic realism is, at bottom, a matter of sensibility, of temperament. It fosters resistance to the militarist definition of activism, which has animated interventionists from the Philippines War to the "war on terror." Though Emerson was no militarist, the anti-intellectual roots of militarist activism can be traced to his aphorism: "Power ceases in the instant of repose."[59] This formula implies that even an instant of stillness can be disempowering; it denies the possibility that action and reflection can coexist. It devalues the need for thoughtfully pondering multiple alternatives and their potential consequences. Power can turn into impotence, it suggests, if powerful men delay decisive action. As always, masculinity and effectuality remain rhetorically twinned.

Twentieth-century thinkers, confronting the nearly unlimited power of the national security state, faced a daunting intellectual task. For them, overcoming the mindless itch for military intervention required rejecting the gendered dualisms of heroism and cowardice. It also depended on a recognition that power resides in the instant of repose as well as the moment of action, and a realization that nothing more fully reveals a powerful nation's greatness than its capacity for restraint. This was pragmatic realism at its most compelling, the realism of Beard but also of Lippmann and Kennan and Fulbright. Nothing could be more foolish than to ignore their collective wisdom.

Sadly, Barack Obama seems intent on doing precisely that. After Obama expanded the Afghanistan War and defended that decision while accepting the Nobel Peace Prize at Oslo, the columnist David Brooks commended the president's Niebuhrian seriousness. "In the past few weeks," Brooks wrote, Obama "has revived the Christian realism that undergirded cold war liberal thinking and tried to apply it to a different world." Brooks had in mind passages like this one from Obama's Oslo speech:

> We must begin by acknowledging the hard truth that we will not eradicate violent conflict in our lifetimes. There will be times when nations—acting individually or in concert—will find the use of force not only necessary but morally justified.... [Despite my admiration for Martin Luther King and other pacifists,] as a head of

state sworn to protect and defend my nation, I cannot be guided by their examples alone. I face the world as it is, and cannot stand idle in the face of threats to the American people. For make no mistake: evil does exist in the world. A non-violent movement could not have halted Hitler's armies. Negotiations cannot convince al Qaeda's leaders to lay down their arms. To say that force is sometimes necessary is not a call to cynicism—it is a recognition of history, the imperfections of man and the limits of reason.[60]

Obama's rhetoric invoked Niebuhr in his least attractive role, as Cold War apologist. The president's inflation of banality into "hard truth," his invocation of a pacifist straw man as the only alternative to violence, and his bogus historical analogy (Hitler's armies and al Qaeda's leaders) all bent toward the perpetuation of that durable fantasy, the reluctant superpower, deploying its military force more in sorrow than in anger. In Afghanistan, as in the Cold War, the rhetoric of tragedy has yet again ennobled military interventionism, allowing imperial elites to do pretty much what they had planned to do anyway, but with furrowed brow and humble mien. Another misbegotten crusade is now well advanced, its final act still to be written.

CHAPTER 6

Toward Transnationalism

Akira Iriye

There are many ways of understanding the "Short American Century." One could view it by noting the dominance of the United States during the several decades following World War II. Such a perspective would delineate how "American" or "Americanized" the rest of the world became during these years. This essay, however, will move in the opposite direction, taking a look first at how the world changed during that period and then considering ways in which those changes had parallels in the United States. Rather than the Americanization of the world, this approach will focus on the globalization of America. The key point is this: during the American Century, the distinction between the United States and the rest of the world became increasingly blurred. This occurred not merely because the United States dominated, influenced, or helped change other societies but also because others in their turn contributed to reshaping American society.

In retrospect, Henry Luce's essay "The American Century" was an audacious, even cheeky, assertion of American influence made in the middle of a global crisis brought about by devastating economic collapse and the rise of totalitarian states in Europe and Asia. The Soviet Union, Germany, and Japan were confidently asserting their respective "new orders," each contending that it would define the twentieth century. For those disillusioned by capitalism or intrigued by antidemocratic thought, the twentieth century seemed well on its way to becoming a Soviet century, a German century, or a Japanese century. (A little over a year before Luce's essay was published, a writer for the *Asahi* newspaper asserted that the twentieth century must become one in which the world would follow Japan rather than the other way around, as had hitherto been the case.)[1] By 1941 the United States had begun to recover from the depth of the Depression but, even so, few Americans would have boldly asserted, as Luce did, that the remainder of the century would see the United States emerge as the richest, most powerful, and most culturally influential nation in the world.

To be sure, in the late 1930s the nation had begun rearming itself and by 1941 had emerged as the one nonbelligerent whose action could determine the outcome of the wars being fought in Europe and Asia. The United States did ultimately become the most powerful nation in the world, its influence far exceeding any that the Soviet Union, Nazi Germany, or imperial Japan had exercised. Yet this amounted to geopolitics as usual, with the balance of power ceaselessly shifting as some nations won and others lost. If the American Century merely signified that the United States was arriving at its moment of preponderance, then Luce's idea would have amounted to simply the next chapter in the ongoing narrative of "the rise and fall of the great powers." The twentieth century might belong to America to the same degree that the nineteenth had been Great Britain's and the twenty-first may prove to be China's. Luce's American Century, however, postulated something much more: a world of economic and cultural resources crossing national boundaries and connecting on the basis of shared ideals, values, and dreams. His vision transcended geopolitics. In that sense, the article had much in common with Franklin D. Roosevelt's "four freedoms" speech of January 1941, with the Atlantic Charter of August that year, or with Wendell Willkie's *One World,* published in 1942. All spoke of the United States bringing into being a world in which shared values and aspirations would supplant national ambitions and international conflict. In short, the world defined solely by sovereign states would give way to something entirely new.

What in fact emerged in the course of the twentieth century were both these worlds, one transnational and the other state-centric. This essay will focus on the former of the two, for Luce's "American Century" makes sense only if we recognize that it looked toward a world of interdependence and universalism. And, indeed, the world during the "American Century" did move significantly in this direction.

A word of caution is in order about the word "transnational." Historians have been using this term with increasing frequency since the 1990s, itself a sign of the transnationalization of the globe. There is no universally accepted definition of "transnational," however, and the word is often used interchangeably with "international." But if the two mean more or less the same thing, there will be no point in using both. Determining where the word "international" ends and where the word "transnational" starts is not always easy, especially since these two types of interactions often work together. Besides, as Josepha Laroche has noted, distinctions between public and private tend to blur in the age of globalization.[2] As used here, the word "transnational" refers to movements and interactions among people, goods, and ideas across national boundaries, as well as to non-national entities (e.g., races and religions). In contrast, the word "international" refers to phenomena in which states and governments are principally involved or where national identities are evident. Trade, for instance, is clearly an international transaction, but those engaged in such activities sometimes form their own cross-border liaisons in pursuit of interests differing from those of a particular country. Perhaps the best way to illustrate transnationalization during the American Century is to cite some specific examples from that period, placing these developments in the framework of transnational, rather than national or international, history.

First, the American Century witnessed large-scale cross-national migrations. The movement of people from country to country, from one region of the world to another, had always existed. In most instances the flow of migrants had been less a national than a private affair; in that sense, therefore, it was a transnational phenomenon. During and immediately after the Second World War, however, large-scale cross-border migrations resulted from international events and national decisions, produced by the redrawing of maps and the establishment of new states. To the extent that geography and history define a nation-state, altering the boundaries of older countries and creating newly sovereign states where none had previously existed meant that hundreds of thousands, even millions, of people moved across borders. Among the most large-scale of such migrations was the exodus of 10 million Germans from their homes in Poland, Estonia, and other parts of Eastern Europe and the Baltic in the wake of the Second World War, a direct consequence of territorial boundaries being redrawn. But the German example was one among many. With the establishment of new states, many of them ethnically defined, large groups moved, or were forced to move, to spaces where they would be among "their own people." The exodus of Muslims from the new state of India and the exodus of Palestinian Arabs after the creation of Israel are two well-known examples. As African countries gained their independence in the 1960s, tribal communities migrated to escape persecution by those who considered them aliens. With the end of empires, metropolitan colonizers returned to their home countries. Yet even some of the colonial population gravitated to the metropoles, as demonstrated by the movement of Chinese from Hong Kong to Britain or of Indonesians to the Netherlands. While most of these migrations were products of postwar national, international, and imperial decisions, the fact remains that millions crossed borders and came to constitute part of the increasing transnational population.

Moreover, war and decolonization were not the only causes of transnational migrations. After the 1960s, tens of millions left their home countries for economic and political reasons. Most of the former were no different from traditional emigrants, such as those who had crossed the Atlantic to find work in North America before the First World War. During the American Century, however, intra-Western migrations were eclipsed by the movement of people from non-Western countries to Europe, North America, and Australia, all of which attracted Asians, Arabs, and Africans looking for better economic opportunities. As these countries began to revise their traditional "whites only" immigration policies, huge numbers of Chinese, Indians, Pakistanis, Turks, Arabs, Algerians, and others came and established their enclaves in European, American, and Australian cities, thus contributing to their ethnic diversity. On the other hand, many who sought refuge abroad from persecution at home for political or religious reasons ended up in refugee camps, living in limbo, often stateless and cared for not by separate countries but by international agencies, especially the United Nations (UN). Combining all these categories of people, by the end of the twentieth century an estimated 5 percent of the total world population consisted of migrants.

Migrants, however, were not the only people crossing national boundaries. During the American Century, the number of people who went overseas not to seek jobs or a new home but to stay temporarily— as tourists, exchange students, or businesspeople on assignments— skyrocketed, providing a second example of transnationalization of the world. After the Second World War, it is true, occupation duties in former enemy countries necessitated the presence of the victorious countries' soldiers and civilians abroad, some of whom stayed even after a formal occupation ended. Their activities were more part of international than transnational history; the bulk of them represented their respective nations and were abroad in official capacity. One important development in the last several decades of the twentieth century, however, was the spectacular rise in the number of individuals and nongovernmental organizations that became connected transnationally. Unlike migrants relocating to another country, these were temporary "sojourners," to borrow Wang Gungwu's phrase.[3] Their number grew by leaps and bounds in the last decades of the twentieth century. For instance, by 1980, some 278 million people were visiting other countries as tourists, making international tourism by 1984 the second largest item in world trade.[4] The number of border crossings by tourists reached 687 million by 2000. Overseas travel, a pastime that not just Europeans and North Americans but an increasing number of Asians and others could now afford, was forging an unprecedented number of transnational connections. Even if on a smaller scale, much the same can be said about students or scholars pursuing educational and research opportunities abroad. Exchanges of this type fostered acquaintances, often lasting a lifetime, on a global scale. Likewise with people sent abroad on business—more and more factories and firms established their branches and sales agencies overseas, resulting in an increasing number of "expats," or expatriates.

The establishment and proliferation of international organizations, both intergovernmental and nongovernmental, offers a third example of cross-border connections. Relief agencies, most notably the United Nations Relief and Reconstruction Agency, provided food and shelter in war-devastated areas of the world and also undertook refugee resettlement. Such international activities vastly expanded the scope of transnational encounters among people of diverse backgrounds. In the meantime, nongovernmental philanthropic organizations, advocacy groups pursuing various causes, and religious institutions (most notably the Catholic Church) were bringing people from various parts of the world into close contact. The number of UN-recognized international nongovernmental organizations reached nearly forty thousand by the end of the century. Some had branches in the remotest corners of the globe.

And then there is the category of indirect encounters and networks across nations, that is, individuals and societies becoming acquainted with one another not so much through personal contact as through goods and ideas. This phenomenon constitutes the fourth example of transnationalization. What is referred to as globalization forged a myriad of such indirect liaisons. Although historians trace the phenomenon of globalization back to the mid-nineteenth century or even earlier, it expanded greatly in scope and intensity during the American Century. For one thing, during this "century" the world's population increased at an unprecedented speed, nearly tripling between 1940 and 2000, from a little over 2 billion to 6.124 billion. The generation born after the war—the "baby boomers"—lived longer than their predecessors not only because there was no third world war but because of the invention and dissemination of penicillin and antibiotics as well as improved sanitary conditions and health care. The vastly increased global population might still have remained in isolation from one another were it not for significant advances in transportation, communication, and information technology. During the second half of the twentieth century, it became much cheaper to fly long distances and to make overseas telephone calls. The volume of international telephone calls, for instance, increased from 12.5 billion call minutes in 1982 to 67.5 billion in 1996.[5] These figures translate into roughly two minutes of international calls per person in 1982 growing to ten minutes by 1996. Although the telephone did not connect everyone, even the poorer regions of the world opened up to such contact as economic globalization proceeded. The spread of computers, in particular the Internet, was even more spectacular. In the early 1990s, when the Internet system of communication began to spread beyond military circles, the "net" included perhaps one hundred thousand computers. Ten years later, that number had jumped to over 100 million. By the end of the American Century, it had reached 1 billion.[6] Such a development dealt a *coup de grace* to isolated communities. Ideas, information, and even gossip crossed borders effortlessly through electronic mail. Geographical distance lost its meaning.

As a consequence, people in all lands came into contact with each other, indirectly if not directly. They purchased goods imported from many countries, availed themselves of banking, investment, and other services in distant lands, speculated in stocks and currencies all over the world, watched foreign movies and television shows, read books published abroad, and obtained information about lands and people overseas. All of this exemplified globalization during the American Century, the scale and variety of which exceeded anything seen before. Although global exchanges of goods and services had accelerated in the nineteenth century, the bulk of such exchanges had been confined to Europe and North America. During the last decades of the twentieth century, globalization became truly global, involving countries outside the West as never before.[7]

The same observation applies to cultural products such as art and music. Artistic and musical exchanges have long existed. However, in the second half of the twentieth century, cultural internationalism became more and more global in scope, transforming itself into cultural transnationalism.[8] Prior to the Second World War, cultural exchanges had mostly taken place within the same civilizational zones, particularly among Western countries. Artists, musicians, and literary figures from outside Europe and North America visited and studied in the West, but the reverse was rarely the case. European music was performed in Asia, and museums all over the world exhibited cultural products from afar. Still, the scope of such transnational activities was limited. (To the extent that exchanges among different civilizations took place, they were primarily promoted within empires, the British

Commonwealth being a notable example.) In the post-1945 years, in contrast, cultural transnationalism grew even as geopolitical divides among powers remained and interstate animosities intensified. Musicians from Russia performed in Western Europe and the United States, Western composers began to incorporate South Asian music into their work, and the United Nations Educational, Scientific, and Cultural Organization promoted the collaboration of artists from East and West to undertake joint projects. (The traditional categories of "East" and "West" began to lose their significance in the cultural landscape of the world, where a Chinese pianist playing a Mozart sonata in South America was neither Eastern nor Western but represented a global cultural asset.) The worldwide popularity of rock music, originating in the United States in the 1950s but swiftly crossing the Atlantic, from Britain to Western Europe and to Eastern Europe in the 1960s, and disseminated elsewhere through indigenous bands, brought young people of all backgrounds together on an unprecedented scale. Through such contacts something akin to universal ideas of beauty, transcending national and regional boundaries, developed. The shared consumption of goods, cultural products, ideas, and even emotions was another aspect of the transnational networking that grew during the American Century.

Fifth, going a step further, there was a growing awareness of worldwide concerns, from nuclear arms to diseases and from human rights abuses to environmental disasters. Previously these issues had elicited responses within the national framework, but in the last decades of the twentieth century they attracted attention as transnational problems, calling for cooperative responses across national boundaries. Governments negotiated arms limitation agreements, and international organizations such as the UN combated communicable diseases such as tuberculosis, cholera, and smallpox while also protecting the natural environment from industrial waste and pollution. Making such actions possible, however, was a shared, transnational awareness of these problems and a determination to protect what in the 1970s came to be called "human security." The collective well-being of humanity claimed attention previously monopolized by the interests of separate states. Phrases such as "human race" and "world citizen" regained popularity, reflecting the awareness of a shared universe of people. So too did "planet earth," an image that gained prominence as a result of space exploration initiated in the late 1950s, spurred by geopolitical competition but producing a new global map devoid of man-made boundaries.

Sixth, the concept of one world did not obliterate but rather strengthened the influence of non-state, supra-state, and even sub-state entities and identities in propelling human behavior. Between separate national identities, on one hand, and the "human race," on the other, alternative self-definitions and group loyalties proliferated, enriching (and complicating) how individuals viewed themselves. Among the most influential non-national identities were race, ethnicity, and religion. All such categories, of course, had existed for centuries, and self-consciousness about them had grown at the end of the nineteenth century, even as transnational encounters were becoming more and more frequent. The predominant tendency at that time and through the 1930s, however, had stressed nationalism and nationality as the overarching framework of identity. This clearly reflected the still preponderant power and influence of the West, consisting overwhelmingly of white Christians. The West's division into nations that were often in conflict with one another did not encourage receptiveness to racial, ethnic, or religious diversity. Within the West, activists committed to enhancing the status of workers or women might pay greater attention to class and gender, but such categories were rarely applied to other parts of the globe.

The acceptance of non-national identities as valid throughout the world emerged only after the Second World War and may thus be seen as another manifestation of far-reaching transnationalization. Even with the creation of many new nations in the decades after the war, non-national identities continued to cut across state boundaries. The "consciousness-raising" that attracted so much attention during the 1960s more often than not referred to racial or ethnic pride. Such pride existed side by side with the idea of human unity so that even as internationalism aimed to bring nations into closer cooperation with one another, non-national solidarities also contributed to the unity of humankind. Human rights promoted both equality and diversity. From around this time, religious self-consciousness also gained strength, sometimes to buttress nationalism but in other instances at the expense of national cohesiveness. Following the Second Vatican Council during the 1960s, the Catholic Church sought energetically to speak for people all over the world in promoting justice and peace, while various Islamic sects sought to integrate their adherents without regard to national boundaries. While most nations remained secular in their official outlook, these religious movements envisaged a parallel, if not an alternative, world order based on faith. All such identities, coupled with the international organizations and transnational movements referred to earlier, further undermined the traditional image of the world as primarily consisting of nations. An accurate map of the globe would now have multiple layers, only one consisting of nations with well-defined borders. The other layers lacked neat boundaries but were nevertheless real and jointly constituted "planet earth."

A seventh manifestation of transnationalism came in the form of newly emerging regional communities. The European Union is, of course, the most ambitious and successful of such regional entities, but there are others, such as the Association of Southeast Asian Nations, Mercosur (a community consisting of South American countries), and the African Union. Even when no formal structure exists, some regional identities have developed, not so much superseding nation-states as existing alongside them. The promotion of an East Asian identity, incorporating China (including Taiwan and Hong Kong), Korea, and Japan, but possibly including Vietnam, Singapore, and some others, offers a conspicuous example. Despite a history of war and colonialism, if Chinese, Koreans, and Japanese can formulate a common identity, the result might eventually lead to the creation of a regional community to match the European Union in importance. In the meantime, other regional identities are finding expression, less institutional than intellectual, including the Atlantic community and the South Asian region. Trade and investment patterns could even produce an all-embracing Asia-Pacific community that could include East Asia, the Antipodes, North America, and even Mexico and Peru.

Eighth, all these developments resulted in an unprecedented degree of intermixing among people of different national, ethnic, social, and cultural backgrounds. Due in part to striking demographic increases, along with advances in transportation, communication, and information technology, but also a consequence of changing attitudes toward "race mixing," the process of what some call "hybridization," that is, the intermixing of people biologically, socially, and culturally, reached unprecedented levels. Although historians such as Martin Bernal have traced hybridization to the ancient Mediterranean world, the scale was now much vaster, denser, and faster, with a larger and increasing number of individuals from different parts of the world mingling with one another, working, living, and studying together in close geographical spaces.[9] Inevitably, such a situation led to the birth of interracial children. Statistics on racial composition are very hard to come by, but it may at least be noted that legal restrictions and social prejudices against "mixed breeds" visibly diminished during the American Century in various parts of the world. The countries formerly constituting the British Empire offer a notable example. There, formerly rigid racial demarcations among Europeans, natives, and "mixed breeds," with their emphasis on maintaining racial "purity" at all costs, have largely disappeared. In Asian countries as well, children of mixed races were traditionally ostracized. Yet such attitudes have steadily diminished as waves of globalization resulted in the transnationalization of people and their habits. Hybridization resulted, and with it the realization that throughout history race mixture had been the norm rather than the exception. In effect, the whole world is in the process of becoming hybrid. One sees this most clearly in food, where ostensibly traditional diets come into contact with imports from other culinary traditions. The result: "fusion" menus.

Crime also became transnational during the American Century, a ninth manifestation of the phenomenon. Much has been written about international terrorism, or about international trafficking in children, women, drugs, and even nuclear arms. Some of these are *international*, in that states actively promote or, alternatively, seek to suppress these activities. Yet there is also a *transnational* dimension, in that criminals of all kinds cross national borders and establish what amounts to a global syndicate. The networks of Islamic terrorists who organize themselves to wage jihad all over the world provide an example. So do criminal entrepreneurs, who take advantage of globalization—the opening of borders, the constant movement of people, ease of communication, deregulation of monetary transactions—to organize themselves transnationally. As a result, both producers and consumers of heroin, cocaine, and other drugs continue to thrive. Against such transnationally organized criminals, international police agencies have formed, notably Interpol and Europol. While the former was initially created in 1923, the number of states represented there vastly expanded after the Second World War and today total 187.[10] Europol, on the other hand, was not established until 1995, as a policing arm of the European Union. These are instances where transnational activities have called forth international responses. But transnational efforts also have been made to combat the roots of such crimes. For instance, nongovernmental organizations dedicated to education, health care, and women's rights seek to dissuade people from turning to illicit drugs and prostitution, while those active in developmental assistance argue that improvements in economic conditions will eradicate at least one cause of terrorism, namely, poverty and unemployment. In any event, the transnationalization of crime stands as yet another emblem of the American Century.

Last, but perhaps not least, the American Century has fostered the transnationalization of scholarship. Of course there is nothing new about academics from various countries carrying on joint research or teaching as exchange faculty, but such phenomena became commonplace only after the Second World War. The community of transnational scholars, as best captured by David Lodge's novels such as *Changing Places* and *Small World,* contributed enormously to confirming that the scholarly arena is global rather than national in scope. Until the middle of the twentieth century, to be sure, such interactions were mostly confined to the Atlantic world; scholarly literature, whether in the natural sciences, social sciences, or humanities, remained predominantly of Western origin. Scholars from other parts of the world imported the products of Western scholarship and made use of them in their own research and teaching. Although such predominance has not ended, during the last several decades researchers from outside the West have increasingly gained recognition as leaders in their respective fields. These fields may still be products of modern Western scholarship, but non-Western scholars contribute not only to enriching but also to reconceptualizing them. Amartya Sen, the winner of the Nobel Prize in Economics in 1998, is a good example. Born in India, he was the first non-Westerner ever to win the prize, recognized for broadening the scope of this discipline by bringing to its purview such factors as society, ethnicity, and civilization. There is little doubt that Sen's upbringing in India had a great deal to do with his broader conception of economics. In other disciplines as well, it became common practice to convene gatherings that included scholars from all over the world. History is no exception. Historians from distant lands come together at academic conferences and collaborate on books. One consequence of such activities has been the realization that even when studying the history of a particular country, a transnational perspective cannot but help. It has long been said that "truth" knows no national boundaries. What the American Century demonstrated was that truth can best be sought through transnational endeavors. (In 1988 I gave a presidential address before the American Historical Association entitled "The Internationalization of History." If I were giving a similar talk today, I would call it "The Transnationalization of History.")

How "American" were these defining features of the American Century? In other words, to what extent did developments within the United States echo the same phenomena? How did the United States contribute to this global transformation?

Demography offers a place to begin answering these questions, with demographic trends within the United States echoing those elsewhere. Although the rate of increase fell below the world's average, the number of people living in the United States more than doubled, from 132 million in 1940 to 288 million in 2005. To the extent that population growth reflects progress in medical science in areas ranging from the eradication of communicable diseases to the reduction of infant mortality, doctors and scientists in the United States played a conspicuous role. One simple measure is the number of Nobel laureates in physiology and medicine, honoring significant contributions to the advancement of medical science. No American won the prize during the first twenty-nine years of its history (1901–1929). However, since 1930, when for the first time an American scientist won the Nobel in medicine, and through 2008, more than ninety Americans (including foreign-born scientists working in the United States) have received the prize, accounting for over half of all the Nobel medical award recipients during that period. This record of achievement is a testament to the significant contributions made by U.S.-based scientific research in developing medical cures such as penicillin and the polio vaccine that have increased life spans not only in the United States but abroad.

The United States also contributed to demographic transnationalism through its reception of huge numbers of foreign immigrants. Restrictive immigration policies instituted during the 1920s had sharply reduced the number of immigrants into the country, and the Depression, the Second World War, and the early Cold War did little to alter the picture. Only after the 1960s, especially after the passage of the new immigration law of 1965, did the United States once again begin to attract large numbers of immigrants, especially from Asia and Central America. Taken together, the European Union (plus Norway and Switzerland, constituting the so-called Schengen group) admitted more permanent immigrants than the United States. In 2005, for instance, while about 1.5 million legal immigrants entered the United States, the Schengen countries hosted more than twice that number.[11] Still, the percentage of foreign-born people in the United States continued to exceed that of any other nation. The proportion of U.S. residents born elsewhere went from 4.7 percent in 1970—the lowest percentage in more than a century—to 12.5 percent in 2007, constituting nearly one-eighth of the total U.S. population. Out of 38 million such people, over 11 million, or nearly 30 percent, were illegal aliens, coming to and living in the country without proper authorization. That, too, reflected the transnational trends within the United States as well as in the world at large.

In addition to attracting immigrants, the United States also continued to host foreign visitors, whether as students, tourists, or businesspeople. American colleges and universities remained the chief magnets for foreign students, whose total number jumped from 34,000 in 1954 (or 1.4 percent of the total U.S. student body) to 623,000 (or 3.5 percent) in 2008. On average, the United States hosted roughly one-third of all college-age individuals studying outside their countries. While the number of foreign students in American colleges declined slightly in the wake of 9/11, this proved to be only a temporary reversal, lasting only four years. By 2006 and thereafter, more foreign students enrolled in American institutions of higher learning than ever before. In terms of tourism, France remained the most popular destination throughout the American Century, but the United States was a close second, visited by 7.5 million travelers from abroad in 1950, out of the world total of 25.3 million, and 133.5 million in 2005, out of 806 million tourists worldwide. That one out of every three travelers chose to visit the United States immediately after the Second World War, whereas only one out of five did half a century later, reflects not simply the time it took for European countries to recover their appeal as tourist destinations but also the diversification of international tourism, with more and more people deciding to visit hitherto less accessible places such as China, Turkey, and South America. For their own part, more and more Americans undertook trips abroad, taking advantage of cheaper costs of travel, consolidating and adding to the networks of travelers.

As for foreign businesspeople residing in the United States, their presence is an integral part of economic globalization, which the United States took a leading part in promoting. The American Century witnessed the opening up of American domestic markets to foreign goods and capital, and in the process merchants, industrialists, and financiers streamed into the United States. Most of these business "sojourners" initially came from Canada and Western Europe, but entrepreneurs from Japan, Korea, and, after the 1990s, China and India soon joined in. For their part, American entrepreneurs went abroad, contributing to the integration of other countries to the global economic nexus. The dollar still remained the main global currency, even after its value began to fluctuate in the 1970s. Especially after the Plaza Accord of 1985, which liberalized currency transactions, more and more foreigners began buying U.S. Treasury bonds and shares in the New York Stock Exchange, as well as speculating in changing rates of exchange.

Needless to say, all such transactions were vastly facilitated by the rapidly advancing information and communications technology. Here lay one of the principal U.S. contributions to the transnationalization of the world. The Internet, begun as a military device but applied to civilian use in the 1970s and the 1980s, had a revolutionary impact, fostered by a socioeconomic system that encouraged private innovation and a style of education that encouraged an open exchange of new ideas. Google, developed in a California garage in 1998, was, within a few years, registering over 1 billion users worldwide on any given day.

Likewise, large numbers of Americans subscribed to transnational concerns such as environmental degradation and human rights abuses. Since the early nineteenth century, Americans had been deeply involved in transnational movements on behalf of universal causes such as peace and the emancipation of slaves. In the first decades of the twentieth century, Woodrow Wilson's distinctively American vision inspired internationalist and anticolonialist agendas all over the world. During the Second World War and the Cold War, the espousal of democracy and freedom served to combine the nation's strategic interests and professed ideals. Quite apart from the geopolitical realm, domestic and external forces meshed to present a powerful coalition on behalf of transnational objectives. For instance, the American civil rights movement was increasingly seen as an integral part of global human rights activism. The UN's 1948 Universal Declaration of Human Rights merged with the struggle for racial equality at home, and civil rights advocates appealed to world opinion for support in the name of universal humanity. Martin Luther King's 1965 trip to Berlin, where he gave speeches in both halves of that divided city, drove home the idea that racial justice is a universal, rather than a national, imperative. For this reason, Americans were particularly active in seeking an end to South Africa's apartheid, an objective finally achieved in the early 1990s. Likewise, Americans had long played a leading role in promoting women's rights. After the Second World War, they worked closely with their counterparts abroad, at the UN, and through nongovernmental bodies in other countries. The Cold War as well as the hot wars in Asia also fueled transnational movements against nuclear and chemical weapons. The movement to ban or at least reduce nuclear armaments transcended national boundaries, and prominent American scientists joined their colleagues from both sides of the Iron

Curtain to promote an antinuclear movement. The introduction of chemical warfare in Vietnam, in particular Agent Orange, a herbicide widely employed to deny hiding places to guerrillas, mobilized American scientists, aware that such agents would do immense damage not only to ecology but to humans as well. Their causes attracted the support of colleagues elsewhere. The movement against what came to be known as "ecocide" was, from the beginning, a transnational one. Working together with activists from other countries, Americans played a leading role in establishing international nongovernmental organizations devoted to environmentalism, such as Greenpeace and Friends of the Earth.

The growth of non-state, non-national identities, another aspect of transnationalization, also had its roots in the United States, which had forged hundreds of thousands of nongovernmental organizations even before 1940. The civil society they represented grew stronger even as the federal government augmented its authority during the Depression and the war. As happened elsewhere, the 1960s and the early 1970s witnessed a serious challenge to the authority of the state, often mounted in the name of "counterculture" and "identity politics." The very idea of America became disaggregated. During the first decades of Luce's American Century, talk of American nationality, American civilization, America's "civic religion," and an American way of life had been commonplace, exemplifying an exceptionalist view of the nation under which class, racial, gender, and other differences within American society seemed unimportant, if not irrelevant. The picture began to change during the 1960s, and this, too, was part of a worldwide phenomenon. In part because of the accelerating tempo of economic globalization but also reflecting cross-border movements of people and ideas, non-state connections across borders grew in importance. The emphasis on diversity at home clearly had its global dimension. Religious or doctrinal assertiveness, exemplified by evangelical Protestant movements in the United States and posing a challenge to the idea of the secular state, had its counterpart in the rise of fundamentalist Islam in the Middle East or the revivalist Catholic Church in South America. Even "neoconservatives" and "neoliberals" in the United States, appalled by the anti-establishment radicalism of the 1960s and the 1970s, were advocates of "small government," calling for reducing the power and authority of the government. In effect, the transnational radicalism of the 1960s elicited a transnational conservative response. Just as "new culture" advocates joined hands across the ocean, so too did "neoliberals" in the United States, Britain, and elsewhere, promoting the deregulation and denationalization of postal, transportation, banking, and other systems. If the public sphere had dominated the private at the outset of the American Century, the private sphere began to assert itself as that century wound down.

In the meantime, hybridization also had a specific American aspect. Whereas before 1940 the foreign-born population had largely originated in Europe, by 2008 30 percent of the foreign born were Mexicans, and another 5 percent Chinese. All of the top ten countries of origin lay outside Europe. Not only were there more and more non-Europeans in the country, but interracial children became increasingly evident as states abolished laws banning interracial marriage during the second half of the twentieth century. Elsewhere, hybridization sometimes produced social tensions and even political crises; in the United States, it evoked little controversy. (Already during the 1990s, about 30 percent of Asian Americans were married to non-Asians.)[12] Accompanying this mixing of people was a mixing of cultures, illustrated in the United States by the mushrooming of "ethnic food" restaurants all over the country, the domestic counterpart to the "McDonaldization" (sometimes referred to as "Coca-colonization") of the rest of the world. With the globe's billions having access to, and seemingly enjoying, all varieties of food—as well as popular music, fashions, and lifestyles—the concept of "pure" traditions lost all meaning. All countries are products of hybridization, the United States, as a consequence of the American Century, perhaps most of all.

The United States also promoted, or became part of, the trend toward regional communities. It is true that the only formal regional structures the nation joined in this period were strategic entities such as the North Atlantic Treaty Organization or trade compacts such as the North American Free Trade Agreement. Less formally, however, the United States cultivated a sense of belonging to the Asia-Pacific region. By the time Barack Obama became president, it had become customary to speak of the Trans-Pacific Partnership, the idea being that countries such as Canada, the United States, Mexico, Peru, Australia, New Zealand, Japan, South Korea, China, and many others constituted as viable and interdependent an economic region as the members of the European Union. With American trade with China and Japan increasing more rapidly than with European countries, and with a constant influx of immigrants and visitors from Asia, the nation's destiny was seen as closely bound up with both the Atlantic and the Pacific.

Although not what Luce had in mind when he contemplated the American Century, the United States has contributed significantly to the transnationalization of crime. The increased American demand for drugs—according to a 2005 governmental survey, nearly half of the nation's population over the age of twelve had used an illicit drug at least once, and 14 percent had done so during the previous year—has certainly promoted the growth of transnational criminality.[13] Criminal syndicates originating in Mexico, Colombia, China, and elsewhere became quite active in the United States, among other things using U.S. banks for illegal financial and monetary transfers. Suffice it to say that in crime, as in all other activities, the nation was an integral part of a world becoming transnational.

One final American contribution to transnationalization relates to the fostering of transnational scholarship. Here, without question, the United States has played the leading role. Virtually simultaneously with the publication of Luce's famous essay, European scholars began flooding American shores, mostly as refugees at first but then later joined by those seeking research and teaching opportunities in the United States in the wake of the Second World War. Not simply researchers in the natural and medical sciences, attracted to envious laboratory facilities, but also those in the social sciences and the humanities found American universities and colleges welcoming, stimulating, and open-minded. Many of them trained the next generations of researchers and teachers, including a large number of those coming from abroad. In time, scholars originating from Asia, the Middle East, Africa, and Latin America diversified higher education in the

United States, turning it into the center of transnational scholarship. Foundations—such as Rockefeller, Ford, and Carnegie—contributed generously to funding international scholarly conferences so that intellectual collaboration across national boundaries became routine. Not surprisingly, the transnational perspective gained currency among historians so that by the end of the twentieth century and the beginning of the twenty-first, it found application even in the study of the United States itself.

Some resisted such a trend. Allan Bloom's *The Closing of the American Mind* (1987), which became a best seller, expressed unhappiness over the transnationalization of American society and culture, particularly as it affected education and scholarship. Bloom bemoaned the growing popularity of economics, an inherently transnational discipline, and the decline of political science, which traditionally took the nation as the irreducible unit of analysis. Above all, he decried the declining emphasis on the West's classical philosophy as the foundation of education and scholarship. But to bemoan the passing of an "American" mind essentially amounted to the swan song of a mind unable to cope with transnationalism. Even as some Americans, concerned over the passing of an age, read *The Closing of the American Mind,* universities and research institutions in the United States were "opening" the minds of scholars and students coming from abroad, while at the same time other Americans contemplated ideas and traditions unconnected with the classical civilization of the West but having equal validity. In that sense, the closing of the American mind was a misnomer. American minds had taken the lead in opening intellectual horizons all over the world to visions of global humanity.

The American Century, then, was a time of intensive transnationalization, both of the world and of the United States, a period in which national boundaries ceased to inhibit the movement of people, goods, money, and ideas, in which different races and cultures amalgamated, and in which claims of national uniqueness began to dissipate. In the American Century, the United States became less "American."

In that sense, the American Century succeeded only too well, albeit with consequences that Henry Luce did not fully anticipate. To be sure, separate sovereign entities remain even today, and nationalism persists, causing friction among people inhabiting different geographical spaces. Yet neither the world nor the United States will ever go back to where they were in 1941. If the Short American Century is to have a successor, it will not be a Chinese century or an Indian century or a Brazilian century. It will be a long transnational century.

CHAPTER 7

From the American Century to Globalization

Jeffry A. Frieden

Today's troubled economic conditions have led many to engage in nostalgic reminiscence about the decades after World War II, when the international economy seemed stable and predictable. The dollar was the world's key currency, trade and investment grew continually, and currency values were practically unchanging. But the international economic order that prevailed from the late 1940s to the mid-1970s was a very unusual creation, never before seen and very unlikely to be reproduced. Neither the United States nor the world is going back to the economic circumstances of that earlier era.

This essay describes the distinguishing features of the international economy during the Short American Century—and, in particular, during the thirty years after World War II. It then explains why the world economy took the form it did in this period, why it evolved as it did, and where we are headed now that the American Century has ended and a new one has begun.[1]

Collapse of the Classical World Economy

The policy makers who constructed the American-led international economic order in the aftermath of World War II worked with the experiences of the decades before 1945 firmly in mind. Even before the war ended, American leaders, and others in the advanced industrial world, had clear ideas about what they wanted to avoid and what they wanted to encourage, as they planned the postwar economic order. Their ideas came from the impressive successes and devastating failures of the international economy's previous hundred years.

One global experience that had a powerful impact on postwar planning was that of the integrated international economy that prevailed in the fifty years before 1914. In that first era of globalization, the movement of goods, capital, people, technologies, and information was freer than it had ever been. Indeed, on a couple of dimensions, the world economy was even more tightly tied together than it has been in our more recent age of globalization. The movement of people—especially of Europeans—was almost completely untrammeled. Some 50 million Europeans left the continent for other lands, largely in the New World, and in most cases they could immigrate almost without documents. Another 50 million Asians also migrated across borders, although their entry to countries like the United States and Australia was more restricted. Nonetheless, immigration was freer than it had been ever before, and freer than it has been ever since.

On a second important dimension, the world was more tightly integrated before 1914 than it is today: almost the entire world shared a common money—gold. At the height of the classical era, every economy of any significance (except China and Persia) was on the gold standard. This was, in some ways, tantamount to having a common currency: while there were separate national monies, they were all easily convertible into gold at a fixed rate. The gold standard made currency values extraordinarily stable and predictable—exchange rates for the major currencies did not change for over forty years, and the gold value of the pound sterling was constant in peacetime for two hundred years. This greatly facilitated trade, investment, finance, travel, and migration across borders, much as the euro has facilitated the greater integration of the economies of present-day Europe.

The world economy of the late nineteenth and early twentieth centuries was not only tightly integrated but also highly successful. The international economy grew more rapidly than it had at any previous time in recorded history—more in seventy-five years than in the previous 750. Many middle-income countries caught up with rich countries; many poor countries caught up with middle-income countries. Although periodic panics and crises occurred, overall macro-economic conditions were quite stable, and world prices changed only gradually, and only very little. To be sure, this was an era of colonial imperialism, of periodic wars and arms races, and of much poverty and brutality. But compared to the economic conditions that came before, this was an extraordinarily successful economic order.

Yet the classical international economic order that had been so successful for generations collapsed in a matter of weeks in 1914. The onset of World War I disrupted international economic relations, which was no surprise. After the war ended, economic and political elites around the world set about trying to revive the prewar economic order—with no success. It turned out that the wartime collapse was no temporary aberration.

For two decades after the end of World War I, the world's political and economic leaders attempted to restore the integrated world economy that had characterized the classical age before 1914—and failed. Despite a bewildering array of conferences, negotiations, treaties, and international organizations, it seemed impossible to rebuild a globalized economy that most governments professed to want to see rebuilt. Not only that, but country after country turned away from the world economy, toward fascism, economic nationalism, and a myriad of anti-internationalist economic philosophies—many of which seemed linked to belligerent and expansionist militarism. The diplomatic lineup that emerged after 1939, in which liberal democracies confronted nationalistic dictatorships, seemed to spell the end of an era in which a consensus in favor of economic integration could be assumed.

As American policy makers began planning for the post–World War II world, they drew some important lessons from the international economic experience of the previous century. The first lesson was that the pre-1914 era had many features worth emulating. It was as close as the modern world had known to an age of generalized prosperity and peace; and whatever the classical system's flaws, it was better than the apparent alternatives. Yet these policy makers recognized that the world could not simply return to the precepts of an earlier era; as Dean Acheson said in 1939, "The economic and political system of the

Nineteenth Century has been for many years in the obvious process of decline. The system is deeply impaired."[2]

The second lesson was that a more open international economy required purposive cooperation among its major participants. A commonly held view during the nineteenth century had been that the classical international economic order was self-regulating and self-equilibrating. But while individual markets might tend toward equilibrium, it seemed clear in retrospect that keeping the world economy open had required substantial, concerted efforts on the part of major governments. This was especially true in times of crisis—and there were periodic "panics" all through the nineteenth and early twentieth centuries. When they hit, the monetary and financial authorities of the major economic powers worked together to stabilize international financial conditions and minimize disruption to international trade and investment. It was precisely the failure of this cooperation after 1929 that had turned a localized recession into a global depression. To avoid any recurrence of this outcome and to rebuild an integrated economy, the governments of the principal economies had to work together.

The third lesson that guided plans for the post–World War II economic order was that for governments to sustain such cooperation they would need strong domestic political support. Mutual efforts to contain international economic problems usually involve national sacrifice, and domestic constituencies needed to be convinced that the costs of compromise and collaboration were worth the benefits. If constituents were unwilling to back the government's efforts to cooperate with its economic partners, cooperation would not be forthcoming—and without cooperation, efforts to rebuild an integrated world economy would fail.

With these three lessons in mind—domestic political support permitting the international cooperation necessary to sustain desirable economic integration—American and British planners went about attempting to construct a world economic order that fulfilled these requirements. And the first question to ask is why, after decades of failures, Anglo-American politicians were successful at reconstituting some semblance of an open international economy in the years after 1945.

Bretton Woods

The international economy that emerged after World War II had a number of striking features. The first was that its broad outlines were, unique among all international economic orders past or present, planned and implemented by government decree. The general contours of the world economy that emerged (at least in the capitalist world) after 1945 were designed while the war was still raging, largely by an American delegation headed by Harry Dexter White and a British delegation headed by John Maynard Keynes. The blueprint was adopted by forty-four Allied governments at an international conference that met at Bretton Woods, New Hampshire, in the summer of 1944. The fact that governments were central to drawing up the postwar international economic system was indicative of the central organizing principles of the new system, which combined a reliance upon free markets with the new tools of government macroeconomic management.

The second defining feature of the Bretton Woods system, as it came to be known, was a broad commitment to open markets at home and abroad. The system's architects were convinced that future economic growth required a restoration of normal patterns of international trade, investment, and payments out of the wreckage caused by two decades of depression and war. They designed a series of international institutions, all of which aimed to oversee the recovery of international economic exchange from its collapse in the 1930s.

The International Monetary Fund was empowered to oversee the reconstruction of the international monetary and financial system out of the ruins of the gold standard and its interwar successor. The Bretton Woods monetary system, as it evolved out of the designs of Keynes and White, was based on a U.S. dollar fixed to gold at thirty-five dollars an ounce, and other currencies whose values were fixed to the dollar but could be changed as policy makers felt necessary. This system of "fixed but adjustable" exchange rates provided what one prominent New York banker had referred to in 1936 as "a union of what was best in the old gold standard, corrected on the basis of experience to date, and of what seems practicable in some of the doctrines of 'managed currencies.'"[3] It provided some of the predictability of the gold standard but without the rigid constraints that had made gold unworkable in the 1930s.

Another Bretton Woods institution, the International Bank for Reconstruction and Development (World Bank), was meant to help restore international investment flows, especially to developing countries. A major obstacle to long-term investment was the inadequacy of the economic infrastructure in many poor societies, with private investors unable or unwilling to finance construction of this infrastructure. The Bank would borrow in the major capital markets, its debts guaranteed by its rich members, and then lend money at attractive rates to developing-country governments for the construction of projects such as power plants and port facilities. This would help smooth the way for private international investors to follow.

Yet another Bretton Woods institution concerned itself with opening world trade. After one false start, the major powers set up the General Agreement on Tariffs and Trade (GATT), a bargaining forum that facilitated the negotiation of reduction in obstacles to international trade. A series of bargaining "rounds" under GATT auspices reduced trade barriers substantially, roughly to where they had been at the height of the era of free trade in the nineteenth century.

In addition to its government origins and its emphasis on liberalizing international economic relations, the Bretton Woods system had a third, very important, characteristic. It was founded on the principle that modern political economies required substantial government intervention in the economy, in particular, active macroeconomic demand management and extensive social insurance policies. In most countries during the age of the pre-1914 open economy, there had been little government involvement in economic affairs: minimal active monetary policy, no fiscal policy to speak of, and barely any social insurance. But after 1918, with the spread of democracy, the rise of organized labor and labor-based political parties, and the development of modern industrial economies, virtually every advanced nation had adopted some form of the social-democratic welfare state. The Bretton Woods system accepted, indeed, attached importance to, this development. Its architects believed both in international economic integration and in the modern welfare state and assumed that the two could be compatible.

As this quick survey indicates, the Bretton Woods system was in almost every way a compromise. Economically, it attempted to find the middle ground between globalism and national economic management, between free markets and government intervention in the economy. Politically, it reflected the class compromises that grew out of the 1930s, among big business, big labor, and the middle classes. Ideologically, it brought together the Center Left and the Center Right against the extremes of fascism and communism.

The postwar economic order also reflected compromise in its gradualism and in the exceptions it allowed for politically controversial measures. In the commercial realm, for example, even as the GATT oversaw a general liberalization of international trade, it avoided confronting the most troublesome areas of world trade. GATT negotiations excluded farm products, for example, as farmers almost everywhere vehemently opposed liberalization. The GATT also exempted developing countries, strongly committed to protectionist methods to encourage industrial development at home. By the same token, the Bretton Woods monetary and financial order rested upon the expectation that governments would limit short-term capital movements in order to maintain a degree of policy independence. Indeed, over the course of the Bretton Woods period, every major participant in the monetary system imposed strict capital controls. This series of arrangements maintained the general commitment to international economic integration but permitted governments wide leeway in their pursuit of national social, political, and economic goals. And this series of compromises was no accident but, rather, a central precept of the system— the belief that the rigidity of the gold-standard classical order had led to its collapse.

Explaining the Postwar Order

What, then, explains the emergence of this international economic arrangement? Attempts to create something similar had failed miserably for twenty years after World War I. What had changed?

The easy answer is that America had changed. American recalcitrance had posed a major obstacle to international economic cooperation in the interwar period. In contrast, the new world economic order built after 1945 was largely designed by Americans and implemented under the leadership of the U.S. government. But what exactly had changed America, and why? The change in American position was not inevitable; and, in fact, it came as a surprise to many informed observers.

After World War I, despite attempts by the Wilson administration to resurrect the international order, the United States had quickly backed away from playing a leadership role in world affairs. In the 1920 elections a Republican Party dominated by its "isolationist" wing swept into power. As a result, the United States did not ratify the Versailles Treaty, did not join the League of Nations, and refused to participate in most of the international economic consultations that were attempting to restore an open world economy. A penchant for unilateralist nationalism—commonly referred to as isolationism—prevailed until 1934, when New Deal Democrats began to dismantle it; yet the Great Depression and war made this reversal largely irrelevant. As World War II came to an end, Americans and Europeans who wanted to avoid another collapse into conflict feared that the United States might repeat its previous trajectory.

In fact, prospects for a major shift in American international economic policy did not appear encouraging. In 1946 the Republicans swept the House and Senate and were widely expected to win the White House in 1948. This was the same Republican Party that had been a stronghold of isolationism twenty years earlier, and it was led by Senator Robert Taft, a conservative anti-interventionist. Public opinion was still wary of American engagement abroad: in 1948, with the Cold War already in full swing, more than one-third of those polled by Gallup agreed that "since the war this country has gone too far in concerning itself with problems in other parts of the world."[4] While there was probably more sympathy for international involvement in 1945 than there had been in 1925, popular enthusiasm for a major American role was muted. This was especially true with respect to economic policy.

Yet U.S. foreign economic policy resumed the generally liberalizing trend that had started during the New Deal, with the United States working diligently to create an open international economic order.

Some suggest that this was due to the lessons of the Great Depression, especially the demonstration that very high trade barriers enacted by the United States in 1930 under the Smoot-Hawley Tariff had worsened economic conditions. However, there is very little evidence for this "learning" hypothesis. Almost all of the support for the Smoot-Hawley Tariff came from Republicans. And when, in 1934, Congress voted on the Reciprocal Trade Agreements Act to reverse this protectionism and begin the liberalizing trend, eighty-four of the eighty-six Republican legislators who had voted for the tariff voted *against* measures to reduce it. Only two Republican supporters of Smoot-Hawley seemed to have learned any particular lesson from its aftermath.[5]

There were two principal reasons for the American commitment to economic openness after 1945, one economic and the other political. On the economic front, the conditions that the U.S. economy confronted in the late 1940s differed fundamentally from those of the 1920s. After the second war, most of the country's potential competitors were in shambles, while the U.S. economy was booming. The world's thirst for American goods seemed endless, and no other country's industries seemed capable of contending with American industry for global markets. American manufacturers who had previously worried more about imports than about exploring markets abroad were now increasingly interested in exports and little troubled by foreign competitors. Indeed, a crucial group of Republican legislators that switched sides from protection to liberalization represented Northern districts in which exports had grown substantially in importance and the threat of imports had faded.[6] Opposition to American involvement in the world economy weakened as America's role in the world economy grew increasingly predominant.

The second source of American interest in international economic integration related to the politics of American national security. Many Americans, and many American politicians, who had previously been hostile or indifferent to international economic affairs came to see them as an important part of the country's foreign relations. After 1947 the world divided into two camps, one capitalist and one Communist. American leadership of the Western camp was, at least at the outset, primarily military and diplomatic. Yet separating military from economic matters posed difficulties. It hardly seemed reasonable for the United States to spend billions helping to rebuild the economies of Western Europe and Japan and at the same time to abandon these countries to their own economic devices. It made much more sense for the Western capitalist coalition to cooperate on economic matters as its members did on military and political ones. Indeed, inasmuch as American security was now closely tied to the strength and stability of its allies, the United States had a powerful incentive to promote their prosperity. Giving America's allies access to American markets and American capital seemed a natural concomitant to providing them with America's nuclear umbrella and diplomatic support.[7]

Both strategic and political factors, each blending ideological with more pragmatic considerations, came into play. There was an intellectual consistency to the argument that an inclusive pro-American, anti-Soviet alliance in the military and diplomatic spheres also needed to be inclusive in the economic sphere—that the United States could not build an integrated Western political bloc without also building an integrated economic bloc. Yet taking this approach also paid off in the domestic political realm. There were Americans who strongly supported economic integration but were not overly concerned about military affairs; and there were those who wanted a strong military alliance against the Soviet Union but were indifferent to economics—in very rough terms, Northeastern economic internationalists and Midwestern anti-Communists. Combining economic cooperation with military cooperation satisfied both groups.

The forging of this domestic consensus goes far toward explaining why the United States was willing and able to take the lead in constructing a new international economic order. And American leadership was crucial. The United States and its allies occupied West Germany, Italy, and Japan, all three essential to the creation of a new world economy, and it dominated the foreign relations of the other major Western powers. But while America's newfound eagerness for international economic cooperation was crucial, so too was European willingness to participate. Strong forces in many Western European countries were less than enthusiastic: Communists in Italy, France, and Belgium; neutralists in Germany. This resistance was swiftly overcome.

European collaboration stemmed in part from new geopolitical realities, as Western governments concerned about the Soviet Union
gravitated toward the American orbit. But this was not all; domestic
political conditions in Europe and Japan were particularly favorable.
World War II and the Cold War had effectively lopped off the political
extremes: the Far Right discredited by its fascist connections, the Far
Left tainted by its association with the Soviet Union. As a consequence,
neither the extreme right-wing nationalism of interwar business and
agricultural groups nor the extreme left-wing redistributionism of
interwar labor could get a hearing. What remained was a centrist consensus that brought together the (largely Social-Democratic) Center
Left and the (largely Christian-Democratic) Center Right. The political forces comprising this coalition of the Center generally agreed
on the desirability of both international economic openness and the
welfare state; they shared a commitment to a gradualist middle
ground that avoided extremism. The Bretton Woods system reflected
this broad trend, a consensus on the desirability of a compromise that
combined the market and the welfare state, both domestically and
internationally.

The result proved extraordinarily successful, both economically and
politically. By the 1960s, with the Bretton Woods system in full swing,
the (capitalist) world economy was booming. World trade and investment took off and international finance revived. International monetary
conditions were extremely stable. All this contributed to the Bretton
Woods system's crowning achievement: the most rapid rates of economic growth in world history—rates that remain unsurpassed even
today. Western Europe's output per person doubled between 1948 and
1964; Japan grew even more rapidly. By 1961, when the advanced
industrial countries created their own club of rich nations, the Organization for Economic Cooperation and Development, its members—
stretching from Japan through Western Europe to North America—
were, for the first time, recognizably similar in their social, economic,
and political organization and in their level of development.

From Bretton Woods to Globalization

The international economy of the Bretton Woods era appeared stable for nearly twenty-five years. But over the course of the 1970s the system ran into difficulties, and eventually it was fundamentally transformed. The result was a virtually global trend toward greater international economic integration.

By the late 1960s a divergence between monetary conditions in the United States and the rest of the industrial world was subjecting the Bretton Woods monetary order to considerable strain. American spending on the Vietnam War and on expanded social programs contributed to a higher rate of inflation in the United States than in Europe, which undermined confidence in the dollar. American austerity measures could have reduced inflation and restored confidence, but the U.S. government hesitated to sacrifice its domestic macroeconomic policy autonomy to maintain the gold-dollar link, even if this link was the centerpiece of the Bretton Woods monetary system. In the event, in August 1971, the United States broke the link and devalued the dollar, ending the Bretton Woods era of fixed but adjustable exchange rates.

Another source of tension in the Bretton Woods system grew, ironically, out of its success in rekindling international financial markets. With the restoration of macroeconomic stability and economic growth, financial institutions rediscovered foreign operations. By the early 1970s international financial markets were large and growing. The increased level of international financial flows helped undermine the fixed exchange rate regime by heightening speculative pressures on some currencies (including the U.S. dollar).

Once the Bretton Woods exchange rate arrangement ended, most major currencies began floating freely against one another. This loosened the previous monetary straitjacket, and a bout of inflationary pressures ensued. On top of this, in 1973, a cartel of oil-producing nations (the Organization of the Petroleum Exporting Countries, or OPEC) quadrupled the price of petroleum, putting further upward pressure on prices. A deep recession in the period 1973–1975 led to an

unaccustomed mixture of high unemployment and high inflation—
"stagflation," as it was called. Another round of OPEC oil price increases in 1979–1980 further aggravated inflation.

Macroeconomic difficulties came to a head after 1979. To slow the
rate of inflation, developed countries began to adopt more contrac-
tionary monetary policies, resulting in extremely high interest rates
and several years of recession. While inflation eased in the advanced
capitalist countries, unemployment remained very high. In this crisis
atmosphere, developed countries gradually moved to recommit themselves to a market orientation and international economic openness.
Governments exercised greater monetary restraint, deregulated many
economic activities, and privatized previously public enterprises. The
trend was epitomized by the policies of the British prime minister
Margaret Thatcher and the American president Ronald Reagan, who
made the case for less government involvement in their respective
economies. Reagan did so, anomalously, while running up enormous
budget deficits in the United States. Nonetheless, and despite such setbacks as a costly American banking crisis, by the mid-1980s the developed capitalist countries had made clear their renewed dedication to
an integrated international economy.

More surprising were trends in the developing countries. After many
decades of economic nationalism and protectionism, they emerged from
the crises of the 1980s with a newfound orientation toward international markets. These crises, along with the accumulated problems of
relatively closed markets in an increasingly open world economy, led
almost every country in Latin America, Africa, and Asia to jettison the
prior inward orientation in favor of much more economic openness to
the rest of the world. Developed and developing capitalist countries
continued to reduce barriers to trade and investment, leading to a char-
acterization of the era as one of "globalization."

The most stunning development on the path to globalization was the
collapse of the centrally planned economies. The economic problems
of the late 1970s and early 1980s eventually drove these countries away
from central planning and toward international markets. China and
Vietnam moved first, in 1979: while maintaining Communist rule,
both governments reoriented their economies toward exporting to

the capitalist world. After 1985 the Soviet Union embarked on an attempt at gradual reform, which was quickly overtaken by events as the country's social and political system unraveled. After the USSR collapsed in 1991, the entire Soviet bloc quickly abandoned central planning and moved toward capitalism at speeds varying from gradual to breakneck.

In a way, the very success of the Bretton Woods order caused its demise. Ever more inclusive patterns of economic integration undermined the gradualism and compromises that had characterized the postwar economic settlement. At the same time, the connection between military and economic interests became less clear as first détente and then the end of the Cold War made the solidarity of the Western bloc seem less relevant. In these circumstances, international markets took precedence over purely domestic considerations, and international economic considerations took precedence over national security concerns. Inasmuch as concern about the Soviet Union and its allies had been a major source of Western political and economic solidarity, the collapse of the Soviet Union and its bloc rendered this particular source obsolete. By the first years of the new century, the international economy had become something very different than it had been between the 1940s and the 1980s, the heyday of the American Century. But what sort of international economic order has arisen in the American Century's wake, and what can we expect of it?

The Contemporary International Economy

Today's globalized international economy is fundamentally different from that spearheaded by the United States in the aftermath of World War II. For one thing, virtually every nation—not just the United States and its closest allies—now engages in the world of international trade, finance, and investment. For another, the principles of compromise and gradualism that characterized the Bretton Woods order have given way to a more unqualified belief in the desirability of removing barriers to international economic exchange, and to a generalized skepticism about heavy-handed government intervention in national economies.

As a result, the international economy of the early twenty-first century is a global, integrated market system. Capital moves far more freely around the world than the Bretton Woods negotiators ever anticipated, and far more countries have joined the World Trade Organization and have committed to limiting their trade barriers than was originally expected in the late 1940s. More than at any time since 1914—and perhaps more than at any time in human history—something approximating a generally open international economy exists.

This evolution toward an ever more tightly integrated world economy has taken place alongside the development of major regional economic blocs. The European Union (EU), which started as a modest league of six nations, now encompasses virtually all of Europe, from Ireland to Bulgaria and from Cyprus to Finland. From a simple customs union, the EU has become a true single market that has eliminated barriers to the movement of goods, capital, and people while harmonizing the regulation of investment, migration, product and production standards, professional licensing, and many other economic activities. A subset of seventeen EU members shares a common currency, the euro, and a common European Central Bank. Meanwhile, the United States, Canada, and Mexico formed a free trade area in 1994, as did Brazil, Argentina, Uruguay, and Paraguay. Similar regional economic arrangements have proliferated elsewhere.

The growth of these regional blocs has contributed to the expansion of economic authority beyond the traditional economic powers. While the United States remains the world's largest economy, it no longer stands alone in terms of economic influence. The United States today has become, in many ways, just another country—subject to the vagaries of international economic trends in a way that Henry Luce would have found bewildering back in 1941.

Many of the new features of the international economic order were illustrated with the economic crisis that began in 2007. The United States found itself in the midst of a debt crisis not unlike those that had typically afflicted developing countries. And even as the U.S. economy and world economies struggled to recover, Americans found themselves heavily reliant on foreigners for goods, capital, technology, and markets. Perhaps even more surprising, chief among the foreigners upon whom America had come to rely was China, which was now a major creditor of the U.S. government and of Americans more generally.

The new economic configurations of the early twenty-first century clearly signaled the end of the American Century. The United States is today one among several major centers of economic power, with other countries gaining ground. In international monetary relations, the dollar's predominance can no longer be taken for granted. America's massive debt to foreigners—hardly a sign of American predominance—has emerged as one of the principal problems in global finance.

The world economy today is, in many ways, far more democratic than it was in the aftermath of World War II. No single country can determine the future course of international monetary, financial, and commercial relations, and none can dictate the characteristics of the international institutions governing those relations. Areas of the world that had stagnated for centuries are now experiencing an unprecedented pace of economic growth and development, lifting hundreds of millions of people out of poverty.

Today's world economy is very much a product of the plans devised during World War II, under American leadership, and implemented, largely with American blueprints, in the years after the war ended. The United States was very successful, during its few decades of global preeminence, in rebuilding an open world economy out of the unpropitious ruins of a failed international order. This success fundamentally changed the way the international economy worked, and these fundamental changes made obsolete many of the original organizing principles devised at Bretton Woods. Today the United States can no longer determine the future of the world economy. America succeeded in creating an economic order largely in its own image, but the subsequent evolution of the world economy helped bring the American Century to a premature end.

CHAPTER 8

Illusions of an American Century

Walter LaFeber

"The American Century," Henry Luce's essay of February 17, 1941, in *Life* magazine, provided many policy makers and observers a rather spectacular title for the new age that, Americans confidently believed, would dawn with the end of World War II. In its believers' minds, the American Century promised to offer the best of the worlds of both God and Mammon: beneficent in its actions and profitable in its results. It did not work out that way, but this particular dream never died. President Barack Obama exemplified the persistence of such a belief when he declared in September 2010, "There's no reason the 21st century is not going to be the American Century just like the 20th century was." Yet as the president spoke, articles and books bearing such titles as "The End of the American Century" were making their appearance. With the post-2001 involvements in Iraq and Afghanistan having helped drag U.S. foreign relations and the nation's economy to their lowest levels since Luce published his famous essay, the American Century seemed to be slinking to an early end, even as the president insisted otherwise.[1]

Unable to capture Osama bin Laden and his closest associates for almost a decade after they had killed nearly three thousand people in New York City, Pennsylvania, and Washington, D.C.; unable, despite efforts that cost thousands of American lives and over $1 trillion, to install cooperative, functioning governments in Iraq after seven bitter years of fighting or in Afghanistan after a full decade; unable to mediate a peace between Israel and the Palestinians after more than two generations of trying; unable to forestall or end an economic downturn that became the worst since the Great Depression of the 1930s; unable to live within its means and instead accruing a debt of $14 trillion, $2 trillion of which was owed to Communist China, a nation on course to eclipsing the United States in gross national product by 2020—all of these contributed to the growing consensus at the end of the twenty-first century's first decade that Luce's American Century would never reach its hundredth birthday.

Yet the real problem was not that the American Century had reached a premature end—it was, contrary to Obama's pronouncement, that it had never begun. It had never existed except as an illusion, but an illusion to which Americans, in their repeated willingness to ignore history, fell prey. Out of that illusion had come the conclusion that the United States possessed such immense power that it might even gloriously "end history," in the widely noted, and perhaps uniquely American, phrase coined by Francis Fukuyama to interpret the final triumph of the United States over the collapsing Soviet Empire in 1989.[2]

That Luce's idea of an "American Century" enjoyed such a long life is evidence of how Americans myopically view their history and place in the world. His essay drew from, and embroidered, a fictionalized account of the nation's past as he attempted to persuade an inward-looking people to embrace global leadership. Luce wrote his essay in part to condemn the American refusal after World War I to join the new League of Nations that, under American leadership, might have brought about the political as well as economic rebuilding of a war-devastated, Communist-endangered Europe. Washington and Wall Street had instead attempted to stabilize Europe through the 1920s and 1930s with informal, shifting, and largely private (and potentially highly profitable) enterprise coalitions that the United States could dominate. This attempt had, of course, produced not the American Century to which Obama referred but the 1929–1931 economic collapse followed by the rise of Adolf Hitler's Third Reich and the ascendancy of Japanese militarists. In 1941 Luce demanded that his nation go to war to defeat Hitler and Japan. Doing so, he insisted, would finally inaugurate the American Century postponed by the errors of the interwar period.[3]

In this regard, Luce's immediate intention in 1941 was not to proclaim immutable principles but to push Americans into an ongoing conflict. He believed, correctly, that by offering aid to Great Britain, President Franklin D. Roosevelt had already informally involved Americans in the conflict. It was one of the few actions by FDR that won Luce's approval. Now, the publisher understood, Congress and the mass of Americans had to be persuaded to enter the war formally and fully. Luce's method was to emphasize feel-good tenets, not to warn of the blood, sweat, and tears that would be wrung from American lives. His hand securely on the country's pulse, Luce had not built the dominant U.S. publishing empire of his time by either ignoring or misreading how to speed up that pulse rate. He knew how to sell. Thus Luce concluded his essay by emphasizing "four areas of life and thought in which we may seek to realize such a vision" of a world transformed by American principles.

This conclusion, to use Arthur Miller's later phrase, was a call to lunch, not a call to sacrifice. Realizing the American Century meant, in the first instance, expanding "free economic enterprise" globally, so that Americans "and our friends" could then go "with our ships and . . . airplanes where we wish, and as we wish." There were to be no curtains, iron or otherwise, to hamper trade and travel. Luce's was an open-door world with no boundaries, but with the usual understanding that those most capable of exploiting opportunities awaiting behind those many doors would be able to enter first and profit most. Extending this "free economic enterprise" system "where we wish" was bait to pull Americans into war. Given the economic horrors they had just endured during the 1930s, including a 25 percent unemployment rate, this bait glistened.

The second "area," Luce went on, involved exporting American "engineers, doctors, movie men, makers of entertainment, developers of airlines, builders of roads, teachers, educators." Thus the publisher defined exporting "entertainment" as equivalent to developing overseas "airlines" and "roads." After 1945 many foreign peoples and governments would disagree with such easy categorization.

Third, he summoned the United States "to be the Good Samaritan" of the entire world. "For every dollar we spend on armaments, we should spend at least a dime in a gigantic effort to feed the world." Luce innocently had no idea how many dollars those "armaments" were to consume in the coming decades as Americans pursued their own "Century." Those interested in finding a "dime" for foreign aid would never be able to keep up.

Finally, he concluded that "all this will fail" without "a passionate devotion to great American ideals," including "a love of freedom, a feeling for [sic] the equality of opportunity, a tradition of self-reliance and independence and also of cooperation"—apparently mere boiler-plate until one notes that Luce was condemning both Hitler's statist ideology and the Soviet Union's Communist system. Four months after Luce published his essay, the Soviets, surprisingly and involuntarily, became a U.S. ally when Germany invaded Russia for the second time in twenty-seven years.[4]

"American Century" has been a term used by many, in various con-texts, and with varying definitions and examples. But Luce was a prime originator of the term and certainly its greatest publicist. He also provided the clearest examples and definitions of what the phrase signified. In the present essay, "American Century" will therefore refer to Luce's use and definition of the term. Resembling many U.S. pam-phleteers and presidents who came after him, Luce carefully laid out his principles against the backdrop of a highly scrubbed version of his own nation's history. Nowhere in his essay would the reader learn that slavery, the Civil War's six hundred thousand dead, and the nearly exterminated Native American tribes had figured among the costs exacted so later Americans could profit from the continental base, eco-nomic promise, and ideological payoffs of an American Century. Lu-ce's argument anticipated the how-to-be-happy-with-small-cost thesis of Norman Vincent Peale's *Power of Positive Thinking,* a runaway best seller that resonated with post–World War II Americans. But Peale's recipe for positive thinking at least seemed to work for some people. The American Century idea was a façade that effectively camouflaged what lay beneath it and thus misled those who accepted Luce's vision.[5]

Reinhold Niebuhr, the most distinguished theologian and influen-tial political philosopher of the mid-twentieth century, had a darker, more realistic view of human nature and, thus, American possibilities.

It was a view, Niebuhr liked to point out, that he shared with James Madison, the most important participant in the writing of the U.S. Constitution. Niebuhr stated flatly that Luce was a classic example of the human propensity for sinfulness: overly proud, hopelessly blind to his own limitations, and lacking historical perspective. The theologian's judgment was severe. "Mr. Luce is to be distrusted," Niebuhr concluded, for "he revels in the new white man's burden. He does not show the slightest indications that our salvation can be worked out only in fear and trembling." Niebuhr differed fundamentally from Luce not over the question of whether to join in the war to defeat Fascism. Instead, Luce's vision of a postwar world bitterly divided the two men. Niebuhr expected, in the words of his biographer, that the United States would be "menaced as much by its own pretensions to virtue as it was by world disorder." Niebuhr deeply feared, and condemned, such "pretensions to virtue," particularly when it was the world's dominant military power that paraded them.[6]

The president initially responsible for dealing with this postwar world disorder was Harry Truman, who suddenly and with virtually no foreign policy preparation became chief executive upon Roosevelt's death in April 1945. Shortly after he moved into the White House, Truman naively rephrased Luce's American Century's objective while retaining its essence when he told close advisers that he might not pry 100 percent of what he wanted from Soviet dictator Josef Stalin (whose armies occupied much of Eastern and Central Europe), but he expected to obtain 85 percent. The new president shared with the publisher a sharp sense of inevitable American destiny.

The supposedly about-to-appear American Century, however, was even then enduring a painful gestation in large parts of Europe and Asia. Soviet armies, which had accounted for the overwhelming majority of both Nazi casualties and Allied deaths, occupied much of Germany, including the capital of Berlin, and virtually all of Eastern Europe. Large Communist parties threatened to take over France and Italy. In Asia, Communists were outmaneuvering, politically and militarily, China's corrupt Nationalist government, which had been allied during the war with the United States. Truman could rightly claim that

Americans produced 50 percent of the otherwise devastated globe's economic goods, held a monopoly on the atomic bomb, and controlled the world's seas with the greatest navy in history. Yet all that could neither unite Europe under an American Century banner nor save China (and some of China's neighbors in Northeast and Southeast Asia) from communism.[7]

The American Century was stillborn. Half the transport of the standing Soviet army was horse-drawn, while Truman commanded the world's most powerful air force with global range and atomic bombs. Even so, that military power could not create an American Century in Central and Eastern Europe, China, or the Soviet Union itself, any more than comparably overwhelming military power some sixty years later could incorporate Iraq, Afghanistan, Ukraine, Georgia, or other parts of the Middle East and central Asia into an American Century.

When U.S. officials set about trying to help reconstruct non-Communist countries in the post-1945 world, it was not Luce's confidence that inspired them but stark fear that the globe might spiral back to the catastrophic 1930s. Truman publicly expressed this fear on March 6, 1947. He told a Baylor University audience that any expansion of closed, state-controlled economic systems (he was obviously referring to communism) would ultimately doom American freedom. The president then effectively drove the point home: "We must not go through the Thirties again." The Baylor speech formed the necessary preface for the message the president delivered six days later to a joint session of Congress.

This speech became known as the Truman Doctrine. Its broad principles guided U.S. foreign policy throughout the Cold War or, in certain cases (as with conflicts in Vietnam and Central America), misguided it. Peoples around the world, the president told the House and Senate, were choosing "between alternative ways of life." Members of a sharply divided Congress consequently had to cooperate in sending vast amounts of military and economic aid to areas threatened by "totalitarian regimes." More precisely, Truman urged Congress—controlled by Republicans determined to pursue an American Century on the cheap by reducing U.S. overseas obligations and slashing taxes—to appropriate $400 million to protect Greece and Turkey against an immediate Communist threat.

The president had dramatically sketched the alternatives: a perhaps open-ended commitment to parts of the world many Americans could not locate on a map, or a return to the 1930s. Faced with that choice, the Republicans surrendered. Fear, not Henry Luce's optimism, forged the resulting Cold War consensus. That fear, in turn, soon led to investigations of those in the government (and private citizens on the outside) whose loyalty to an anti-Communist crusade was questionable. Lacking an adequate understanding of the way the world works, Americans reflexively attributed troubles beyond their borders to nefarious forces at home. So the dream of an American Century became instead the nightmare of another Red Scare.[8]

Truman quickly followed his doctrine with the Marshall Plan, which ultimately provided $13 billion over five years to save two groups: West Europeans—from succumbing to communism, and U.S. producers and exporters—from losing irreplaceable European markets. In 1949 the United States worked with West European allies to establish the North Atlantic Treaty Organization. Familiarly known as NATO, this alliance served as a military bulwark that protected or, more accurately, reassured nervous Europeans worried about a replay of the 1919–1920 American abandonment.

Truman's Doctrine, the Marshall Plan, and NATO formed cornerstones of U.S. policies for the next forty years. What immediately ensued, however, was not an American Century but a series of disasters. In the spring of 1949 Communists finally gained control of the world's most populous country, China, as the remnants of the U.S.-supported Nationalist regime fled for safety to the offshore island of Taiwan. In September 1949 Truman announced, as calmly as he could, that the U.S. monopoly of the atomic bomb had ended considerably earlier than many experts had predicted. The Soviets had successfully triggered an atomic device. In the late winter of 1950 Senator Joseph McCarthy (Rep.-Wisc.) declared he knew why these historic setbacks had occurred: Communists and their sympathizers had infiltrated the U.S. government, particularly the State Department. McCarthy provided Americans with a ready-made explanation for why Luce's promised American Century had metastasized into the Cold War. Not for the last time, grand expectations nourished by bad history resulted in dangerous demagoguery.

"I hold in my hand" solid evidence of Communists in high places of government, McCarthy famously proclaimed. When the evidence proved worthless, most of his Senate colleagues ignored him, at least for a time. Then in June 1950 the five-year civil war between a Communist regime in northern Korea and a U.S.-supported government in the south erupted into an all-out conventional conflict when the Communists attacked across the 38th parallel separating the two Koreas. United Nations armies under the command of World War II military hero General Douglas MacArthur finally drove back the Communist forces by early autumn. Truman and his secretary of state, Dean Acheson, then committed one of the gravest errors of the Cold War. MacArthur had assured them that he could cross the 38th parallel and destroy the enemy, march to the Yalu River, which separated Korea from China, and forcefully reunite Korea. Containment of communism would magically transform into liberation from communism, thereby providing a glimpse of a revived American Century on the very borders of the People's Republic of China. The general assured the president that he would have the troops home by Christmas.

Faced with McCarthyism at home and contemplating the rich possibilities MacArthur held out, Truman and Acheson approved the general's plans. In late September 1950 U.S. forces quickly moved north until advanced units could see the Yalu. First hundreds, then thousands, then 250,000 Chinese troops swarmed across the river into Korea. These "volunteers" drove MacArthur's army not only away from the border but deep into southern Korea itself. Thousands of retreating U.S. troops froze to death in the bitter 1950–1951 winter. Trumpeting his reinvigorated search for the Communists in Washington who must have brought about such a humiliation, McCarthy became a major force in U.S. politics. Even Dwight D. Eisenhower, the most lauded American World War II hero and 1952 Republican presidential candidate, found it necessary to defer to the Wisconsin senator. When a desperate MacArthur pleaded for a series of atomic bombs to be dropped on bases inside China, Truman refused. Among other problems, the president could not be confident that the United States possessed enough such weapons to stop the Chinese invasion.[9]

As Truman prepared to leave office in 1953, the American-created utopia that Luce had forecast a dozen years earlier was nowhere in sight. Crises, not confidence, defined the temperament and policies of the time. Instead of celebrating a triumphant American Century, the departing president had found himself attempting to maintain bankrupt French colonialism against a nationalist, Communist uprising in Vietnam; dispatching U.S. troops to NATO to protect a vulnerable Central and Western Europe; reluctantly pledging to commit American lives to defend the remnants of the Nationalist Chinese regime on Taiwan; and nearly quadrupling U.S. military spending, from $13 billion to over $50 billion in just thirty months. The U.S. economy and foreign policies were increasingly shaped not by American Century principles but by a "military-industrial complex," as President Eisenhower would later accurately phrase it. Relations with China entered a highly dangerous, twenty-year era of cold, and at times shooting, war. In mid-1950 Truman and Acheson had toyed with transforming their policy of static containment into dynamic liberation. A later Discovery television network documentary revealed the actual results: Discovery called its film about the 1950–1953 Korean War "Our Time in Hell."

Once in the White House, Eisenhower moved rapidly to halt the now stagnated war in Korea. He had to free his hands so he could deal with multiple outbreaks in the so-called Third World. In oil-rich Iran, a nationalist movement led by Mohammad Mossadegh had come to power in 1951. As prime minister, Mossadegh challenged both the young shah, who ruled Iran, and the British-controlled Anglo-Iranian Oil Company, which extracted Iran's oil and then sent the largest share of the profits not to Iranians but to the company's shareholders and the British government. Luce's *Time* magazine proclaimed Mossadegh its "Man of the Year" for 1951. (Luce, not surprisingly, preferred MacArthur for the title but finally deferred to his editors.) Less enthralled by the prime minister's actions, Eisenhower and Secretary of State John Foster Dulles were determined to teach a lesson not only to Mossadegh but to other nationalists around the globe contemplating neutrality rather than joining the anti-Communist camp. Working in mid-1953 with British intelligence and Iranians who were bought off or voluntarily joined the Americans, Central Intelligence Agency (CIA) personnel helped direct the overthrow of Mossadegh. The young shah was restored to his throne. Control of Iran's oil fields, once entirely British controlled, was reapportioned: five U.S. companies now gained access to 40 percent of Iranian oil production.[10]

The American Century seemed finally to be coming into its own, complete with the rewards for private enterprise that Luce had applauded in 1941. The evidence, however, proved illusory. Over the next twenty-five years, SAVAK, the shah's secret police, brutally moved to silence political opponents. U.S. officials bolstered his regime with massive military aid, sophisticated aircraft, and other weapons. By the early 1970s President Richard Nixon termed the shah one of the most important of U.S. allies. In a public speech on New Year's Eve, 1977, President Jimmy Carter flattered the shah for "the admiration and love which your people give you." Only months after Carter spoke, a popular revolution, finally led by Ayatollah Ruholla Khomeini, overthrew the shah. When the United States provided refuge for the deposed monarch, who was dying of cancer, Iranians seized the U.S. embassy in Tehran and held fifty-three Americans hostage, a humiliation that continued until—and helped bring about—the end of Carter's presidency in January 1981. The temporary loss of Iran's oil during this crisis drove up world petroleum prices 60 percent. It also triggered an inflationary spiral in the United States that exacted a heavy toll on Americans whose wages could not keep pace with the skyrocketing prices of groceries and gasoline. The Soviets, Chinese, Koreans, Vietnamese, Latin Americans, and now Iranians had taken turns raising fundamental questions about Luce's vision.[11]

Nikki R. Keddie, a noted scholar of Iran, concluded her study of the revolution by indirectly passing judgment on some assumptions of Luce's American Century. The rise to power in 1979 of the religious ayatollahs was, she argued, not at all consistent with Iran's increasingly secular political thought. To comprehend how radical was the change in 1979, Keddie believed, "we must remember the concurrent intensification of [the shah's] Westernized despotism, closely tied to [its] dependence on the West, and especially the United States."[12]

The putative success of the CIA operation in Iran during 1953 led U.S. officials to believe they could repeat that success elsewhere. Eisenhower and Dulles next overthrew a democratically elected Guatemalan government. This government had moved to help its land-starved people by giving them 178,000 acres long claimed, but little used, by the Boston-based United Fruit Company. United Fruit had dominated for over half a century both Central America's banana exports to the United States and the region's communications systems—particularly its railroads, which had been built for carrying bananas, not Guatemalans. As Dulles moved to mobilize much of the hemisphere, Eisenhower ordered secret CIA training for a group of Guatemalan exiles. The government in Guatemala City, fearing that it might follow Mossadegh into oblivion, acquired nineteen hundred tons of arms from Communist Czechoslovakia for self-protection. The CIA-sponsored exiles then struck in June 1954 and, with critical last-minute U.S. help, replaced the Guatemalan government with a military regime. Dulles announced that good Guatemalans had overthrown the bad.[13]

The story, however, did not end there anymore than it had ended in Iran during 1953. Over the next three decades, Guatemala's military rulers racked up the worst human rights record in the Western Hemisphere. Government forces killed some seventy-five thousand of their own citizens. Despite, or because of, these horrific conditions, the United States funneled more economic and military aid to this small country than to any other Latin American nation. A not surprising result was the rise of anti-U.S. revolutionary movements not only in Guatemala but also in nearby Nicaragua, El Salvador, and Honduras. These accelerated in the late 1970s (notably just as the Iranian Revolution gathered speed). President Ronald Reagan's administration responded by expanding military aid to the besieged governments. Supporting ruthless oligarchs and military strongmen was presumably not what Luce had in mind when he called on the United States to serve as the world's Good Samaritan.

An estimated two hundred thousand people died during the Central American uprisings against the U.S.-supported military rulers in the 1980s. Most of the deaths occurred in Nicaragua, where "Sandinistas"—named after Augusto Sandino, who had fought the U.S. occupation of

Nicaragua from 1926 to 1933 and was then murdered by the U.S.-installed Somoza dictatorship—had overthrown the last of the Somoza family in 1978. Cuba and later the Soviet Union sent aid to the Sandinistas, but that help was not decisive. The Soviets, for example, spent much of the 1970s supporting the laughable Nicaraguan Communist Party, which the growing Sandinista movement could ignore or exploit. Indeed, non-Communist suppliers, particularly Mexico and Western European nations, sent the Sandinistas more aid in the post-1978 years than did the Communist bloc. Beginning in 1981 the Reagan administration attempted to overthrow the Sandinistas by funneling military supplies and advisers to the "Contras," whose forces included remnants of the Somoza dictatorship. Rather than fulfilling Luce's optimistic vision of a prosperous, peaceful American Century, Central America—affectionately known as the "backyard" of the United States—became a blood-soaked site of guerrilla warfare. "On the whole," the secretary-general of the Organization of American States declared in 1986, "the region is worse off now than it was twenty-five years ago."[14]

As early as 1954 a top-secret CIA analysis had explored how "to arrest the development of irresponsible and extreme nationalism, and [the Latin American] immunity from the exercise of U.S. power." The answer: "long-standing American concepts of 'fair play' must be reconsidered." "Fair play" had apparently become an obstacle to realizing the American Century. Unfair play could mean ignoring the solemn U.S. pledge made in the Charter of the Organization of American States (1948): "No State or group of States has the right to intervene, directly or indirectly, for any reason whatever, in the internal or external affairs of any other State." The CIA's complaint about unwanted restrictions was tantamount to an admission of failure: Washington's many military interventions over the previous half century in Mexico, the Caribbean, and Central America had not brought equitable economic development and stability. Latin American hopes that the promised American Century might end such Yankee habits were soon crushed. Luce apparently knew nothing of this CIA report, but he might have been disturbed by the claim that his principled, powerful American Century was unequal to the task of handling Guatemala, a country the size of Tennessee, and that it instead had to be done by forgetting about "fair play."[15]

The CIA report's conclusion applied far beyond Central America. The Cold War took a fundamental turn in the mid-1950s. During the first decade of the conflict, the two superpowers had consolidated their blocs. Americans employed economic pacts and military alliances with Latin America and Western Europe, while the Soviets did the same with Eastern Europe and China. But in the 1950s, as the two blocs began to fragment, each superpower relied on coercion, often direct military power, to shore up its authority. U.S. covert interventions in Iran and Guatemala were paralleled by Soviet military actions in East Germany (1953) and Hungary (1956). These were merely the preliminaries. With some thirty new nations born in the 1950s out of collapsing colonial empires, large areas of Asia and Africa not only freed themselves but often invited the two superpowers to bid against one another for their support. The appearance of these new states ended the U.S. dominance in the United Nations that Americans had taken for granted since 1945. In late 1960 Adlai Stevenson, the newly appointed U.S. ambassador to the UN, explained what had happened to this supposedly important venue of the American Century: "Due to the admission of so many new countries, the United States and the Western countries no longer control the United Nations. Our position is much more difficult."[16]

This second Cold War went off in new directions. Fissures began to split each superpower's bloc, which in turn led to new possibilities for Soviet-American confrontation. By 1957–1958 U.S. officials began to recognize (but not acknowledge publicly) that the growing rivalry between the USSR and China was inexorably splintering the Communist camp. Then an even more shocking division occurred: Cuba, ninety miles from Florida and under *de facto* U.S. control since 1898, fell to Fidel Castro's revolutionary forces on New Year's Day, 1959. Castro quickly opted out of anything resembling Luce's American Century.

Americans were stunned. They had long, and usually easy, relations with Cuban rulers. In 1952 Fulgencio Batista had seized power. Two years later he conducted an election that gave him 87 percent of the vote. (When Mossadegh obtained 95 percent of the vote in an Iranian election, Eisenhower took it as proof that the prime minister was Communist; when Batista received 87 percent, Eisenhower apparently simply assumed he was popular.) In 1955 Vice President Richard Nixon visited the island and in effect welcomed Batista as a member of the American Century by comparing the dictator, "a man of humble background," to Abraham Lincoln. U.S. domination of the nation's sugar industry and the control of Havana's roaring night life by Cosa Nostra, the U.S. crime syndicate, seemingly cemented Cuba to the United States. Yet if Batista had apparently kept the lid on revolutionary activities, it came at a high cost: John F. Kennedy, during his 1960 presidential campaign, charged Batista with killing "over 20,000 Cubans in 7 years." In reality, those killings fueled the Castro uprising and a revolutionary worldview. Indeed, to assert genuine control over Cuban affairs, Castro believed the island had to be fully independent of Washington. He set out to break free from U.S. economic and political controls.

By early 1961 the outgoing Eisenhower administration had cut off diplomatic relations with Castro's government and was secretly training Cuban exiles for a rerun of the 1954 Guatemalan intervention. Having closely studied the Guatemalan affair, Castro ensured that his army, unlike the Guatemalan, would remain utterly loyal. Meanwhile, once in the White House, Kennedy changed his campaign rhetoric. He ordered that Eisenhower's invasion plans go forward but withheld crucial U.S. air and naval support of the exile invasion force. Kennedy hoped at least to give the appearance of abiding by the U.S. nonintervention pledges made years earlier in the Organization of American States' charter. Such pledges, after all, were supposed to indicate the Free World's ethical and political superiority over the Communist bloc—an important advantage, as dozens of new nations were declaring their independence from European colonialism. Kennedy's concern for the appearance of U.S. noninvolvement resulted in a disaster for his administration. In April 1961 Castro's forces destroyed the exiles' invasion at the Bay of Pigs. U.S. involvement (the training and direction of the exile forces) was immediately apparent to all. Few events in the Cold War matched the Bay of Pigs in exposing the contradictions in the claims of an American Century.[17]

Cuba and the United States became locked in mutual hatred, and then, with the help of the Soviets, nearly tripped the world into nuclear war during October 1962. Meanwhile, the CIA recklessly sought to deal with Castro's challenge by assassinating him. In one plan U.S. agents worked with American mobsters Sam Giancana and Santo Trafficante, the latter Cosa Nostra's top boss in Havana. But the Cuban leader's security forces blocked such efforts. Washington finally settled for trying to contain Castro. Over the next half century, the U.S.-Cuban confrontation continued, sometimes bloodily in Central America, the Caribbean, and even in Africa. That a neighboring island so locked into the promises of the American Century might want to drop out had, before 1959, been virtually unthinkable. That the island could defy U.S. policies for more than fifty years (often helped by extensive economic aid from such American allies as Canada, Mexico, and Western Europe) revealed starkly the limits of Washington's authority. And Castro's regime was not the only new government that opted out of Luce's American Century.[18]

In 1954 Paris officials finally abandoned their failed military efforts to return Indochina to what little remained of France's former colonial empire. Despite massive military aid sent to French forces by Truman and Eisenhower, Ho Chi Minh and his Vietnamese followers had prevailed. An international agreement hammered out in Geneva, Switzerland, formally removed the French and scheduled elections to be held throughout Vietnam by 1956. Fearing that Ho with Soviet and Chinese support would easily win any national election, the United States refused to sign the Geneva agreements and instead deployed six hundred American "advisers" to help establish a pro-Western regime in South Vietnam. During his abbreviated presidency, Kennedy quietly increased the number of these advisers to sixteen thousand. The South Vietnamese regime nevertheless continued to lose ground to Ho Chi Minh's forces. In the autumn of 1963 the desperate Kennedy administration conspired with the South Vietnamese military to overthrow the government Eisenhower had put into place in 1954. That coup succeeded. Three weeks later Kennedy himself was dead. In Saigon, meanwhile, political uncertainty loomed, along with North Vietnamese military advances. President Lyndon Johnson tried to control both by committing U.S. combat forces. Although by 1967 the number of U.S. troops reached 550,000, the numbers seemed to make little difference. GIs won battles but could not win the war.

As the conflict dragged on, U.S. casualties rose dramatically. The war's economic costs spiraled upward. The American economy could no longer support the once mighty dollar that since 1945 had undergirded much of the non-Communist world's development and trade while also defraying the costs of expanding U.S. military commitments and bases. Antiwar groups rapidly grew in number and, working increasingly alongside a vibrant civil rights movement (both movements embodied by 1967 in the charismatic figure of Martin Luther King), launched mass demonstrations in major cities and on college campuses. In 1968 the deeply unpopular Johnson finally had to drop out of his reelection race.

Now at the end of his life, Luce watched his quarter-century-old hope of an American Century recede even farther into gloomy historical mists. He responded by uncritically supporting the U.S. commitment to South Vietnam and by using *Time* and *Life* to try to reverse the spreading antiwar sentiment. The effort failed miserably. Luce had spent his childhood as the son of a missionary family in pre-Communist China. His hatred of the People's Republic of China and anyone cooperating with the Communist regime was bottomless. Luce concluded that the war had to be won because China was aiding the North Vietnamese. "China is the real enemy in Asia, and the greatest threat anywhere [*sic*] to world peace," he wrote, so escalating the war in Vietnam "would be to risk a confrontation with China in the right place at the right time."[19]

Luce believed that Ho Chi Minh's North Vietnam was the willing instrument of a Communist China that was seeking to take over all of Southeast Asia. Shared by policy makers in the Eisenhower, Kennedy, and Johnson administrations, this view tragically misread, or ignored, centuries of history in which the Vietnamese and Chinese had been mortal enemies. (Indeed, in 1979, four years after the United States exited South Vietnam, the Chinese and Vietnamese were again at war with one another.) Richard Nixon did not make that error. Elected president in 1968, he began restoring relations with China as part of his effort not only to extricate the United States from Vietnam but to try to stop American decline.

As Nixon told a Pittsburgh audience in 1971, he had come to the conclusion that "the United States no longer is in the position of complete pre-eminence or predominance [and] that is not a bad thing." He predicted that "in 5 years, 10 years . . . , but in any event within our time," U.S. hegemony would be replaced by five "leading powers": the United States, the Soviet Union, Japan, China, and Western Europe. The president dismissed any idea that an American Century was on the horizon: "I think of what happened to Greece and Rome, and you see what is left—only the pillars." As "the great civilizations of the past . . . have become wealthy, as they have lost their will to live, to improve, they then have become subject to decadence that eventually destroys the civilization. The U.S. is now reaching that period." Nixon's historic decision to open relations with Communist China (after he had made a political career of condemning anyone who believed they could profitably deal with Communists) was at the center of this policy—a policy of trying to stop an accelerating American decline by playing the other four "leading powers" against one another, especially the Chinese against the Soviets. Luce had died in 1967, so he never had to deal with the Vietnam War's final consequences: fifty-eight thousand Americans killed, along with an estimated 2 million Vietnamese dead, climaxing in a U.S. defeat and an American president flying to Beijing to pay homage to leaders of a China that Luce had once loved and now despised.[20]

For those who still clung to Luce's vision, its unraveling seemed never-ending. The U.S. economy, undermined by the 1960s military budgets and Americans' refusal to pay for the needs of their supposed Century with more taxes, became less competitive, particularly when pitted against the new, highly efficient manufacturing plants of Germany and Japan. In 1945 the United States had controlled more than half of the world's gold holdings, thus making the dollar as good as gold. By the 1960s, declining trade balances and accelerating defense spending overseas had depleted those holdings, thus weakening the dollar's power and attractiveness. Americans, moreover, had begun investing large amounts of dollars in Europe, Asia, and Latin America so they could operate behind tariff walls, stake out holdings in oil and other raw materials, and exploit cheap labor. The nation's manufacturing complex, which had dominated world markets for a century, had entered an era of gradual but relentless decline. In early 1973, after several failed attempts to stabilize the dollar, President Nixon was forced to take the greenback off the gold standard, thus allowing the dollar's value to float and thereby exposing it to the vagaries of the market and the betting of speculators.[21]

Historians and other scholars and journalists might laud the so-called Americanization of the world. American fast-food franchises flashed around the globe, with the golden arches of McDonald's arriving by the late 1980s even in the Soviet Union. Foreign basketball players wore Nike sneakers, and American investors penetrated the world's most promising market, Communist China, to the level of $50 billion by 2010. But this "Americanization" also produced the destruction of key parts of long-vital U.S. industry (such as clothing and steel); wage increases for American laborers between 1970 and 2010 that did not keep up with inflation-driven prices; and, increasingly, unfavorable balances of trade that forced the United States to borrow ever larger amounts from abroad (principally China, Europe, and Japan) to pay for both the lifestyle to which Americans had become accustomed and the military forces to which Washington leaders and their think-tank allies were becoming addicted.[22] By the 1970s, therefore, the nation's economic building blocks, the necessary foundations for an American Century, were deteriorating.

In 1973 war erupted between Israel, a U.S. ally, and Egypt, backed by Arab oil-producing states. To punish nations viewed as pro-Israeli, major oil producers, particularly those now working together in the Organization of the Petroleum Exporting Countries, sharply cut oil exports. Gasoline prices quickly doubled at U.S. pumps. Americans were shocked. In Luce's vision the United States was supposed to call the shots, not take them—especially from regimes in the still "developing" world. The resulting inflation of the oil shocks that struck between 1973 and 1981 caused American interest rates to soar to the highest levels since World War II. As U.S.-made products consequently increased in price, they became even less competitive abroad.

In a historic turn that would be fully appreciated only a decade or more later, at this same time (1973–1981) the Chinese government demonstrated unexpected ideological flexibility. It began to loosen the Communist Party's control over the nation's economy. One billion Chinese offered a huge, cheap, and disciplined workforce. U.S. multinational companies began to move into China and, in too many instances, close up century-old bastions of American manufacturing in the Carolinas, New York, Massachusetts, and Ohio. When new corporations did appear in these regions, particularly in the Midwest and South, they were as likely to be European or Japanese as American. This was especially true in the case of automobile makers such as BMW, Honda, and Toyota, which were lured by massive tax breaks and a nonunion workforce. For working-class Americans, dreams of an American Century defined by good jobs, good wages, and the prospect of a good retirement were becoming increasingly dim. In mid-1975 *Time* magazine simply asked, "Can Capitalism Survive?"[23] Elected the following year, Jimmy Carter was the first president victimized by these post-1960s economic shifts. Not that his predecessors had left office riding waves of success. Johnson had been drummed out of the White House by war and the civil rights protests; Nixon had resigned in disgrace; and Gerald Ford, the nation's only unelected chief executive, had no chance of overcoming the anti-Washington animus enveloping the country, so in 1976 lost to Carter, the Georgia governor little known beyond that state. The new president quickly ran into difficulties at home, but his loss in the 1980 election resulted largely from his inability to control crucial overseas events, the kind of control that true believers in the American Century could expect him to impose.

Carter did mediate an agreement between Israel and Egypt to end their thirty-year conflict. He also negotiated and pushed through the Senate a treaty that promised to return the U.S.-built and operated Panama Canal to the Panamanians in 1999. The treaty removed a long-festering sore from Washington's declining relationship with Latin America. But Carter could neither save the shah of Iran nor stop the Soviet Union's invasion of Afghanistan in 1979–1980—although he secretly moved to short-circuit the Russian attack with covert aid sent through CIA channels to the Afghans who opposed the invasion. His efforts to rescue U.S. hostages held by the new Iranian revolutionary government collapsed amid desert sandstorms and broken-down U.S. helicopters. Carter's final two years in power became a case study of Washington's inability to control revolutions, the limits of its military reach, and the proof of Niebuhr's warnings about the need to examine American pretensions with "fear and trembling." A deeply religious man, Carter probably knew something about Niebuhr's warning, but like presidents before and since, he concluded that it was preferable to take a chance on the illusions of an American Century's supposed reach, especially with a tough reelection campaign looming.

Carter's policies in Cambodia raised particularly painful questions in regard to a supposed American Century. Caught in the middle of the Vietnam conflict, and devastated by U.S. bombing intended to stop North Vietnamese troops from using this supposedly neutral sanctuary, Cambodia after 1975 fell under the control of one of the great murderers of the post-1945 era—Pol Pot, who slaughtered millions of his fellow citizens in a vain attempt to consolidate his rule. The Soviets tried to work with a now united Communist Vietnam to overthrow Pol Pot. Carter, however, was on guard against any such expansion of Vietnamese and possibly Russian influence. When Pol Pot was finally overthrown, the president supported a Chinese attack on Vietnam in 1979 that also aimed at returning to power the Cambodian murderer. Carter's policy was consistent with his pro-Chinese, anti-Soviet policies. But it was, to say the least, inconsistent with his speeches trumpeting the importance of human rights. Supposed realism now took precedence over principles that ostensibly had shaped Luce's American Century.[24]

Proclaiming it was "morning in America," and implying that the dawn of the American Century lay just ahead, Ronald Reagan defeated the luckless Carter in 1980. The former movie actor became one of the most popular twentieth-century presidents. Many Americans believed Reagan, and continued to do so a generation later, even though the American Century idea has resembled not the rising sun but the distant horizon that recedes as one tries to approach it. In an April 1982 speech the new president quoted one of Luce's writings of twenty years earlier: "We're the country of the endless frontier, of the big sky, of manifest destiny, of unlimited resources, of 'go west young man,' of opportunity for all . . . gung ho and can do." It soon appeared, however, that America's "endless frontier" and "manifest destiny" did not seem to extend to, among other places, the Middle East.[25] In 1982, to try to end the chaos triggered by an Israeli invasion of Lebanon, Reagan dispatched U.S. troops to Beirut. There they remained until a terrorist bombing in October 1983 killed 241 American soldiers. To distract attention from this debacle, although ostensibly in response to a growing Communist threat in the Caribbean, Reagan immediately ordered the invasion of Grenada. Not even the invasion of this small island, however, accorded with American Century standards: Operation Urgent Fury required almost a week for six thousand U.S. troops to overcome opposition consisting of local police and eight hundred Cubans, some of whom were soldiers and some laborers who had been building airport runways. Nineteen Americans, seventy-one Cubans, and at least forty-five Grenadians died in the fighting.[26]

Meanwhile, Reagan pulled out all the stops in attempting to bring about an American Century in revolution-torn Central America. He deployed CIA operatives, economic coercion, U.S. military advisers, and large amounts of military aid to stop insurgents who were attempting to overthrow U.S.-supported authoritarian regimes in El Salvador, Honduras, and Guatemala. In Nicaragua, the president increased support to the Contras who were fighting the Sandinistas. In doing so, Reagan ignored both U.S. congressional legislation that tried to prevent Washington's interference in the civil war and U.S. public opinion that consistently opposed becoming involved.

The Reagan administration resorted to changing the metaphor from the American Century to the popular and often used domino theory: if the Sandinistas made a go of it, El Salvador and Guatemala would be the next victims of left-wing revolution, and governments would then fall from Panama to the U.S.-Mexican border. But the domino theory, which had been rolled out by President Eisenhower as early as 1954 to justify U.S. involvement in Vietnam, with unhappy results, had little relevance to Central America. Vietnam was eight thousand miles away, but Central America was, as the phrase went, the U.S. "backyard" and had been under Washington's informal control ever since the United States began building the Panama Canal in 1903. The region was also impoverished, governed by small elites (in El Salvador they had long been simply identified as the Thirty Families) who monopolized land ownership and commerce, and saddled with corrupt, ineffective institutions that had been further misshaped by decades of U.S. meddling. The problem was not a Communist-triggered domino theory but regimes that had little, if anything, in common with accountable politics and competitive capitalism that Luce's hopes for an American Century had assumed.[27]

Reagan's efforts to bring Central America to heel produced results too often associated with the post-1945 quest for an American Century. Frustrated by opposition from Congress and important elements of public opinion (notably Roman Catholic priests and nuns deeply experienced in Central America who condemned U.S. intervention), Reagan administration officials secretly tried to circumvent restrictions imposed by Congress by funding the Contras through the diversion of profits gained from covert arms sales to (of all places) Iran. No one could recite the script about an imagined American Century more compellingly or colorfully than Reagan when he took the presidential stage. But while his back was turned, the curtain parted to reveal what was going on backstage: an administration engaged in blatantly illegal dealings—and with none other than the hated Iranian ayatollahs who were secretly providing funds to help the Contras. The despised Iranians had covertly become an ATM machine providing the cash that enabled the Reagan White House to ignore U.S. law. When revealed in a Middle East newspaper in late 1986, the Iran-Contra affair led to the prosecution of top Reagan administration members and the nadir of the "Great Communicator's" presidency.

"Morning in America" was turning into a dangerously stormy evening. By the mid-1980s more than $1 trillion of government debt had built up as a result of both the president's $300 billion annual military spending and the large tax cuts that overwhelmingly benefited only the wealthiest 5 percent. American producers, the cutting edge of Luce's free-enterprise Century, had grown increasingly less competitive so had moved their plants to cheaper labor areas such as Mexico and Asia. Trade deficits consequently hit record highs. These official deficits did not take into account the illegal drug trade, which reached an estimated $100 billion a year, with perhaps one-quarter of that amount going to drug producers in Latin America and Asia. The globe's leading creditor when Reagan moved into the White House, the United States sank below Mexico to become the world's greatest debtor nation by the time he stepped down in 1989. New economic powers, led by Japan (which the United States had atomic bombed, defeated, and occupied four decades earlier), were not only outselling the grand symbol of American assembly-line prowess, the Detroit-made automobile, but were using their profits to purchase U.S. manufacturing plants, famous California golf courses, and even New York City's iconic Rockefeller Center.[28]

Yet Americans remember Reagan less for these historic economic shifts, Central American revolutions, or the criminality of the Iran-Contra humiliation than for reversing his own fervent anti-Soviet rhetoric to begin historic discussions with Mikhail Gorbachev, the new Russian leader, who assumed power in 1985. Reagan supported Gorbachev's attempts to try to change Soviet communism by opening its system and, Gorbachev fervently hoped, thus resurrecting its moribund economy. Advised by Secretary of State George Shultz, who astutely handled the day-to-day dealings with Moscow and accurately conceptualized why and how the new Moscow leader would have to reduce Cold War tensions, Reagan stunned global observers by patiently, and at times joyfully, working with Gorbachev to overcome nearly seventy years of Soviet-American hatred. Among those stunned were some of the president's own top officials. Caspar Weinberger, secretary of defense, Richard Perle, Weinberger's top aide, and Robert Gates, the deputy chief of the CIA, were among those convinced that Gorbachev was an old-line Communist intent only on deluding Reagan and Shultz.

These dissenters failed to make the turn that history was taking in the late 1980s. Gorbachev understood that the Russian economy had disastrously stalled (it endured a zero percent growth rate during some years of the 1980s), and that it hopelessly trailed far behind the West in developing computers and other electronic inventions that were transforming the world's economies—and militaries. The Soviet leader understood that a more open Russian system was the prerequisite for the effective adoption of the new technology. Gorbachev was not applying for membership in Luce's American Century. He devoutly believed his changes would revive and strengthen the Communist system. Jack Matlock, U.S. ambassador to the Soviet Union, underlined the main point in early 1989: Moscow's "foreign policy will be heavily— and often decisively—influenced by domestic needs and imperatives."[29] The same could be said of U.S. foreign policy.

Reagan and his successor, George H. W. Bush, made historic contributions by working with Gorbachev, while marginalizing such doubters as Weinberger, Perle, and Gates. As Soviet control of Eastern and Central Europe began to disintegrate rapidly in 1989–1990, Bush worked quietly behind the scenes to help Chancellor Helmut Kohl of West Germany absorb Communist East Germany. The British, Italian, and Dutch governments, initially supported by Gorbachev, strongly opposed such unification. All of them, particularly the Russians, had suffered catastrophically in two world wars against Germany. Nor did they relish the thought of the economic powerhouse that a united Germany could again become. Gorbachev understood this, but he also understood that East Germany was artificial, and that an unhappy, divided Germany would be a highly expensive distraction for the Soviet Union. Bush helped by assuring Gorbachev that a unified Germany would be integrated into, and thus closely watched by, NATO and the European Union. The Russian leader finally agreed to unite the two Germanys under Kohl's leadership. Gorbachev, for his own purposes—not those of Reagan, Bush, or an imagined American Century—emerged as the indispensable statesman, the catalyst, in the ending of the Cold War.[30]

The Soviet Union officially disappeared on Christmas Day, 1991. The Cold War was over. But the following decade did not produce the "end of history," that is, the final triumph of American-style democracy and capitalism, the American Century fully revealed. Instead, the decade produced an easing of global tension between the two superpowers and, partially as a consequence, growing disorder within the new, post-Communist Russia along with other parts of the world that had earlier been held together by the tensions and demands of the

Cold War. As a result, regions long frozen in place fragmented. Areas turned dangerously unstable, and the United States, with its overwhelming supremacy, responded with fresh bursts of military and/or economic interventionism in the Philippines, Somalia, Haiti, Yugoslavia (several times), Mexico, parts of Africa (particularly Sudan and Kenya), and the borders of Russia itself (notably Latvia, Lithuania, Estonia, Georgia, and Ukraine) to put out—or exploit—the fires. Attempting to justify this unmatched deployment of U.S. power during peacetime, Madeleine Albright, secretary of state under President Bill Clinton, anointed her country "the indispensable nation." It was a one-dimensional updating of Luce's 1941 prophecy and, like that prophecy, was soon fundamentally questioned. France and newly reunited Germany, close U.S. allies in the Cold War, now condemned America's expansive use of its "hyperpower" and its "lacking in sensitivity." Samuel ("Sandy") Berger, President Clinton's top White House national security adviser, accurately identified the dilemma created by efforts to resuscitate the American Century idea. Although describing what he called "the 'indispensable nation' thing" as "a little too triumphalist," Berger insisted that when facing fragmentation and disorder "America has to lead," even if fulfilling this responsibility makes the United States look like "the biggest rogue state in the world."[31]

Amidst all the insular celebrations of the supposed triumphs of American culture, democracy, military power, and multinational corporations, Berger had perfectly defined the trap in which the United States found itself during the 1990s—and after. In the two decades that followed the end of the Cold War, the United States carried out more military interventions than it had during the previous forty-five years of waging that war. The results, particularly Berger's accurate observation that the United States might appear to be "the biggest rogue state in the world," certainly did not signal the arrival of an American Century. Filipinos sent the United States packing from important bases it had occupied since 1898. Somali warlords killed eighteen American soldiers and then dragged their bodies through the streets before the world's television audiences, thereby convincing President Bill Clinton to abandon a mission that had begun as an effort to feed Somalis. Clinton's advisers had persuaded him that the United

States could destroy powerful Somali clans and put that country on the path of living happily ever after. Instead, a long-term civil war resulted. Haiti, the poorest nation in the Western Hemisphere, even after the United States had begun intervening periodically as early as 1915, became poorer and more unstable and remained impervious to another round of U.S. ministrations in 1994–1995. Mexico, which was rapidly integrated into the U.S. economy after the 1980s, suffered a massive currency crisis that threatened its stability until Washington sent billions of dollars to prop up a financial system on which Americans as well as Mexicans depended.[32]

The Soviet Union meanwhile fragmented into nearly a dozen sovereign countries. Russia itself, counseled by prominent American economists, suffered severely as its former Communist system morphed into a corrupt, murderous, private enterprise system. Some of its leading businesses, especially the nation's rich mineral resources, fell under the control of robber barons who bought and sold Russian bureaucrats and politicians. The life expectancy of Russian males then plummeted from sixty-four to fifty-seven years, the only such decline recorded in the developed world after 1990. For Russia, either during or after the 1990s, Luce's American Century ideas proved singularly unhelpful. Vladimir Putin, who assumed power in 2000, increasingly reached for authoritarian tactics to stabilize the country. Helped by historically high oil prices, Putin steadied the economy, successfully checked U.S. efforts to take over important strategic and economic stakes in the former Soviet territories of Ukraine and Central Asia, exploited and increased Europe's dependence on Russian gas and oil, and in 2008 brutally punished the former Soviet state of Georgia, which had begun to align itself with the United States—all without any effective response from Washington. These were among the reasons some observers concluded by 2010 that the supposed American Century was over.

Actually, it had never begun, certainly not in Luce's version. Americans like to talk about their "City on a Hill," "Manifest Destiny," and "American Century," but they invariably choose facts that fit their patriotic predispositions and ignore those that do not—a tendency that corrupts some high school history texts as well as foreign policies. Those with a taste for irony will appreciate the role played by one of the

American Century's privately generated offshoots—the grandiloquently titled "Project for the New American Century"—in generating many of the assumptions (along with more than a few of the personnel) that persuaded President George W. Bush to invade Afghanistan and Iraq after the tragedies of 9/11. By 2011 those decisions had led to an ongoing eleven-year war in Afghanistan and a continuous nine-year war in Iraq (by far the longest wars ever fought by Americans), which cost more than six thousand U.S. lives and well over $1 trillion. With the tenth anniversary of 9/11 approaching, Secretary of Defense Robert Gates, no longer the hawkish cold warrior, drew one conclusion: "I've got a military that's exhausted. Let's just finish the wars we're in and keep focused on that instead of signing up for other *wars of choice*." Gates had earlier implicitly condemned Bush's post-9/11 policies by telling West Point cadets, "In my opinion, any future defense secretary who advises the president to again send a big American land army into Asia or into the Middle East or Africa should 'have his head examined,' as General MacArthur so delicately put it." (Bush had appointed Gates as secretary of defense in 2006.) By the time it quietly disbanded in 2006, the "Project for the New American Century" had therefore left a notable legacy: it had helped destroy any lingering hopes for an American Century.[33]

In early 2011 mass movements demanding the replacement of authoritarian rulers with democratic reforms suddenly, and quite unexpectedly, erupted in Tunisia, Egypt, Bahrain, Jordan, Libya, Syria, and Yemen. Observers dubbed these surprising developments the "Arab Spring." Earlier, proponents of democratic change had often used the United States as inspiration; in 1989, for example, Chinese demanding more democracy pointedly brought Statues of Liberty to their demonstrations—before they were brutally put down by China's Communist government. "The Arab Spring" demonstrators, however, avoided such references to any such inspiration from the United States. The American-led invasions of Iraq and Afghanistan and the long, bloody wars that resulted soured many Arabs on any idea of associating themselves with the United States. A foreign policy expert in Qatar said flatly, "No one in the region is pro-American anymore." A similarly experienced observer and adviser to protesters in Jordan told a reporter, "I don't think America appeals to the younger generation. I'm cautious not to present them with the American example because there's a negative attitude to America, a disappointment." An international relations expert in Lebanon declared, "Nobody's listening to America anymore. It's become irrelevant." Something had gone fundamentally wrong with Luce's hope for an American Century, but U.S. policies after 9/11 had only accelerated a trend that had begun decades earlier.[34]

Guided by some historians, Americans have remained convinced they never had an empire. Leading Founders of the nation in 1776 and the Framers of the Constitution in 1789, however, including George Washington and Thomas Jefferson, easily referred to the "empire" they were building. The process of going from thirteen states to fifty did not occur without, at times, the coercion and, in notable instances, the bloodshed that characterize empire building. Yet Americans associated the term with the British, French, and German empires that they feared and sometimes fought in the nineteenth century, and then with fascism, Nazism, and communism in the twentieth century. It became important, as well as patriotic, to drop the term as it applied to U.S. history. And to be fair, *informal empire* became a more accurate phrase anyway, particularly given Washington's policies in the Western Hemisphere and Asia after 1898.[35]

Luce's vision of an American Century fits neatly into this tradition of informal empire, notably in his four themes outlined at the beginning of this essay. Yet unprecedented levels of military spending were a significant additive to that vision. Military budgets began to mushroom when it became clear by late 1950 that the quest for an American Century, in this case along the northeastern and southwestern borders of China, had become a highly combustible enterprise.

As President Obama's statement in 2010 indicated, the American Century phrase will continue to find use, as will other similar terms such as "manifest destiny." That older phrase, dating from the 1830s and 1840s, has been revived since 9/11 by those who argue that understanding and avoiding any further recurrence of the failed interventions of the Cold War, the 1990s, and the early twenty-first century will require first coming to terms with some two hundred years of American expansionism.[36]

But critics of "manifest destiny" or Luce's "American Century" will have little influence in policy-making circles. Instead, advocates of ever-increasing military spending will join interventionists, promising that this time, unlike the last, some proposed U.S. intervention will succeed quickly and cheaply—not, in other words, as it was done in Korea, Iran, Cuba, Vietnam, Central America, Lebanon, Somalia, Iraq, and Afghanistan. As long as Americans believe such pledges, they will remain oblivious to the lessons and consequences of persisting in Luce's dream—a dream that was, after all, conjured up in order to persuade them to go to war.

CHAPTER 9

The Heavenly City of Business

Eugene McCarraher

✦

Nancy Mitford, in her novel *The Blessing* (1951), inserted a priceless vignette that captures the essence of the American Century. Grace Allingham, the novel's heroine, is hosting a dinner party. Among her guests is a pompous American politician, Hector Dexter, who discourses about the marvels of American business. Dexter caps his harangue with this visionary flourish:

> When I say a bottle of Coca-Cola . . . I mean an outward and visible sign of something inward and spiritual, I mean it as if each Coca-Cola bottle contained a *djinn,* and as if that *djinn* was our great American civilization ready to spring out of each bottle and cover the whole global universe with its great wide wings. That is what I mean.[1]

Hector Dexter's fictional bloviation, clearly intended as satire, finds a remarkable real world counterpart in these words, written by *New York Times* columnist Thomas Friedman in the spring of 1999:

> For globalization to work, America can't be afraid to act like the almighty superpower that it is. The hidden hand of the market will not work without a hidden fist. McDonald's cannot flourish without McDonnell-Douglas, the designer of the F-15, and the hidden fist that keeps the world safe for Silicon Valley's technology is called the United States, Army, Air Force, Navy, and Marine Corps.[2]

Friedman, energetic huckster of globalization, thereby recycles Dexter's epiphany, ordnance now added, thereby showing that when it comes to business America very much means business. Yet note the religiosity that pervades both passages. Like Hector and his dinnertime homily, Friedman salts his edict in unmistakably religious language. In these passages we glimpse an eschatological vision; view the commodity as a sacramental token, material conveying the essence of the American spirit; understand corporate expansion culminating in judgment rendered and punishments administered. With their extravagant faith in a corporate future underwritten by our money and arms, such statements convey the essence of what Henry Luce dubbed "the American Century."

In an effort to dissect the American Century, this essay will examine the eschatology of corporate business. One crucial and enduring element in America's quest for global supremacy has been the extraordinary hubris of our corporate managerial and professional elites. That hubris stems from a steadfast faith that American capitalism represents the highest stage of human achievement, the end of history itself. Eschatology, Terry Eagleton reminds us, remains "the grandest narrative of all"; and just as millions of Americans continue to believe in some version of Christian eschatology, many—especially among the upper echelons of politics and business—adhere to an allegedly more secular mythology. Even before Henry Luce coined the phrase, belief in a perpetual American Century has formed the grandest narrative of our corporate intelligentsia. As the grandest narrative of corporate capitalism, the American Century was and remains a heavenly city of business.[3]

Eschatology is always a narrative of longing for a just and beloved community, ample with delight, innocent of violence, and complete and unceasing in fulfillment. We long, as Augustine put it, for a "heavenly city," but all our attempts to construct that metropolis achieve magnificent but perverse imitations—"earthly cities," facsimiles of heaven that sometimes achieve imperial dimensions. Corrupted by the lust for domination, our "earthly cities" are inevitably grotesque distortions of our heavenly desire; art, commerce, technology, and politics become illustrious but disfigured products of our desire for communion. Sin cannot beguile or enslave without offering some promise of heaven.[4]

Offering its own story of human fulfillment, capitalism is an eschatological tale as well as a form of political economy. Relying on the instrumental reason inscribed in business, science, and technology, capitalism is often considered an agent of secularization. Yet while Max Weber taught us that capitalism is a culprit in the "disenchantment of the world," many historians now doubt the demise of enchantment. As Marx perceived, commodities are fetishes, mementos of errant desire, symbols of longing. (Think of Hector Dexter's Coca-Cola bottle.) And as Friedman's image of the Almighty gendarme of globalization suggests, capitalism substitutes one mythos of redemption for another: *extra agoram nulla salus*—outside the market, there is no salvation.[5]

Friedman affirms the corporate state as a wrathful God of Battles; Mitford points to the enchantment of the American corporation and its products. Since the end of the Civil War, corporate business culture, however "secular" its veneer, has sought to convert unbelievers to a covenant theology of wealth. Luce's essay offered a latter-day mission statement of imperial corporate modernity, but the genealogy of the American Century stretches back into the early seventeenth century. Though culminating in the architecture of national security and corporate industry erected after World War II, the American drive for global dominion was not some fall from a state of republican grace that occurred after 1945. The roots of the modern American Century lie in an indomitable conviction, first articulated in Puritan theology, that business success was a sign of God's providence and a token of benediction for mastery over others. From John Winthrop to Ralph Waldo Emerson and from Walter Lippmann and Woodrow Wilson to Francis Fukuyama and Barack Obama, American proponents of modernization have espoused some historical teleology that concludes with a business civilization. In other words, there have been several "American Centuries." Some form of capitalist eschatology has long been central to American identity; for the "Redeemer Nation," salvation implies inclusion in a worldwide marketplace. Indeed, "American exceptionalism"—the belief that this nation has been charged with a mission to uplift and lead the world—has been inseparable from the capitalist passion to construct a heavenly city of business. Understood as a fervent eschatological hope—an "end of history" in a beloved community sponsored by corporate business—the American Century was and remains a beatific vision, a form of capitalist enchantment.

"God's American Israel"

Luce's American Century had a long if not venerable pedigree. Its historical origin lies in the Puritans' "errand into the wilderness," their quest to convert or vanquish the heathens and claim the land for the gospel. As Anders Stephanson has argued, "any genealogy" of American expansionism must begin with the Puritan belief in their "predestined, redemptive role [as] God's chosen people in the Promised Land: providential destiny revealed." The Puritan clergy, the first cultural elite in American history, wrote the initial script for expansionism. According to the terms of the Puritan "covenant theology," the elect accepted a sacred mission to build a godly commonwealth, a "city on a hill" whose radiance would reveal the majesty and power of the Almighty.[6]

In the ensuing historical drama, the Puritans enacted the role of new Israelites, with Native Americans consigned to the part of new Canaanites, idolaters whose degenerate customs reflected their election for God's wrath. Indian economic culture in particular struck Puritans as unnatural and abhorrent. The Indians' conception of property, value, and exchange struck the saints as wasteful and unproductive. Confronted with such prodigal iniquity, God's chosen had a right, and in fact a duty, to clear the land of its slothful inhabitants and put the soil to profitable use. Well before John Locke justified dispossession and colonization for the purposes of "improvement"—the use of land and other resources for the production of exchange value—John Winthrop had already sketched a theology of ethnic cleansing. Writing to his father after his first trip to America in 1628, the young Winthrop faulted "the Natives of New England," who "inclose noe Land, neither have any settled habytation, nor any tame Cattle to improve the Land by." Since, by divine decree, rights to land and animals entailed their profitable exploitation, the saints, he resolved, must not "suffer a whole Continent as fruitfull and convenient for the use of man to lie waste without any improvement."[7]

Thus the "city on a hill" was a citadel of wealth as well as an abode of the elect, a place in which Christian (read Protestant) proprietors could enjoy what one Puritan divine called "the Blessings of Time and Eternity." Providence and the Protestant work ethic fused in a covenant theology of economics. "The gospel hath brought in its right hand Eternal Salvation," one minister exulted, "and in its left hand, Riches with Protection and Deliverance from Enemies." Conceding that it was "rare" in history for "religion and profit [to] jump together," the clerics were convinced they skipped happily in the towns and villages of New England. As Sacvan Bercovitch archly noted, "the wheel of fortune and the wheel of grace revolved in harmony." If the elect adhered to the covenant, the new Israel would be unto Him a kingdom of merchants, both holy and prosperous. Enlisting scriptural exegesis and homiletic ingenuity in the service of commerce, Puritan clergy preached the first gospel of modernization in American cultural history.[8]

The Puritans were conquistadores in Protestant garb. Yet their errand did not mandate endless territorial expansion. With the withering of Calvinist devotion, the errand into the wilderness underwent a profound transformation. By the First Great Awakening of the 1730s and 1740s, the *Puritan* errand had become an *American* project of global revitalization. "'Tis probable," reflected Jonathan Edwards, the premier theologian of the Awakening, "that the world shall be more like Heaven" very soon. In Edwards's eschatology, business enterprise and technological progress were preparing the way for the return of Christ. Edwards anticipated the arrival of "better contrivances for assisting one another through the whole earth by more expedite, easy, and safe communication between distant regions than now." "The whole earth," he predicted, "may be as one community, one body in Christ." Edwards saw portents of this millennial state in the religious revivals sweeping New England. The growth of material wealth in the colonies foreshadowed "what is approaching in spiritual things, when the world shall be supplied with spiritual treasures from America." From its trove of riches, America would effect, Edwards prophesied, "the most glorious renovation of the world." Edwards enlarged the scale of Winthrop's blueprints for a city on a hill. Thus did American business activity take on world-historical significance, agents of American commerce and industry touched by God's finger even as they did God's work.[9]

Over the eighteenth and early nineteenth centuries, even as Calvinist theology waned, an eschatological residue persisted. With the Anglo-American Enlightenment, the Protestant language of millennialism was joined by liberal republicanism, the hodgepodge of acquisitive individualism and classical virtue still pervading American political discourse. One popular and rousing example was a "Song on Liberty," written by Joseph Warren, physician, orator, and Son of Liberty. Published in the *Massachusetts Spy* in May 1774—a little over a year before Warren fell at Bunker Hill—the "Song on Liberty" disavowed overt imperial aspirations. Having "led fair Freedom hither, when lo the Desart smil'd," Americans could take pride that "a paradise of pleasure was open'd in the Wild." Calling on his countrymen to defend their paradise from British "tyranny," Warren concluded with this masterful expression of the will to power:

> The land where Freedom reigns shall still be masters of the main,
> In giving laws and freedom to subject France and Spain;
> And all the isles o'er ocean spread shall tremble and obey
> The prince who rules by Freedom's laws in North America.[10]

Warren's imperial doggerel received a theological imprimatur from Reverend Ezra Stiles, Congregationalist minister and president of Yale. In his renowned 1783 oration to the new General Assembly of Connecticut, entitled "The United States Elevated to Glory and Honor," Stiles proclaimed an eschatological herald of riches. The Puritan theology of racial cleansing remained, implacable as a gravestone: the attrition of the Indians, and their replacement by whites, was "God's good providence." With the red menace removed by the hand of the Almighty, "the political welfare of God's American Israel" was assured, and its victory over both the Indians and the British was "allusively prophetic of the future prosperity and splendor of the United States." "God hath still greater blessings in store for this vine which His own right hand hath planted," Stiles predicted. Portraying the United States as a heavenly city of proprietorship, Stiles noted the "sweet and attractive charms" of "liberty, civil and religious" and dilated on the passions of acquisition and the pleasures of mastery. "The rewards of [liberty], with property, have filled the English settlers in America with a most amazing spirit. Never before has the experiment been so effectually tried, of every man's reaping the fruits of his labor and feeling his share in the aggregate system of power." By expelling the Indians and throwing off the yoke of English monarchy, Americans had overcome the last remaining obstacles that "obstruct the progress of society towards perfection." If left to an unimpeded and relentless expansion, American institutions of economic and political liberty promised the "inevitable perfectibility of man."[11]

Other luminaries concurred. In his Federalist Paper #10, James Madison insisted that Americans would need to "extend the sphere" of their dominion, acquiring the space necessary for proprietary enterprise. Endorsing a kind of "frontier thesis" long before Frederick Jackson Turner, Madison counted on expansion to reduce social friction and enlarge the scope of commercial activity. Thomas Jefferson agreed, maintaining that westward expansion would create an "empire for liberty," an imperium of yeomen farmers and artisans. (Jefferson paid homage to the Puritan covenant when he proposed that the Great Seal of the United States depict the people of Israel following a divine light.) With Jefferson, Madison, and Stiles, the city on a hill was becoming a homestead on a plain, and the company of saints was morphing into a herrenvolk order of white small-scale producers.[12]

By the middle of the 1840s—after the Second Great Awakening and the "Market Revolution"—covenant theology had been recast in terms of republican moralism, proprietary labor, and evangelical Christianity. The predestination of the elect now evolved into the "Manifest Destiny" of all. Alongside "prophets of prosperity," such as the economists Francis Wayland and Henry Carey, ministers such as Lyman Beecher preached the evangelical gospel of empire. In his *Plea for the West* (1835)—a notorious broadside that mixed expansionist brio with anti-Catholic vitriol—Beecher called upon Americans to mobilize their "pecuniary and moral power to evangelize the world." Admonishing his eastern readers that the West prefigured the future of America—"her destiny is our destiny"—Beecher trumpeted the "young empire of mind, and power, and wealth." But the West-as-America was also a portent for the redemption of the globe, prefiguring "the joy of the whole earth" and rising in "the majesty of her intelligence, and benevolence, and enterprise, for the emancipation of the world." A decade later, the Democratic journalist John O'Sullivan echoed Beecher's augury, coining a memorable and contagious phrase in the vernacular of empire. Writing in the *United States Magazine and Democratic Review,* O'Sullivan argued that the annexation of Texas into the Union was required by the search for American lebensraum. It was, he modestly proposed, "the manifest destiny of the United States to overspread the continent allotted by Providence for the free development of our yearly multiplying millions."[13]

Yet living space for the white republic was not the only concern of Providence. As O'Sullivan had contended in an earlier essay for the same periodical, this "manifest destiny" embraced not only the continent but the rest of the world as well. In "The Great Nation of Futurity" (1839), O'Sullivan had echoed Edwards and Stiles in staking out the terms of an American era. With its democratic institutions and material prosperity, the United States, he asserted, demonstrated "the excellence of divine principles"; and as other nations hurried to emulate our example, "the boundless future will be the era of American greatness." This generous account of American expansionism found favor with the Whig politician William H. Seward, governor and senator from New York and later secretary of state. In his Whig restatement of the covenant theology, Seward observed that the nation that "fabricates the most, and sells the most of productions and fabrics to foreign nations, must be, and will be, the great power of the earth." In pursuing their vocation, Americans would reveal "the secret of the ultimate regeneration and reunion of human society throughout the world." Commerce and capitalist modernity were paving the road to beatitude. To Seward as to O'Sullivan, the Manifest Destiny of America was more than American; in the unfolding narrative of God's design for the redemption of humanity, America served purposes larger than mere territorial aggrandizement. Yet the Great Nation of Futurity would itself remain a herrenvolk democracy—white, Protestant, and Anglo-Saxon. Enveloped in a Christian penumbra, the covenant theology of expansion remained a volatile blend of property accumulation, racial superiority, and international idealism.[14]

As an ardent Jacksonian expansionist, O'Sullivan complained that the American intelligentsia was indifferent to the nation's destiny. "Why cannot our literati comprehend the matchless sublimity of our position amongst the nations of the world?" he asked. Ralph Waldo Emerson both echoed his lament and sought to meet his challenge. In his 1844 essay "The Young American"—another precursor of Luce's "American Century"—Emerson called upon the cultural elite to affirm that America was "the country of the Future." "In every age," Emerson declared, "there has been a leading nation, one of generous sentiment, whose eminent citizens were willing to stand for the interests of general justice and humanity"—even if they risked the obloquy of being denounced as self-seeking, "chimerical and fantastic." Emerson chastised the nation's political and cultural leaders for their failure to cultivate an expansionist sentiment. "I find no expression in our state papers or legislative debate, in our lyceums or churches, specially in our newspapers, of a high national feeling." Despairing of the establishment, Emerson looked to a new generation for a culture of manifest destiny. "Who should lead the leaders, but the Young American." As the sage of the Market Revolution, Emerson pointed to merchants and manufacturers as the vanguard of the American age. In the "new and anti-feudal power of Commerce," Emerson detected the beneficent hand of "that sublime and friendly Destiny by which the human race is guided." Eschewing both Calvinist and evangelical theology while appealing to the machinations of "Destiny," Emerson updated the eschatology of American expansionism by divorcing it from Christianity.[15]

Herman Melville was more ambivalent about the American Future. Sensitive to the brutal delusions of American messianism, Melville discerned the sublimity and sham bound together in the national eschatology. In *White-Jacket* (1850), for instance, the title character delivers an exhilarating oration on the destiny of America. In exemplary jeremiad fashion, White Jacket upbraids a people doubtful of its mission to establish a benevolent dominion. "Long enough have we been skeptics with regard to ourselves," he asserts portentously. "[W]e Americans are the peculiar, chosen people—the Israel of our time," "predestinated" for greatness. Unlike the Persians, Romans, or other imperial peoples who conquered only to subdue and exploit, "with ourselves," he proclaims, "almost for the first time in history, national selfishness is unbounded philanthropy; for we cannot do good to Americans but we give alms to the world." Whether or not Melville believed this fustian is ultimately beside the point. In a passage that anticipated the spirit of Luce's "American Century," he captured the vainglorious and exuberant bravado of Manifest Destiny.[16]

Yet elsewhere in his writings, Melville expressed another view. The typical American, he observed in *Israel Potter* (1855), was "intrepid, unprincipled, reckless, predatory, with boundless ambition, civilized in externals but a savage at heart." Exposing "the metaphysics of Indian-hating" in *The Confidence-Man* (1857), Melville hinted that the dreams of expansion were fantasies of powerlust. However crude and violent, the backwoodsman was a "captain in the vanguard of conquering civilization," a figure akin to "Moses in the Exodus, or the Emperor Julian in Gaul." The more polite and devious market society that followed in his wake reflected the same will to power. Well versed in self-delusion, the Confidence Man would have known what to make of White Jacket.[17]

"Lift your eyes to the horizons of business"

After the Civil War, the United States grew in opulence and power, as the Union victory released the energies of industrial capitalism. As the voracious appetite of industry grew—and as the continental frontier for territorial expansion receded—the architects of postbellum foreign policy sought to acquire markets and resources beyond North America, especially in Latin America and Asia. The hunger for markets derived not only from the need for profitable investment opportunities but from a fear of class war at home. Especially after the frontier was declared officially closed in 1890—thus depriving the nation of its preferred palliative for social discontent—prominent Americans concluded that the only solution to underconsumption and social conflict lay in overseas economic expansion. Shortly after the Pullman and Homestead strikes of the early 1890s, Henry Cabot Lodge warned that unless the nation discovered new markets it would be "visited by declines in wages and by great industrial disturbances." Fueled by such fears, what Walter LaFeber has politely dubbed "the American search for opportunity" required both heavy diplomatic pressure and overseas military ventures. Even before the Spanish-American War in 1898, the United States, LaFeber observes, was already becoming "the new empire."[18]

If the United States was a "new empire," the old expansionist eschatology lingered, expressed now in Darwinist terms. Prominent imperial ideologues writing at the turn of the century saw American expansion as an episode in natural history, a case of the fittest surviving in the global arena of capitalist competition. Brooks Adams (brother of the melancholy Henry) typified the Darwinian turn in expansionist eschatology. By expanding economically and militarily, the United States "only obeys the impulsion of nature," Adams wrote in *America's Economic Supremacy* (1900). In the "battle for life" among nations, America was "fitted to survive in the contest of the twentieth century." With Britain fading in wealth, power, and vigor, the laws of Darwinian cosmology meant that the United States was destined to surpass its imperial predecessor. "The expansion of the United States is automatic and inevitable." For Adams, the process of natural selection displaced Providence in the old covenant theology of expansion. America's path to imperial supremacy was "determined by forces which override the volition of man."[19]

Adams's Darwinian eschatology was less popular than the more Christianized Darwinism of Josiah Strong and Albert J. Beveridge. In his best-selling *Our Country* (1885), Strong—a Congregationalist minister and secretary of the American Evangelical Alliance—predicted that the world was entering a new and final phase of history: "the final competition of the races for which the Anglo-Saxon is being schooled." Strong's racialist eschatology was Manifest Destiny on steroids: having filled North America, Protestant whites would descend upon Latin America, swarm over Africa, and move on to Asia, displacing or "civilizing" the native inhabitants. In his saner and more benign moments, Strong envisioned lesser breeds being Anglo-Saxonized through elevation of their consumer tastes. "What is the process of civilizing but the *creating of more and higher wants?*" For the evangelical clergyman, religion and profit could still jump together as they had for his

Puritan forebears. If "the millions of Africa and Asia are someday to have the wants of a Christian civilization," Americans would have to rise to the occasion. "With these vast continents added to our market," Strong concluded, America would become "the mighty workshop of the world."[20]

Similarly, Beveridge—Republican senator from Indiana, stalwart ally of President Theodore Roosevelt, and Progressive reform politician—urged his countrymen to undertake the tasks imposed by a wise and Anglo-Saxon Providence. In widely read speeches, Beveridge expounded a more benign but nonetheless coercive eschatology of Anglo-Saxon predominance. Telling a packed Senate chamber in 1900 that God had "marked us as His chosen people, henceforth to lead the regeneration of the world," Beveridge denied that the quest for empire had anything to do with avarice. Indeed, he prayed that "Mammon and the love of ease" would not "debase our blood" and weaken American resolve to exercise worldwide dominion. Still, like the Puritans, Beveridge saw abundance as a fitting remuneration for performing the mandate of heaven. "The divine mission of America," he assured his fellow senators, held "all the profit, all the glory, all the happiness possible to man." Providence and capital went hand in hand. As Beveridge told an audience just after the end of the Spanish-American War, America's "march toward the commercial supremacy of the world" was inseparable from its accomplishment of "Heaven-directed purposes." True to God's call, Americans—"sprung from the most masterful blood of history"—would "reap the reward that waits on our discharge of our high duty." Among those rewards were "new markets for what our farmers raise, our factories make, our merchants sell." The annexation of the Philippines represented, Beveridge declared, the moment when "the empire of our principles" could be "established over the hearts of mankind."[21]

Beveridge's hope that colonized peoples might be "touched by the fingertips of modern methods" points to the importance of corporate expertise in the nascent imperial eschatology. The new self-consciously imperialist expansionism grew out of a corporate reconfiguration of American capitalism. What Alan Trachtenberg once dubbed "the incorporation of America" recast American life in accordance with the requirements of large-scale capitalist enterprise. On the domestic scene, incorporation entailed the remaking of American elite culture. Where proprietary covenant theology had relied on the rhetoric of republicanism and evangelical Protestantism, a new covenant needed forms of cultural and political authority that ratified the managerial, professional, and technical cadres spawned by corporate capitalism. The modern capitalist corporation displayed two key features: the separation of legal ownership from daily control of the workplace, and the division of mental and manual labor in production. Corporate managers and professionals appropriated the knowledge and organizational prowess formerly possessed by artisans and farmers. If agrarian and artisanal skills had been the foundation of herrenvolk democracy, professional and managerial expertise now legitimized corporate hegemony. At the same time, the lexicon of professionalism and efficiency helped brace the moral spines of men tempted by the allure of consumer culture. To be sure, the new terms of hegemony coexisted uneasily: ever-increasing abundance both demonstrated the power of corporate expertise and threatened its moral foundations. Still, the idiom of expertise served, Jackson Lears observes, to "redefine the old republican vision of the public good in corporate and technocratic terms." Transforming the terms of authority from proprietary-Protestant virtue to corporate expertise, the incorporation of America created a new modernizing elite.[22]

As Lears has amply demonstrated, this civilizing mission among the new elites was bound up with longings for "regeneration": projects to assuage pervasive fears of effeminacy among men, racial deterioration among whites, and enervation among the middle and upper classes. Yet regeneration also took shape as "corporate liberalism": the renovation of liberal principles, formerly associated with the proprietary order, to accommodate the realities of corporate enterprise. Conceived or undertaken by a motley array of business and labor leaders, reform politicians, academics, and journalists, "corporate liberalism" has, from the 1890s to the present day, attempted to rationalize the accumulation of capital: corporate administration of markets, more or less grudging concessions to workers, farmers, and other subaltern groups, and more or less stringent state regulation of corporate activity. Taken up with questions of management, bureaucracy, efficiency, and engineering, corporate liberalism portrays itself as a thoroughly empiricist and secular mode of thinking. But corporate liberals have also been pugnacious and romantic internationalists, seeking to revitalize the sense of American destiny by linking it to the dynamism of corporate expansion. When they were "Progressives" committed to a broader crusade for social justice and moral renewal, corporate liberals attributed a numinous power to the business corporation, seeing it as a vanguard of peace and plenty. Indeed, like their Puritan and evangelical predecessors, corporate liberals have been beholden to an eschatology: the global achievement of beloved community underwritten by corporate expertise and largesse. Though "secular" insofar as they avoided explicitly religious (meaning Christian) language, corporate liberals have employed a rhetoric of "fate," "destiny," or kindred terms. Much more than a mere ideological screen to veil exploitation, corporate eschatology was and remains a millennial vision, a mythology of history's final consummation.[23]

Corporate eschatologists agreed with Lenin that imperialism was the highest stage of capitalism. Indeed, as Martin Sklar has pointed out, American social scientists rather than European Marxists were the pioneers of modern imperialist theory. Well before J. H. Hobson, Karl Kautsky, Rosa Luxemburg, and Lenin—in fact, before the Open Door policy and "dollar diplomacy"—economists and political scientists such as Charles A. Conant understood that imperialism was a strategy for the investment of surplus capital. But corporate imperialists aspired not only to exploit resources but to modernize the institutions of colonized areas. Imbued with missionary zeal, the corporate clerisy wanted to introduce—if need be relying on bloodshed and intimidation—capitalist property relations, liberal political ideas and institutions, and consumer culture. In part, of course, "modernization" facilitated exploitation. Yet at the same time modernization revived the missionary impulse. As Conant put it, "the United States shall assert their right to free markets in all the old countries which are being opened up to the surplus resources of the capitalistic countries and thereby given the benefits of modern civilization."[24]

Meanwhile, political elites also waxed philosophic about the moral education afforded by American capital investment. In his instructions to American diplomats at the Algeciras Conference in 1905, Secretary of State Elihu Root—formerly the nation's premier corporate lawyer—included a brief meditation on the civilizing aspects of the Open Door policy. Moroccan society needed to be changed, he wrote, in order for Moroccans to benefit from American capitalism. "Intercourse with that country," he wrote, "demands the existence of internal conditions favorable thereto. Security of life and property; equality of opportunities for trade with all natives . . . improvement of the condition of the people that will enable them to profit by the opportunities of foreign traffic . . . People shall be made in a measure fit and able to profit by the advantages" of inclusion in a global economy. A year later, speaking at a business convention in New York, Root extolled the corporate missionary project. Noting that Latin Americans had a less assiduous work ethic than their northern neighbors—"we have less of the cheerful philosophy"—Root contended that Anglo-Saxons could help them cultivate "the inventive faculty which strives continually to increase the productive power of men."[25]

Root's boss, President Theodore Roosevelt, exemplified the spirit of Progressive corporate liberalism. For Roosevelt the warrior-prophet, the effort to regulate corporate monopolies was tantamount to a holy war. "We stand at Armageddon and we battle for the Lord," he thundered at the Progressive Party's convention in Chicago in 1912, thereby capturing the eschatological fervor of many Progressive intellectuals and reformers. Roosevelt's allusion to the Book of Revelation should remind us of Progressivism's deeply religious character. Ranging from Christian apostles of the Social Gospel to more secular reformers, Progressives featured what Robert Crunden has called an "innovative nostalgia": a humane reconstruction of industrial society inspired by memories of small-town Protestant community. Faith in a providential American mission formed part of that inheritance, with many Progressives steeped in the covenant theology of expansionism. Whether or not they retained their youthful Protestant faith, many Progressives assigned to corporate business a central role in the new eschatology. Progressives (as well as later "liberals") were not inveterately hostile to corporations. Indeed, Progressive intellectuals saw the advent of a global corporate capitalism as an auspicious chapter in the history of America and the world. As the *New Republic*'s Walter Weyl opined,

American imperialism foreshadowed "a certain phase or form of an inevitable development, the creation of an economic unity of the World." Weyl's *New Republic* colleague Herbert Croly used even more explicitly religious language, though he drained it of theological specificity. For Croly, the corporate era was an arduous but liberating "pilgrimage" toward a "holy city" or "consummate community." As enlightened pilgrims, adherents of "progressive democratic faith" dwelled in a love that—"like that of St. Paul"—signified, to Croly, "an expression of the mystical unity of the human race." United by this "common faith that sanctifies those who share it," the people of the corporate era could draw upon a "spiritual heritage," a "fund of virtue" conserved and enlarged by a modern clerisy—"learned or holy men" exemplified by the "democratic administrator" and the "scientific manager." In the Holy City of Progressives, the benevolent expertise of corporations was heir to the divinity of Protestant clergy.[26]

Of course, like the Puritans, Progressives like Croly claimed the inalienable right to admonish and smite the heathen. In *The Promise of American Life* (1909)—the *ur*-text of Progressive political thought—Croly made clear that an international order of peaceful trade and production would require American supremacy and, on occasion, intervention. Pointing to unrest and insurrection in Latin America, Croly judged that "no American international system will ever be established without the forcible pacification of one or more such centers of disorder." Later, in *Progressive Democracy,* Croly explained the eschatological rationale for U.S. interventionism. In a volume redolent with post-Protestant religiosity, Croly did not shy away from the coercive and imperialist import of the new liberal eschatology. Like proselytizers for any faith, Progressive democrats were obliged to bring "pressure to bear" on the "less emancipated or more stubborn." While Croly hoped that they could exert this pressure "not necessarily by force," he admitted that imperial violence was "probably necessary." The beloved community of corporate capital would require legions as well as priests.[27]

Progressive corporate liberalism's most influential cleric was Walter Lippmann, a colleague of both Croly and Weyl at the *New Republic.* Icon of the Washington-New York "punditocracy," Lippmann was a virtuoso of grave and well-mannered opinion that affirms the wisdom of power. From the 1910s until well into the 1930s (and even beyond), Lippmann lauded the sagacity of economic and political executives. In *Drift and Mastery* (1914) he portrayed corporate managers as mandarins, philosopher-rulers who combined the expertise of the specialist with the wisdom of the humanist. If greed had driven "the old chop-whiskered merchants" of an earlier day, the "civilizing passions" of science and public service moved the modern manager. Separated from stockholders by salary and speciality, the manager was a "relatively disinterested person," beholden to "stubborn and irreducible facts" and less bound by "the acquisitiveness of immaturity." Insulated from both the avarice of capital and the envy of labor, corporate managers and professionals were poised to "revolutionize the discipline, the incentives, and the vision of the business world." Having dispelled "the old sanctities of private property," the steward-clerics of corporate property could promote innovation and foster a cosmopolitan sensibility—"modern communion," in Lippmann words, a recovery of that "old sense of cosmic wonder" to which "the old religions could point as their finest flower." "Modern communion" echoed Croly's Holy City, and both notions reflected the hope Progressives placed in the potential of corporate business.[28]

Lippmann's panegyric to the modern corporation lay behind his defense of imperialism. "Modern communion," he soon maintained, must embrace all the peoples of the world, and only America could sponsor it. If, as he wrote in 1915, American business activity promoted the "interrelation of peoples," then "any real friend of mankind" must be "passionately devoted to the regeneration of those territories which constitute the stakes of diplomacy": China, Africa, the Balkans, and other "backward" areas of the globe in need of capital investment. Two decades later, Lippmann's forecast of a *pax corporata* prefigured later auguries of "globalization." Lippmann acknowledged the brutality of imperialism but offered exculpatory evidence. Wherever it set up shop, corporate business, he asserted in *The Good Society* (1937), advanced "the regime of law and order" and achieved "a stupendous improvement in the standard of life." Offering an apologia for empire, Lippmann took the long view: the price of progress might be paid in the currency of human misery, but the outcome would justify the anguish of those born too early to benefit. Like the earlier Puritans and Indian haters, violence figured among the start-up costs for business. "Though their work has been stained with blood, cruelty, and injustice," Lippmann mused, "the men who open the world to economic development are completing the work of the explorers who set forth at the end of the fifteenth century." The true successors of Columbus, Magellan, and Diaz were the disinterested managers and professionals, the new captains of modern industry. By bringing the cornucopia of goods and knowledge to the impoverished and benighted, corporations were forging "a satisfactory organization of mankind." And, as Lippmann insisted, freedom was mandatory. Anticipating Margaret Thatcher, he admonished any putative dissenters that there was no alternative to corporate capitalism. "In the end no nation can fail to enter this system"; if it is unwilling to make itself "secure for the new economy," then "its certain destiny is to be conquered." Corporate eschatology admitted of no option to refuse the offer of salvation.[29]

Many Europeans agreed that American corporate hegemony was unstoppable. Visitors such as Andre Siegfried, G. K. Chesterton, and W. T. Stead both marveled and shuddered at the impending ascendancy of American capitalism. Stead bluntly predicted *The Americanization of the World* (1902). Surpassing the British Empire in population, resources, and vitality, the United States, Stead contended, now led "the providential mission which has been entrusted to the English-speaking Race." Indeed, Stead leavened his book with providentialist, millennial fervor. American primacy exemplified "the great law which presides over the evolution of human society," and Stead urged his countrymen to "cheerfully acquiesce in the decree of Destiny." What Stead dubbed "the principles of Americanism"—which prominently included capitalist business practices—were, he thought, illustrative of a divine order, "part and parcel of the sacred deposit of truth." Throughout, Stead marveled that peoples around the planet were embracing American commodities and techniques. From typewriters, cigarettes, and sewing machines to blast furnaces, photographic equipment, and management methods, the industrial cornucopia of American capitalism enriched a thankful world. Stead considered American global dominance a peaceful brand of imperialism, with production and trade supplanting bullets and warships. Still, even as he thought the Americanization of the world irresistible, Stead conceded that the road to Destiny could be harsh and ugly, concluding his book with the biblical question: "What shall it profit a man to gain the whole world, and lose his soul?"[30]

Woodrow Wilson, a devout Presbyterian and accomplished scholar, knew the answer: one could gain one's soul *and* gain the whole world, while turning a handsome profit to boot. From the New Freedom to the League of Nations to his interventions in Central America and the Caribbean, Wilson's domestic and foreign policies exuded a high-minded and often haughty moralism that could put off both friends and opponents. "Wilsonian internationalism" in particular is often interpreted as a secular version of the Puritan errand, the quest to build a city on a hill becoming, with Wilson, the imposition of liberal values on the world. But Wilson wrought no "secularization" of the covenant theology of expansion. For him, business activity was inextricably bound up with idealism, not antithetical to it; American corporate modernity was, to his mind, a model of virtue and a providential assignment. Business did not undermine the crusade for freedom; business embodied that crusade. Echoing Puritan covenant theology and Manifest Destiny, Wilson's providentialist conception of America suggests that Wilsonians considered the pursuit of economic and geopolitical advantage a moral goal in itself. Fusing prophecy and profits, Wilsonian internationalism was a potent rendition of corporate eschatology.[31]

Although Wilson usually avoided overt references to religion in his public speeches and writings, the specter of predestination loomed whenever he dwelled on America's history and future. "I believe very profoundly in an over-ruling Providence," he once confided to a friend. As Providence directed the course of history, Wilson echoed the Puritan sense of an unsought but sacred and ennobling mission. "We did not of deliberate choice undertake these tasks" of "promoting freedom and prosperity throughout the world," he asserted in 1901. "The great pressure of a people moving always to new frontiers, in search of new lands, new power, the full freedom of a virgin world, has ruled our course and formed our policies like a Fate," he wrote in the *Atlantic Monthly* a year later. "Fate," to Wilson, was another word for God. From his days as a professor of political economy at Princeton, Wilson held

that God worked through our mercenary ways his redemptive wonders to perform. He was not being a vulgar materialist when he told
students in 1898 that "in the main, the conduct of men is determined
by economic motives." As products of those motives—fashioned, he
thought, "by operation of irresistible forces"—corporations represented
"another chapter in the natural history of power and of governing
classes." The laws of that "natural history" had been decreed by a wise
and munificent Providence. In a subsequent essay, also appearing in
the *Atlantic Monthly,* Wilson reflected that, in the face of the global
power exerted by corporations, "every man knows that the world is to
be changed—changed according to an ordering of Providence."[32]

Painting in broad eschatological strokes, Wilson portrayed the arrival of a beloved world community as a commercial millennium. "As
if part of a great preconceived plan," Wilson wrote in 1901, the world
was approaching "a single vicinage; each part had become neighbor to
all the rest," people everywhere to be included in "the universal world
of commerce." That republic of trade bore the image and likeness of
Euro-American capital, the rest of the world having no choice but to
submit to the regime of economic freedom. Wilson echoed Lippmann
and Croly when he declared that "the East is to be opened and transformed," and that "the standards of the West are to be imposed upon
it." Like other corporate liberals, Wilson resolved this paradox of com-
pulsory freedom by resorting to eschatological comedy. All will be
well, he assured himself, because American business was providing,
"in the spirit of service, a government and rule which shall moralize
them by being moral." If the Puritans had moralized the Pequots with
muskets, modern liberals would moralize the world with goods and
services. This faith in the civilizing promise of capitalism helps explain Wilson's ultimate political failure. When, as president, Wilson
presented the Versailles Treaty to the Senate in July 1919, he professed
the same eschatological conviction. "The stage is set, the destiny dis-
closed . . . the hand of God [has] led us into this way . . . We can only
go forth, with lifted eyes and freshened spirit, to follow the vision . . .
America shall in truth show the way."[33]

Wilson expressed the same faith when he spoke directly to business
audiences. Although he professed to loathe the "dollar diplomacy" of

his predecessor William Howard Taft, his homily to the World's Sales-manship Congress in Detroit in July 1916 shows how central corpo-rate business was to Wilsonian internationalism. Sounding rather like George Babbitt at an Elks Club meeting, Wilson told the salesmen that they were marketing not just commodities but the "democracy of business." Wilson exhorted his audience to embark on a "peaceful con-quest of the world," since "permanent peace can grow in only one soil": the "actual good will" generated through commercial camaraderie. Wilson charged the salesmen to "go out and sell goods that will make the world more comfortable and more happy, and convert them to the principles of America." "Lift your eyes to the horizons of business," Wilson urged, "carry[ing] liberty and justice and the principles of hu-manity wherever you go." Salesmen were missionaries preaching the gospel of corporate liberal internationalism.[34]

"This vastly stirring Civilization of Business"

Wilson failed to sell the Senate on the League of Nations, and his in-ternationalist vision would have to wait for a more auspicious political moment. Besides, as labor unrest after World War I indicated, Ameri-can workers were not "more comfortable and more happy," and so corporate business needed to re-brand the system for a disgruntled domestic clientele. The corporate intelligentsia responded with new visions of capitalist destiny, corporate eschatologies resonant with hopes of a country and a planet united under the auspices of American capital. During the 1920s, prominent business leaders—typified by Gerard Swope of General Electric, Walter Teagle of Standard Oil, and Myron Young of AT&T—espoused what *Forbes* dubbed "the New Cap-italism," recasting the capitalist economy as a consumer culture offer-ing higher wages and more harmonious relations between corporate capital and labor. The spiritual aspirations contained in this corporate humanism were unmistakable. Just after the Armistice, *Forbes*—the flagship journal of the New Capitalism—forecast that "business here-after will be conducted on a higher plane." The postwar era promised a "reformation and rebirth in the business world," with capitalists "set[ting] a new value upon the things of the spirit."[35]

"New Capitalist" thinking had its own eschatology, exemplified in two of the period's most audacious corporate visionaries: the merchandising mogul Edward A. Filene and the advertising executive Earnest Elmo Calkins. Filene was a renowned philanthropist and "social entrepreneur" who authored several best sellers on social and economic matters, while Calkins wrote frequently for the *Atlantic Monthly* and other middle-class journals of opinion. Both men believed that the Machine Age augured a glorious new stage in human history—a "business millennium," as Calkins put it. In *Successful Living in This Machine Age* (1931), Filene asserted that by fostering interdependence through trade and technology, corporate business was sponsoring "a more inclusive loyalty, a sense of the oneness of all humanity." That "oneness of all humanity" was a planet of commodity democracy, a plebiscite of purchases. Filene even envisioned the business millennium as a new form of religious life. "The right and power to buy must lead to a great new religious awakening," Filene proclaimed, "a religious experience such as humanity has never had an opportunity to know before." Free from traditional dogmatic restrictions, the religious culture of a mass production society would be "a seven-day religion" of "constant, creative participation in human life"—"participation" defined almost exclusively in terms of commodified leisure and entertainment.[36]

Calkins waxed more romantically than Filene. In *Business the Civilizer* (1928) he depicted corporate enterprise as a "Field of Gold" offering opportunities for faith, conquest, and heroism. The managerial, scientific, and technological employment provided by corporations afforded "the glory that in the past was given to the crusader, the soldier, the courtier, the explorer, and the martyr." This could be easily dismissed as bunkum, but Calkins was genuinely impatient with the corruption and ineptitude of organized religion, and he ended *Business the Civilizer* with a daring assertion of corporate ambition. "That eternal job of administering the planet must be turned over to the business man. The work that religion and government have failed in must be done by business."[37]

This vision of a corporate superintendence of the world also transfixed Henry Luce, who was engaged in erecting the journalistic apparatus that would announce "the American Century": *Time* (1923),

Fortune (1930), and *Life* (1936), his River Rouge complex of cultural production. Born in China to Presbyterian missionaries, Luce blended literary flair with mercenary skill. Although he published his celebrated essay in a February 1941 issue of *Life,* it marked the culmination of aspirations nurtured earlier in the pages of *Fortune.* Aimed at a professional and managerial audience seeking both business news and cultural savvy, *Fortune* played a leading role in the moral and imaginative education of the corporate elite. Fusing iconoclastic business journalism, corporate liberal social thought, and aesthetic modernism, *Fortune* represented the most ambitious attempt yet to make the corporate intelligentsia into an American *clerisy* and *avant-garde.* Its contributors included a roster of American arts and letters, from James Agee and Margaret Bourke-White to Dwight Macdonald and John Kenneth Galbraith. The magazine incorporated modernist aesthetic principles into its ads and illustrations. And although Luce himself was a Republican who backed Wendell Willkie in 1940, *Fortune* provided a venue for corporate liberals, from "industrial statesmen" such as Swope, Young, and Teagle to the Business Advisory Council and the Council for Economic Development, two leading forums for the reception and dissemination of Keynesian economics.[38]

Luce envisioned *Fortune* as a monthly herald of the business millennium. In the summer of 1929, while hustling to mobilize the start-up capital for *Fortune,* he circulated a prospectus to potential investors and contributors that sketched out an illustrious corporate epoch. Luce promised that *Fortune* would "portray Business in all its heroic present-day proportions" and convey "a sustained sense of the challenging personalities, significant trends, and high excitements of this vastly stirring Civilization of Business." Addressed to "the aristocracy of our human civilization," *Fortune* would reconcile art and commerce, broker a deal between the classes, and conclude an alliance between the warring fiefdoms of Wall Street and Greenwich Village. An ad for the advertising firm of Young and Rubicam captured the splendor of Luce's corporate mythology. "No longer is business a column of figures, or work a daily grind," the ad proclaimed. "Here is epic enterprise, a panorama of romance, adventure, conquest—with beauty in factories and derricks." Over the 1930s and 1940s, *Fortune* regularly profiled business leaders who displayed a cosmopolitan sensibility, employed sophisticated management methods, and exuded enthusiasm for scientific and technological progress. Thus Luce spoke for and to many in what Thomas Ferguson has called the new "hegemonic bloc" of the New Deal coalition: investment firms, capital-intensive industries, mass merchandisers, and internationally oriented commercial banks.[39]

If Luce aimed *Fortune* at the corporate elite, he preached to the humbler faithful in *Life,* whose larger circulation gave him optimal range for his homiletic talents. "The American Century" is Luce's Epistle to the Americans, one of the boldest eschatological visions in American history, a scripture of revelation that announces the advent of a business kingdom on earth, the essay leavened from beginning to end with biblical allusions. Like an evangelical pastor preparing his flock for the troubles preceding the *eschaton,* Luce rallied his readers for what he called "the great test" when destiny arrived at its American moment. With an array of vexations in mind—especially the Great Depression and the rise of fascism—Luce reassured his readers that "in all our trials and tribulations of spirit" they could discern a transformative episode, when "the meaning of our time" would be brilliantly revealed as the bestowal of "an authentic 20th century—our Century." But the most portentous mite of millennial imperialism comes early on, when Luce audaciously avers that the mission of the United States is a salvific enterprise, "lifting the life of mankind from the level of the beasts to what the Psalmist called a little lower than the angels."[40]

Like previous imperial projects, the American Century required artisans, proconsuls, priests, and legions, Luce situating the political and moral economy just below the level of the seraphim. With the United States at its "dynamic center," a "vital international economy" would pave the way for "an international moral order"—a Civilization of Business like the one championed in the pages of *Fortune.* This corporate order would supply "the skillful servants of mankind." These humble servants included "engineers, scientists, doctors, movie men, makers of entertainment, developers of airlines, builders of roads, teachers, [and] educators," Luce fully expecting the world to greet these technical and cultural specialists as liberators, with the United States "eagerly welcomed" as a "good Samaritan" by the backward and wretched of the earth. Indeed, Luce observed, "there is already an immense American internationalism," a planetary culture tied together by commodities that embodied the American spirit. To Luce, corporate culture *was* international culture, an emporium of goods that united far-flung peoples in a harmony of consumption. "American jazz, Hollywood movies, American slang, American machines and patented products, are in fact the only things that every community in the world, from Zanzibar to Hamburg, recognizes in common." Here was Filene's "oneness of humanity" as well as Calkins's business executives repairing what the priests and politicians had bungled. Here also was Winthrop's "city on a hill," now extending its environs to the outermost limits; Edwards's "most glorious renovation of the world"; and Stiles's American Israel "Elevated to Glory and Honor." Here was O'Sullivan's "Great Nation of Futurity" and Emerson's "sublime and friendly Destiny"; Lippmann's "modern communion" and Wilson's "democracy of business."[41]

Luce hoped that the products of American industry would betoken a peaceful consummation, but he hinted that the Good Samaritan would on occasion have to act as the American Centurion. As the "powerhouse from which ideals spread around the world," we must be ready, he wrote ominously, to "exert upon the world the full impact of our influence, for such purposes as we see fit and by such means as we see fit." Launching into jeremiad mode, Luce lamented that, preoccupied with the Depression, apprehensive about events in Europe and Asia, and fearful of global responsibility, Americans had not "accommodated themselves spiritually and practically" to their power, stature, and destiny. Suffering from "the virus of isolationist sterility," the nation could not complete its redemptive mission unless there coursed "strongly through its veins . . . the blood of purpose and enterprise and high resolve."[42] With strapping sinews and blood that flowed without contagion through the national vessels, the United States could either sell a Pax Americana or impose it like previous imperial powers. Either way, neither America nor the rest of the world could resist the trajectory of history. As the grandest undertaking in the history of capitalist enchantment, the American Century would be a long, victorious, and lucrative march toward the heavenly city of business.

"The American Century" was not the only epistle to emerge from Luce's clerical presses. Exactly ten years later, in February 1951, special projects editor Russell Davenport and his colleagues at *Fortune* published "U.S.A.: The Permanent Revolution," a de facto appendix to "The American Century." The editors' appropriation of Trotskyite rhetoric underscored their belief that American capitalism, or "The American Way of Life," best represented the aspirations of the postcolonial world. Yet "The Permanent Revolution" was also a manifesto for domestic cultural rearmament. Echoing Luce's dismay at the apparent lack of moral leadership, Davenport and his fellow rebels accused unnamed political, religious, and cultural luminaries of sowing "intellectual and spiritual confusion" at a time when clarity was needed. Following the lead of "military and business leaders" (also unnamed), *Fortune* resolved to probe "the meaning of America," elucidating the "metaphysical" principles on which the nation stood: freedom, prosperity, and progress. In a manner that Will Herberg would later condemn as a parody of religion, *Fortune* intoned that "the American Way of Life embodies a mystery which is common to all men," namely, "the mystery of the human spirit." Since all peoples partook of that "mystery," all desired, deep down, to participate in corporate modernity, and so "the question of Americans thrusting themselves on anybody can never really arise." Here was the blankest of checks ever printed and written to the account of American imperialism. If postcolonial people aspired to be Americans, those who had already entered that beatific state resided in an "industrial democracy," *Fortune* contended. In articles on labor relations, management, and technology, *Fortune* surveyed a promised land of production and consumption in which class antagonisms had been happily resolved. The millennium, it seemed, had arrived.[43]

With their beatific vision of a Civilization of Business, "The American Century" and "U.S.A." were *Fortune*'s ur-texts of postwar corporate hegemony, mapping the range of global ambition and sanctifying domestic arrangements. Especially along the Wall Street-Washington axis, the *Fortune* version of the American Century idealized this political economy. It bestowed the mandate of history on what Robert Griffith has dubbed "the corporate commonwealth": a consumers' and producers' republic, lasting roughly from 1945 to 1975, characterized by a tenuous truce among corporate management, organized labor, and the state; the military-industrial complex that Charles Wilson of General Electric dubbed "the permanent war economy"; the maturation of Fordist mass production and management techniques, epitomized in the work of Peter Drucker, *Fortune* editor and management guru; international financial arrangements constructed at Bretton Woods; and a structure of corporate governance in which stockholders deferred to managers and executives—"managerial capitalism." Belief in an American Century united business leaders as disparate as H. L. Hunt and J. Howard Pew on the extreme right and the more moderate executives on the Committee on Economic Development such as Ralph Cordiner of General Electric, who told students at the Columbia School of Business in 1957 that American business life was a "people's capitalism." It lent credibility to the declaration in 1946 of Leo D. Welch, treasurer and later chairman of Standard Oil of New Jersey, that the United States must "assume the responsibility of the majority stockholder in this corporation known as the world." And twenty years later, W. W. Rostow, theorist of "modernization" and special assistant for national security to President Lyndon Johnson, provided yet another technocratic imprimatur. Writing while napalm was lathering the jungles and hamlets of South Vietnam, Rostow envisioned "a new day in which organized violence finally ends." Since "aggressive impulses diminish in technologically mature economies," the spread of corporate technology and expertise would usher in peace as poor countries experienced the "take-off" to a "high-mass consumption economy."[44]

Fortune's Civilization of Business was a domestic idyll as well as a globalist eschatology. Three of the most influential postwar writers on business, social mores, and politics emerged from the curial offices of *Fortune*. Drucker, for instance, authored several books that blended management theory, moral philosophy, and social thought in an extended panegyric to corporate capitalism. The corporation, Drucker wrote in a renowned 1946 study of General Motors, was "our representative social institution," one that provided "the standard for the way of life and the mode of living" for Americans. Indeed, Drucker considered corporate managers "a genuine aristocracy." "There has never been a more efficient, a more honest, a more capable and conscientious group of rulers than the professional management of the great American corporations." Though usually included among the roster of critics of suburban "conformity" and corporate bureaucracy, Drucker's fellow editor William H. Whyte was no antibusiness prophet. Whyte's *The Organization Man* (1956) is routinely listed as an indictment of corporate life, but it is easy to overlook his fundamental affirmation of the managers and professionals he studied. Whyte himself offered a disclaimer that "this book is not a plea for nonconformity," and he proves it at one point by concluding that, because of the "Social Ethic" of his Organization families, "none has been so well equipped to lead a meaningful community life." Whyte's seal of approval became a world-historical pronouncement with Daniel Bell, who declared "the end of ideology" in a book by that title (1960) after ten years as *Fortune*'s labor editor.[45]

The Golden Arches at the End of History

But in the thirty years after Bell's announcement, the gray-flanneled millennium faded, as a number of forces eroded the foundations of the corporate commonwealth. Rising energy costs and increased international competition both obliged and enabled corporations to abrogate the social truce with organized labor, breaking unions and enforcing stringent wage and benefit restrictions. Computerized production and communication technologies permitted management to accelerate automation and introduce more intensive labor practices. New management and production practices—"post-Fordism"—emphasized the flexibility of labor (i.e., lack of unions) and decentralized organization. Already weakened by these developments, the postwar managerial regime of capitalism came under assault from mutual fund directors and other institutional investors eager to break all accumulative shackles. Managerial capitalism gave way to "investor capitalism," marked by a virulent reassertion of shareholder interests and by the primacy of financial institutions in the governance of other capitalist firms. The "industrial democracy" touted by *Fortune* looked more and more nakedly plutocratic.[46]

Out of this maelstrom two new and interrelated mythologies emerged—"the computer" or "the Internet" and "neoliberalism" or "globalization." Separately and in tandem they comprised post–Cold War brands of American Century eschatology. In digital millennialism, computer technology has emerged as the agent of global harmony and beatitude. The founding father of digital eschatology was Marshall McLuhan, the Canadian academic who became a fixture in the media firmament in the 1960s. McLuhan's fame as a techno-prophet was somewhat ironic, as he had launched his career with a witty critique of *Fortune* and "the Ballet Luce" in *The Mechanical Bride* (1951). Calling *Fortune* "a Bayreuth festival in the megalomaniac style," McLuhan also perceptively characterized its hosannas to the Civilization of Business as "a major religious liturgy celebrating the feats of technological man." A devout Catholic, McLuhan promised to be an incisive religious critic of the American Century: corporate business culture, in his view, was "a secular adaptation of some of the most striking features of medieval scholastic culture." Alas, soon after the publication of *The Mechanical Bride,* McLuhan assumed the chairmanship of the Ford Foundation's Seminars on Culture and Communication, one of the leading corporate-sponsored sites for A-list intellectuals. Sure enough, in *The Gutenberg Galaxy* (1962) and especially in *Understanding Media* (1964), McLuhan looked for salvation in the spread of technological literacy and the enlightenment of corporate elites. *Understanding Media* in particular abounds with hyperbolic eschatology. Worldwide computer networks, McLuhan announced with rapture, "have extended our central nervous system itself in a global embrace, abolishing both space and time as far as our planet is concerned." Indeed, as he told *Playboy* in a 1968 interview, computers would conjure "a Pentecostal condition" of unity in diversity. "The computer," he continued, "holds out the promise of . . . a state of absorption in the logos that could knit mankind into one family and create a perpetuity of collective harmony and peace." Recalling Jonathan Edwards's postmillennial vision of the world as a "body of Christ," McLuhan's much-ballyhooed "global village" was a digitalized beatitude, a heavenly city of corporate technology. Thanks to his timely fusion of technical savvy and vatic pronouncement, McLuhan swiftly became a guru of middlebrow hipness, popular among the reading and televisual public. Despite his professed aversion to capitalism, McLuhan inspired a rising generation of business leaders eager to join in what Thomas Frank has called "the conquest of cool," the embrace of the counterculture by corporate image and managerial professionals.[47]

McLuhan's work foreshadowed the convergence of the cool with the "cyberculture." As Fred Turner has demonstrated, the cyberculture, a new conception of human relationships as vast, interlocking information networks, is a form of techno-humanism that dovetailed nicely with post-Fordist corporate culture. Drawn from cyberculture, business culture, and the globalism of the "American Century," post-Fordist business eschatology emerged from the ranks of ex-hippie technophiles, New Right ideologues, and entrepreneurial visionaries. In this literature of cyber-eschatology, electronic information technologies—sponsored by corporations and protected by military power—augured the erosion of bureaucracy and the rise of global yet intimate organizations. From Alvin Toffler's account of "Third Wave" digitalized business organizations to Bill Gates's celebration of a global "friction-free capitalism," techno-business millennialism envisioned a planetary community of dot-com start-ups and info-glutted consumers, while microchips and fiber-optic cables joined the sacramental inventory of the American spirit. This mythology reached its zenith in the 1990s, when techno-business magazines such as *Wired* and *Fast Company* featured articles wrapping digital technics and turbo-capitalism in a lissome New Age spirituality.[48]

Many of the premier techno-millennial ideologues—Toffler, Gates, George Gilder, Nicholas Negroponte, Kevin Kelly, Esther Dyson, and Newt Gingrich—celebrated computer technology not only as a vehicle of radical democracy but as a vessel of moral and ontological sublimity. Though less given to religious hyperbole than McLuhan, Toffler—a freelance journalist and autodidact historian—was no less visionary. In *Future Shock* (1970) and, later, in *The Third Wave* (1980), coauthored with his wife, Heidi, Toffler outlined a future dominated by worldwide business organizations more flexible and libertarian than the gray-flanneled combines of old. The global economy would feature "great globe-girdling syndicates" whose primary commodity was symbolic knowledge: Toffler dubbed them "psych-corps," companies specializing in information and entertainment. Employing educated and cosmopolitan workers, "Third Wave" corporations were more respectful of employees' freedoms, talents, and idiosyncrasies—they were "adhocracies." Negroponte, director of MIT's Media Lab and an avid evangelist for the techno-millennium, predicted in *Wired* that the Internet would "flatten organizations, globalize society, decentralize control, and help harmonize people." Two years later, in a lecture at the Getty Institute in Los Angeles, Negroponte went further, exulting that digital technology would perform Christ-like miracles of healing. "Within the next few decades, with the aid of computer chips, the blind shall see, the deaf shall hear, and the lame shall walk."[49]

As the *ubergeek* of the digital age, Gates sketched out a paradise of global commercial transparency in *The Road Ahead* (1995) and *Business @ the Speed of Thought* (2000), the latter's very title implying a transcendence of physical reality. Gates visualized a future in which technology would confer semidivine power on consumers, giving people "the power to do what they want, where and when they want, on any device." Besides enhancing profits, technology would fulfill ancient longings for omnipresence and omnipotence. A "friction-free capitalism" would end class conflict, international rivalries, and commercial impediments. Relations between classes, countries, and vendors and customers would be utterly transparent, mediated by the Internet as "the ultimate go-between, the universal middle-man." The emancipation of commerce and technology depended, he argued, on reimagining the new global marketplace as a gargantuan digital organism, with computer networks as its "digital nervous system." Like other contributors to the souped-up business literature of the 1990s, Gates passed off gnomic platitudes as fresh insight and revelation: "information technology and business are becoming inextricably interwoven." The end of conflict among classes and nations was no fantasy, and when Gates sketched out a world of abundance—"all the goods in the world will be available for you . . . it will be a shopper's heaven"—he spoke to enduring millennial dreams of material felicity.[50]

Yet Gates's "friction-free capitalism" was not the purest ideological fantasy to emerge from the techno-millennial milieu. Shortly after an

August 1994 conference of Gingrich's Progress and Freedom Foundation in Aspen, Colorado, several of the luminaries—Gingrich, Dyson, Toffler, and George Keyworth, a former science adviser to President Ronald Reagan—issued a manifesto entitled "Cyberspace and the American Dream: A Magna Carta for the Knowledge Age." For these clerics of the cybernauts, digitalized capitalism was a metaphysical and political revolution. "The central event of the 20th century is the overthrow of matter," they proclaimed. "The powers of mind are everywhere ascendant over the brute force of things," and the exploration of cyberspace was now "civilization's truest, highest calling." Since these "powers of mind" were embodied in the techno-professional cadres of info-capitalism, this assertion echoed the conceits of earlier modernizing cultural elites, from the Puritans to the Progressives. Indeed, even though the "Magna Carta" claimed that cyberspace now offered the opportunity "to empower every person," it quickly identified personal empowerment with the deregulation of the computer and telecommunications industries. "Obstructing such collaborations," the authors warned, "is socially elitist." The document explicitly linked the cyber-right to the lineage of corporate liberalism. Freed from Second Wave fetters, cyber-capitalists would reinvigorate the American Dream and restore "the promise of American life."[51]

The imperial trajectory of techno-eschatology found its political champion in Gingrich, whose combination of acerbity, geekiness, and political opportunism made him a formidable point man for techno-eschatology. An enthusiast and friend of the Tofflers, Gingrich put a crusading spin on their techno-millennial vision, implying that the Third Wave was the highest stage of American corporate imperialism. In an interview he gave to Dyson for the August 1995 issue of *Wired*, Gingrich anointed corporate cybernauts as the vanguard of a revitalized American Century. Comparing the conquest of "the bio-electronic frontier" to the founding of America, Gingrich went on to repackage the old covenant theology, telling Dyson that "this is a society permeated by a belief that we have a mission, that our mission relates to God, and that our powers relate to God." That mission—outlined in the Contract With America, the program of sweeping right-wing social and economic reform offered by House Republicans in 1994—was defined primarily as business deregulation, the final unfettering of those forces responsible for the toppling of matter and the ascendancy of mind. But Gingrich further implied that the Contract with America prefigured a Contract with the World, an errand to the globe undertaken on orders from a Truer, Higher Mind. "We have to lead the planet," he informed Dyson. "We're the only country capable of leading the human race." If the overthrow of matter was the twentieth century's most significant achievement, then the nation that had sponsored the metaphysical revolution now had to export that revolution. Like earlier prophets of an American millennium, Gingrich identified corporate imperatives with eschatological purposes.[52]

Gingrich's pugnacious support for free global markets marked him as a neoliberal, and other neoliberals were no less enchanted by visions of historical consummation. Neoliberalism—or "neoconservatism," its more bellicose twin—arose from anxiety over the prospect of the American Century ending. Shaken by the turbulence of the 1960s and the economic crisis of the following decade, American mandarins across the political spectrum detected a waning of imperial hegemony. So the imperial intelligentsia ensconced in venues such as the American Enterprise Institute, the Brookings Institution, the *New York Times,* and the *Washington Post* set out to restore the nation's economic supremacy and strengthen its domestic resolve. The achievements of Margaret Thatcher in Britain and Ronald Reagan in the United States did much to revive the moral legitimacy of capitalism; and with the collapse of the Soviet bloc in 1989, the final impediment to a robust reassertion of imperial dominance fell away. Corporate capitalism, it seemed, had won a final victory, crushing or discrediting all other possibilities for social and economic life: as Thatcher had (in)famously declared, "there is no alternative" to the reign of capital. By the 1990s, intellectuals already enveloped in the piety of the "American Century" had developed the "Washington Consensus": unfettered global trade, privatization of public services, and deregulation of corporate finance and industry. A renewed obduracy marked the political elites of the American Century: as President George H. W. Bush told the Earth Summit in Rio de Janeiro in 1992, "the American way of life is not negotiable." The eschatological import of the Washington Consensus was not lost on its proponents. In the millennially titled *A Future Perfect* (2000), John Micklethwaite and Adrian Woolridge, Washington correspondents for *The Economist*, wrote with no apparent irony or embarrassment of the "broad church" of neoliberalism. Forecasting an "empire without end"—directed by an elite of nerdy "cosmocrats"— they aligned the sway of the United States with the grain of history and Providence, citing Sir Robert Peel's invocation of "the beneficent designs of an all-seeing Creator."[53]

In neoliberal millennialism, God and History competed for the role of premier eschatological force. President Bill Clinton, for instance, alluded to Scripture when he told a meeting of the World Trade Organization in Geneva in May 1998 that the demise of communism and the end of the Cold War had ushered in "the fullness of time"—a biblical phrase denoting the birth of Christ. In the same year, speaking in Hong Kong, Clinton shifted from divine to secular modes of imperial vindication, asserting that the worldwide spread of free markets demonstrated that the United States was on "the right side of history." Neoliberal imperial eschatology was impeccably bipartisan, shared by Republicans such as Condoleezza Rice. Writing in *Foreign Affairs* in early 2000—a year before she became George W. Bush's national security adviser—Rice bluntly asserted that "the United States and its allies are on the right side of history." Rice's use of Clinton's phraseology demonstrates that while liberal opinion routinely mocked Bush's invocations of God or "history," his evangelical eschatology of empire differed in style but not in substance from the views of his ostensibly more cosmopolitan critics. Bush's evangelical braggadocio dressed the Washington Consensus in neo-Puritan drag. When the president asserted, in his post-9/11 sermon at the National Cathedral on September 14, 2001, that the United States had a "responsibility to history" to "rid the world of evil," the specters of Winthrop and other Calvinist warriors hovered over the ecumenical gathering. When Bush observed, in his second inaugural address in January 2005, that history "has a visible direction, set by liberty and the Author of Liberty," he echoed the postmillennial piety of Joseph Warren and Ezra Stiles. And when his first press secretary, Ari Fleischer, proclaimed that "the American way of life is a blessed one," he staked a claim to divine favor that Wilson, Luce, or Clinton could have endorsed.[54]

Bush, Rice, and Clinton were echoing policy intellectuals such as Francis Fukuyama, a former official in the Reagan State Department who became an instant celebrity when he declared "The End of History" in 1989. Expanded and published in book form three years later, Fukuyama's essay encapsulated the neoliberal sense of insuperable triumph. What had ended, Fukuyama explained, was not history as discrete events but history as "a single, coherent, evolutionary process." Indebted to Hegel, Fukuyama provided a phenomenology of the spirit of neoliberal corporate enterprise. As the most sophisticated and productive expression of *thymos*—the drive for prestige and recognition that defines the essence of human nature—multinational corporate capitalism had won the "ultimate victory as the world's only viable economic system." Fukuyama envisioned a "universal consumer culture," an imperial emporium signified by the VCR—the heir to Dexter's Coca-Cola bottle, a sacramental vessel for neoliberal principles. Though wary of the moral shabbiness of consumerism—the "Last Man" of the title was Nietzsche's figure of spineless, soulless affluence—Fukuyama reflected in the first-person Beltway plural that "we cannot picture to ourselves a world that is *essentially* different from the present one, and at the same time better."[55]

To foster policies designed to eternalize the end of history, Fukuyama, together with other Beltway "neoconservatives," joined the Project for a New American Century (PNAC), founded by *Weekly Standard* editor William Kristol in 1997. PNAC was cultivating a hegemonic bloc well before the attacks of September 11, 2001, lent its views a new credibility. The signatories to PNAC's "Statement of Principles" comprised a roster of military specialists, right-wing intellectuals, and corporate chieftains, among them Elliott Abrams, William J. Bennett, Dick Cheney, Midge Decter, Steve Forbes, I. Lewis Libby, Norman Podhoretz, Donald Rumsfeld, Paul Wolfowitz, and Fukuyama himself. To "promote the cause of political and economic freedom," PNAC's members advocated increased defense spending, accelerated weapons procurement, a more interventionist and unilateralist foreign policy, and the "pre-emptive" use of military force.[56]

Yet PNAC's aggressive wonkery promoted not only economic and military supremacy but an eschatological vision: a business millennium extended and protected by U.S. diplomacy and arms. An intoxicating sense of omnicompetence came to pervade both policy and military circles, culminating in 2002 with the publication of *The National Security Strategy of the United States of America*. An expanded version of a policy paper first prepared by Wolfowitz and Libby for President George H. W. Bush in 1992, this document joined unilateralist realpolitik to Fukuyama's End of History. Although best known for committing the United States to a doctrine of "preventive war," the younger President Bush's strategic blueprint draws its moral and intellectual energy from the spirit of capitalist crusade. Citing President Bush's assertion at the National Cathedral, the document defined the eradication of evil not as the fruit of contrition or as the Second Coming of Christ but as the triumph of a liberal capitalist globalism. With hubristic flourish, it declared that there is but "a single sustainable model for national success: freedom, democracy, and free enterprise." The United States would assist any nation to achieve this goal, but developing nations would not receive economic aid—and might well invite something worse—if they failed to "govern themselves wisely." Wisdom consisted in "opening [their] societies" to "free markets and free trade," and by "follow[ing] responsible economic policies and enabl[ing] entrepreneurship." Here was Luce's Civilization of Business— without the Presbyterian cadences—as well as Luce's military "powerhouse," now more than ever committed to attaining omnipotence and omniscience. As General Tommy Franks observed in 2004, the new technologies of surveillance and destruction give U.S. military forces "the kind of Olympian perspective that Homer had given his gods." Thus the Pentagon's grasp for "full spectrum dominance"—complete U.S. control over air, sea, land, and outer space—is not simply the hyperbole of intimidation; it is the serious goal of a warrior class commissioned to patrol the global agora.[57]

So Thomas Friedman's invocation of an "almighty superpower" to police the global marketplace was no mere wild metaphor. The technoutopian and neoliberal currents of new American Century thinking converge in Friedman, who, like Luce, has been one of the business millennium's high-profile prophets and missionaries. Friedman's three best sellers on globalization—*The Lexus and the Olive Tree* (1999), *The World Is Flat* (2005), and *Hot, Flat and Crowded* (2008)—comprise an illuminating trilogy of corporate eschatology. Though Friedman swans among the Davos Olympians of executives, entrepreneurs, and diplomats, his volumes are on the syllabi of history, civics, and business classes in numerous public and private secondary schools. Thus his work affords insight not only into what passes for thinking among the business and political intelligentsia but into the moral economy of a sizable swath of the contemporary middle classes.[58]

Though Friedman usually bristles at the charge that he considers the United States a paradigm for the rest of the world, he frequently implies, and sometimes clearly states, that America is an apotheosis. "Deep down the rest of the world envies American optimism," he writes in *The World Is Flat*. "It is one of the things that help keep the world spinning on its axis." In *The Lexus and the Olive Tree*, the vaunted "Electronic Herd" of leading financial and manufacturing corporations is overwhelmingly American: Merrill Lynch, General Electric, IBM, Intel, and others. Elsewhere, Friedman is helpfully, if not quite refreshingly, blunt. "In so many ways, globalization is us," he concedes; it "wears Mickey Mouse ears, eats Big Macs, drinks Coca-Cola or Pepsi and does its computing on an IBM PC." His grand theories of global conflict prevention—the "Golden Arches" and the "Dell"—are both cast in American corporate terms. Occasionally, Friedman drops whatever reserve he can muster and tells us what he really thinks. America, he preaches in *Lexus*, is "a spiritual value and a role model" for a "healthy global society." Just as there is no alternative to global corporatism, "there is no better model for this [healthy global society] on earth than America."[59]

Friedman's exaltation of American capitalism as a "spiritual value" puts him squarely in the tradition of the American Century and in the lineage of covenant economics. Of course, his explicit excursions into religion are often embarrassing. "Is God in cyberspace?" he asks in *Lexus*. ("He wants to be," Friedman assures us.) His metaphors, mixed, inapt, and belabored as they can be, reveal nonetheless a commitment to the faith. His eschatological vision recalls the city of Revelation, redesigned as an emporium on a hill, accessible only to those who undertake the forced march of freedom. Not usually considered a neoconservative, Friedman nonetheless endorsed the fundamental tenet of the Bush 2002 *National Security Strategy.* "If you want higher standards of living in a world without walls, the free market is the only ideological alternative left," he intones. And there is only "one road. Different speeds. But one road." Understood almost exclusively in business terms, America becomes the apogee of creation, the missionary of capital, and even the Almighty itself. In one excruciating passage in *Lexus,* Friedman imagines a "visionary geo-architect" who, having been asked to design a country able to "compete and win" in a globalized economy, would have come up with "something that looks an awful lot like the United States of America." From their consumerist apotheosis, Americans venture into the wilderness on an errand of salvation as "apostles of the Fast World, the prophets of the free market and the high priests of high tech." Like the missionaries of old, the Fast Worlders embark on their errand protected by benevolent military force: the United States is, for Friedman, the world's "ultimate benign hegemon-enforcer," like a wrathful God, swift and remorseless in punishing whoever wanders off or forsakes the Road.[60]

"The Ultimate American Frontier"

To at least some observers, events appear to have discredited Friedman's swaggering and at times malicious bluster. In this view, the prolonged U.S. debacles in Iraq, Afghanistan, and elsewhere, together with the turmoil in the global economy since September 2008, suggest that the era of American global dominance has reached or is approaching its impending end. While there is plenty of evidence to support this view—economic sluggishness, ecological crisis, the hemorrhage of human and financial resources to maintain the American Empire—Friedman's continued popularity indicates that Americans will ferociously resist their imperial decline. For even if the American Empire is indeed in the first days of its senescence, faith in the business millennium remains widespread and intractable, and the eschatology of corporate business still enchants the popular moral imagination. The reaction to the economic crisis of 2008 is illustrative. While politicians and pundits fumed with populist umbrage about the government bailout of finance capital, there has been little if any serious reflection about a new way of life to which Goldman Sachs would be irrelevant. Americans complain about corporations, but they remain incapable of imagining life without them. Among the "grass roots," the hegemony of empire as a way of being overcomes anxiety about its costs. The moral economy of most Americans remains that of a consumers' republic—or, perhaps better, in Chalmers Johnson's words, "a consumerist Sparta" that fuses emporium and imperium. As Andrew Bacevich has summarized, "the chief desire of the American people, whether they admit it or not, is that nothing should disrupt their access to goods, oil, and credit. The chief aim of the U.S. government is to satisfy that desire."[61]

Given the strength of that desire, any hope for "change" within the parameters of the American Empire qualifies as delusional. Many had believed that the election of Senator Barack Obama to the presidency in November 2008 portended, at the very least, a new sense of realism and modesty. Such hopes were always misplaced—in part because Obama's vision of the future has never departed from the capitalist eschatology of the American past. Despite the sensitivity he displays to the concerns of the postcolonial world, President Obama has done nothing to curb the drive for global hegemony—nor does he intend to, for he has always subscribed, in his lissome and idealistic way, to the tenets of covenant economics. When candidate Obama told *Fortune* in June 2008 "I still believe that the business of America is business," he was both announcing the ideological foundation of his presidency and proclaiming his faith in the Civilization of Business. No one who bothered to consult the ample record of Obama's votes, publications, and interviews should have been surprised by his fealty to finance capital, his escalation of the wars in Afghanistan and Pakistan, or his reassertion of imperial prerogative when he claimed the Nobel Peace Prize in Oslo—the latter being the one indisputably audacious act of his career. As a senator, as a candidate, and as chief executive, Obama has never strayed from the central assumptions of empire as a way of being: the right and duty of the United States to control events around the world, and the centrality of corporate capitalism to the promise of American life.[62]

The opening lines of President Obama's inaugural address should have snuffed any hopes still nurtured by liberal *bien-pensants:* "We will not apologize for our way of life, and we will not waver in its defense." Declaring, like the first President Bush, that the American way of life is not negotiable, Obama signaled his unwillingness to reexamine the claims and prerogatives of empire. To be sure, there have been glimmers of repentance and sanity in Obama's remarks on foreign and military affairs, among them his June 2009 address to Muslim religious and political leaders at Cairo University. In this speech, Obama acknowledged U.S. complicity in coups such as the one that toppled Iranian Prime Minister Mohammed Mossadegh in 1953 and reinstalled the shah to the Peacock Throne. A few months later, explaining his escalation of the war in Afghanistan to cadets at West Point, Obama alluded to fiscal constraints on the projection of U.S. power: "We simply can't afford to ignore the price of these wars." Yet despite the price, he chose to expand the war, demonstrating his determination to perpetuate the American Century. Indeed, in two of the rhetorical milestones of his career—the West Point and Oslo speeches, separated by a week and a half—Obama affirmed the exceptionalist tale essential to imperial eschatology. Transposing some of his remarks almost verbatim from one oration to the other, Obama related the Sacred Narrative of American Destiny. Crediting the United States with having "underwritten global security for six decades," while shouldering "our special burden in global affairs," Obama offered his own rendition of American imperial innocence. "We have borne this burden not because we seek to impose our will," he told the Nobel assembly; "unlike the powers of old," he lectured the cadets, "we have not sought world domination." The United States, Obama contended, had reluctantly assumed its burden "out of enlightened self-interest"—the pursuit of "a better future" for America and the rest of the world, defined in the most generic terms of "freedom and prosperity." Having recited the latest version of the Sacred Narrative, Obama assured the world of the Reluctant Empire's continuing resolve. In accepting the Nobel Peace Prize, Obama emphasized his readiness to make war: "I—like any head of state—reserve the right to act unilaterally if necessary to defend my nation"—a right whose exercise by, say, Iran the United States would unhesitatingly condemn.[63]

Militant rhetoric coming from the lips of George W. Bush had met with disdain, and rightly so. Yet when uttered by President Obama, it has been greeted, on the whole, as the poetry of statecraft—"a sincere product of serious deliberations," according to Frank Rich in the *New York Times*. Eager to believe that righteousness and reason have returned to the Oval Office after the Bush regime, intellectuals benignly disposed to Obama have obscured his fidelity to the imperial creed. Garry Wills takes refuge in the Tragedy of It All. "A president is greatly pressured to keep all the empire's secrets," he observes. Clearly trying to convince himself of Obama's honorable but thwarted intentions, Wills apologizes for his hero's reversion to imperial presidential form. "Turning around the huge secret empire built by the National Security State is a hard, perhaps impossible task," he muses ruefully.[64]

If Wills desires a restoration of republican virtue, why "turn around" the empire? Why not dismantle it? President Obama has no intention of charting a course that differs from that of his neoliberal predecessors. In foreign as in domestic policy, Obama has no "progressive" agenda that is somehow being blocked by the national security apparatus. Instead, epitomizing the business culture that reigns among today's professional and managerial elites, Obama offers the American Century a new lease on hegemony. Educated at elite universities and enmeshed in international business networks, members of today's corporate patricianate are far more "open" than their gray-flanneled or chop-whiskered predecessors of yesteryear. Indeed, to the extent that corporate capitalism has opened its meritocracy to all racial and ethnic groups—"merit" defined chiefly as the talent for making money—it has arguably produced, or at least clearly augured, the first multiracial ruling class in American history. Rejecting the moralism of a Winthrop or the racism of a Beveridge, they share the faith in a Democracy of Business propounded by Wilson and Luce; and having been sensitized to the exclusions and indignities once imposed on racial minorities at home and colonized peoples abroad, they define discrimination, not exploitation, as the most fundamental and grievous injustice imaginable. Inclusiveness is the beatitude of neoliberalism; as Slavoj Žižek has put it, the ideology of "multiculturalism" is "the cultural logic of multinational capitalism."[65]

As the first African American president, Obama appears to herald the arrival of this meritocratic paradise, and thus he represents the crowning vindication of the neoliberal American Century. He is well positioned to rewrite the exceptionalist tale. By revising the Sacred Narrative to take account of racism and brutality in the past, Obama demonstrates that the Washington Consensus can accommodate a partial revision of American imperial history. His ideological strategy appears to be that a selective admission of fault can strengthen imperial moral authority—if the business of America remains business, acknowledging occasional past missteps can repair and even enhance the company's reputation. If Obama's confession of American sins can charm international opinion—witness the starstruck and credulous silence of the dignitaries at Oslo—then the present imperial structures can persist under cover of a promise to be wiser. Thus President Obama can speak, with a pride born of historical amnesia, of "an architecture of institutions—from the United Nations to NATO to the World Bank—that provide for the common security and prosperity of human beings." And thus does Obama's American Century end in a Civilization of Business.[66]

Obama's fulsome homilies enable Americans to postpone an inevitable disenchantment with their "blessed way of life," for the decline of imperial hegemony will be the pivotal episode of the twenty-first century. The horsemen of this apocalypse are already visible and galloping at an accelerating speed, with mounting levels of personal, corporate, and government debt; military overextension that cannot be sustained without unpopular conscription, further fiscal indenture, and greater damage to an already disfigured world image; ecological destruction whose repair is routinely subordinated to the imperatives of business; and an economy whose injustice and indignity become ever more glaring and pernicious. Still profoundly enchanted by empire as a way of life, Americans and their leaders may try—with pecuniary ingenuity and perhaps with great violence—to prolong the imperium of consumption. Yet even if they appear to succeed, their victory will be brief and pyrrhic, for they will have purchased their triumph in the currency of fear, denial, and death. In the end, other peoples—perhaps even many Americans themselves—will not abide the expenditure in money and lives required to extend the American Century. With a degree of rudeness directly proportional to the level of our evasion, we will discover that our way of life is neither charmed nor nonnegotiable.

A generation ago the historian William Appleman Williams posed this question: "Is the idea and reality of America possible without empire?" If one answers *yes*, Williams wrote, then one is a "pioneer on . . . the ultimate American frontier," a successor of those "who said *no* to empire as the only definition of democracy."[67] The creation of a post-imperial identity could be the most liberating adventure for Americans in the twenty-first century. What would Americans make of the country's future—not to mention its past and present—if they lost their conviction of divine anointment and eschatological mission? What would replace the eschatology of business? Preparing for the end of the American Century will be difficult, if not impossible, given the profound and pervasive enchantment of imperial dominion. As the popularity of Christian conservatives such as Michele Bachmann and Sarah Palin suggests, many Americans still affirm the tenets of American exceptionalism in its crudest and most bilious form. The spirit of Manifest Destiny thrives in the soul of American Evangelicalism. But for those who see the impending twilight of empire as a way of life, the decline of our power should be openly embraced as a moment of possibility, a moment when the scales could fall from our eyes and the world would stand revealed. The corporate order would appear in all its true enormity of perniciousness, a regime that robs us not only of the fruits of our labor but of politics, leisure, and delight. It seduces and exploits the very marrow of our beings; and, like any undertaking, in what Augustine called *libido dominandi*—the lust for domination that arises from perversion of the deepest sources of our lives—the desire to erect a heavenly city of business corrupts and disfigures what is finest. That paradise of avarice has been the utopian ideal for the project of American empire; and if Americans could see the very real benefits of relinquishing their imperial dreams, they could greet the erosion of their hegemony with a sense of deliverance, even jubilation. Once redeemed from the burden of empire, and dispelled of the illusion that the world cannot survive without American money, weapons, and leadership, we would surely be weaker, but we would also be wiser, freer to arrange our affairs by a truer and saner standard.

By the standards of Caesar and Mammon, such a deliberate renunciation of the will to mastery is lethal and improvident folly. The patricians and clerics of the corporate state will cling to the fantasy of a global emporium for they have faith in nothing else. Among the many still entranced by the dreams of empire and the hallucination of riches, resistance to the passing of American imperium will be adamant—and possibly violent. But the only alternative to peaceful decline will be perpetual and unavailing war. Sooner or later, Americans must embark on a journey toward a world without America at the center. Like Abraham, they will have to go out, not knowing whither they go; they will have to wander in the wilderness without an errand or a manifest destiny. For the first time, they will have to truly dwell in hope.

CHAPTER 10

Not So Different After All

Andrew J. Bacevich

In Henry Luce's day and in our own, the abiding allure of the American Century (one to which even non-Americans can prove susceptible) stems from the conviction that the United States as a great power differs from every other great power in history. It stands apart: unique, singular, *sans pareil.*

In that sense the American Century is American Exceptionalism manifested on a global scale. It represents potential realized, promise fulfilled, and responsibility finally and willingly accepted. With America's arrival at the summit of world power, humankind's journey toward freedom, destined to culminate in the universal embrace of American values, reaches its decisive phase. If history, as George W. Bush proclaimed in 2005, "has a visible direction, set by liberty and the Author of Liberty," then the American Century defines the moment in which Liberty's Author has chosen to complete His work, thereby accomplishing "the mission that created our Nation."[1]

As Bush's choice of language suggests, that mission has sacred overtones. Speaking in 1919, Woodrow Wilson, another war president, emphasized this point. The doughboys who had left American shores to fight on the western front, he declared, "were crusaders."

> They were not going forth to prove the might of the United States. They were going forth to prove the might of justice and right, and all the world accepted them as crusaders, and their transcendent achievement has made all the world believe in America as it believes in no

> other nation. . . . [T]he moral obligation that rests upon us . . . [is] to see the thing through . . . and make good their redemption of the world.[2]

Seeking neither dominion nor empire, the United States uses its power to advance the cause of all humanity. Wilson emphatically believed this; since U.S. entry into World War II, those following him to the White House have routinely endorsed that view. Even—perhaps especially—when the United States employs armed force, its purposes are by definition beyond reproach. To the extent that the pursuit of interests shapes U.S. policy, satisfying those interests points to the building of a better and more peaceful world. Speaking in 1965, President Lyndon B. Johnson put it this way: "We fight for values and we fight for principles, rather than territory or colonies. [Therefore], no nation need ever fear that we desire their land, or to impose our will, or to dictate their institutions."[3] Although referring specifically to Vietnam, Johnson was expressing sentiments shared by the presidents who preceded him and those who followed him in the American Century. Greed, hubris, and ambition might motivate others to wield the sword, but Americans fight for a Just Cause to Restore Hope in pursuit of Enduring Freedom.[4] More than simply compatible, U.S. interests, American ideals, and the well-being of humankind all converge at a single point. To paraphrase the Eisenhower-era defense secretary Charles E. Wilson, what's good for the United States is good for the world as a whole, and vice versa.

To many Americans, even to question this proposition is intolerable. Note the furor unleashed in 2009 when Barack Obama offered a less than categorical endorsement of his nation's special standing. "I believe in American exceptionalism," the president remarked in response to a reporter's question, "just as I suspect that the Brits believe in British exceptionalism and the Greeks believe in Greek exceptionalism."[5] To critics, such cultural equivalence was cause for outrage. "President Obama may be the first American president to lack faith in our special history, our special spirit and our special mission in the world," a commentator for *Forbes* complained.[6] A *National Review* cover story accused Obama of proposing "to abandon our traditional sense of ourselves as an exceptional nation" while throwing overboard America's "unique role and mission in the world."[7] Mike Huckabee, former Arkansas governor and presumed presidential hopeful, concurred. Obama's "world view is dramatically different from any president, Republican or Democrat, we've had," he charged. "To deny American exceptionalism is, in essence, to deny the heart and soul of this nation."[8] Sarah Palin likewise took Obama to task. "Sad to say," wrote the former governor of Alaska, "many of our national leaders no longer believe in American exceptionalism." Palin continued:

> They . . . think America is just an ordinary nation and so America should act like just an ordinary nation. They don't believe we have a special message for the world or a special mission to preserve our greatness for the betterment of not just ourselves but all of humanity.[9]

To dismiss such criticism as crudely ethnocentric boosterism laced with partisanship would be a mistake. Obama's off-the-cuff remark attracted inordinate attention because he had carelessly violated a cherished norm—it was as if the pope had casually questioned the divinity of Jesus Christ. Wrapping themselves in the mantle of American Exceptionalism, Obama's critics could claim a surer grasp of the nation's prevailing self-image. To liken the United States to any other country (Israel possibly excepted) is to defile a central tenet of the American civil religion. In national politics it is simply impermissible. So the complaint lodged against the president resonated. He had laid open a vein, which his critics willingly tapped. Here, it seemed, was conclusive evidence confirming suspicions that Barack Hussein Obama might be less than fully American.[10]

Such exceptionalist sensitivities help explain why even those oblivious to the provenance of the phrase "American Century" nonetheless remain deeply committed to its perpetuation. To doubt the feasibility of America's redemptive mission—to allow that the American Century has never quite lived up to expectations (or worse still, that it never existed in the first place)—would be, in effect, to concede that American Exceptionalism is an illusion or an outright fraud. To declare the American Century defunct would be tantamount to lumping the United

States among all of the other powers that have paraded across history's pages purporting to erect a new order for the ages before falling short of that goal. The insistence that "we" differ fundamentally from "them" would thereby become unsustainable. So for those devoted to the proposition that the United States is different and special—a group likely including a majority of Americans—celebrating the American Century becomes something akin to a civic duty.

Yet incorporating the actual events of the era into a suitable narrative poses a challenge, simply because exertions undertaken to benefit ourselves and all humanity have so often produced unforeseen, unintended, and even perverse consequences. After all, Wilson's crusade to launch an American Century before Henry Luce even coined the phrase proved something of a bust. U.S. intervention in the war to end all wars consumed over 116,000 American lives but did nothing to avert, and in some respects laid the groundwork for, an even more catastrophic conflict a mere two decades later. Much the same can be said of LBJ's misbegotten vision of exporting New Deal-style reforms to transform Southeast Asia, harnessing the Mekong River to "provide food and water and power on a scale to dwarf even our own TVA." Fifty-eight thousand Americans died; the mighty river rolled on, unimpressed and unaffected. As for George W. Bush, although his defenders might argue that it is too soon to render a definitive verdict, the prospects of the United States "ending tyranny" anytime soon, as Bush had promised, appear less than promising. Preventive war has proven to be something other than the panacea envisioned by the enthusiasts who once confidently promoted it. Whatever democracy's prospects in the Islamic world, they depend not on what Washington prescribes and attempts to enforce but on what Arabs, Iranians, Afghans, and Pakistanis demand and struggle for.

Yet these previous failures to export democracy (along with sundry other errors and disappointments along the way) say nothing essential about the United States or about its ability to direct the course of events, so defenders of the American Century insist. To support their case—and to rebut the naysayers who contend that trying to remake the world in America's own image is a fool's errand—they cite the results of World War II and the outcome of the Cold War.

Luce himself had expected U.S. entry into World War II to vault the United States to a position of global preeminence. The so-called Good War did just that, with circumstances by 1945 serving as both apparent vindication and forecast. Several decades later, the Cold War's abrupt conclusion on terms favorable to the United States, an outcome that few in Washington had foreseen or expected, seemed to prove that 1945 was no fluke.

Framed as chapters in a longer narrative of liberation, these two events invest the ambitions inherent in the vision of an American Century with a modicum of plausibility. Yet sustaining that narrative requires the careful selection and arrangement of facts, with inconvenient or uncomfortable truths excluded, suppressed, or simply ignored.

With regard to World War II, those facts-that-don't-fit include the following: in achieving the destruction of Nazi Germany, U.S. forces played at best a supporting role, with Stalin's Red Army—the vanguard of a totalitarian police state—doing the lion's share of fighting, killing, and dying; as a result, the price of liberating Western Europe included delivering Eastern Europe to Stalin and his henchmen. Meanwhile, in its aerial bombing campaign directed against German and Japanese cities, the United States engaged in the conscious, intentional, wholesale slaughter of noncombatants. In the aftermath of the European war, the victorious allies collaborated in enforcing a massive involuntary transfer of populations, that is, a policy of ethnic cleansing. When they found it expedient to do so, U.S. officials allowed Nazi war criminals—rocket scientists, for example, and intelligence officials—to escape justice and to enter the service of the United States. Then there is this: at no time prior to or during the war did the United States make any substantive effort to prevent or even disrupt the Nazi persecution of Jews that culminated in the "final solution." In Washington the fate of European Jewry never figured as more than an afterthought. As much or more than the promotion of American ideals—that "sharing with all peoples of our Bill of Rights, our Declaration of Independence, [and] our Constitution" that Luce dearly hoped to see—these choices and decisions, along with the priorities they reflect, laid the basis for the interval of American primacy that followed.

Yet most American citizens and virtually all American politicians choose to airbrush such matters out of their own preferred historical account. This "Disneyfication" of World War II, to use Paul Fussell's term, now finds its counterpart in the Disneyfication of the Cold War, reduced in popular imagination and the halls of Congress to Ronald Reagan demanding "Mr. Gorbachev, tear down this wall!" The Soviet leader meekly complied, and freedom erupted across Europe as a consequence. Facts that complicate this story—assassination plots, dirty tricks gone awry, cozy relations with corrupt dictators—provide endless fodder for scholarly articles and books but ultimately get filed under the heading of things that don't really matter. The Ike that Americans like even today is the one who kept the Soviets at bay while presiding over eight years of peace and prosperity. The other Ike—the one who unleashed the CIA on Iran and Guatemala, refused to let the Vietnamese exercise their right to self-determination in 1956, and ignored the plight of Hungarians who, taking seriously Washington's rhetoric of liberation, rose up to throw off the yoke of Soviet power—remains far less well known. Similarly, Americans today continue to cherish John F. Kennedy's charisma, wit, and eloquence. When it comes to the Bay of Pigs, Operation Mongoose, and the murder of Ngo Dinh Diem, they generously give the martyred president a pass.

Granting in American memory a privileged place to World War II and the end of the Cold War keeps the American Century simple and uncluttered. The *way* that Americans choose to remember those two events—evil overthrown thanks chiefly to the United States—invests the American Century with reassuring moral clarity.

To be sure, an uncluttered, morally uplifting version of the past has on occasion served the national interest. Clinging to the concept of an American Century has facilitated efforts to deny the existence of an American Empire. Fixing December 7, 1941, as the start date of the Japanese-American struggle for Pacific dominion, for example, helped mobilize popular support for what had by then become a fight to the finish. In reality that struggle had been engaged long before. Yet after Pearl Harbor, no room remained for second thoughts or might-have-beens, certainly none for seeing the Pacific War for what it actually was: a clash emanating from two rival and irreconcilable visions of empire. With the onset of hostilities, the long train of events that had laid the basis for conflict collapsed into a single "day of infamy," with the Japanese aggressor thereby saddled with responsibility for all that followed. The high-handedness of Commodore Matthew Calbraith Perry in coercing Japan to open itself to the outside world, nearly a century earlier; systematic American discrimination directed against Japanese immigrants, codified in insulting state and local laws; Washington's refusal to acknowledge a Japanese sphere of influence in East Asia, while asserting American primacy throughout the Western Hemisphere; and, more immediately, the impact of U.S.-imposed sanctions intended to strangle Japan economically: For Americans, Pearl Harbor had rendered all these irrelevant—a carefully scrubbed account of all that had gone before justifying a conflict that it had now become imperative to win.

The problem for the United States today is that sanitizing history no longer serves U.S. interests. Instead, it blinds Americans to the challenges that they confront. Self-serving mendacities—that the attacks of September 11, 2001, reprising those of December 7, 1941, "came out of nowhere" to strike an innocent nation—don't enhance the safety and well-being of the American people. If anything, the reverse is true. The Disneyfication of the Iraq War—now well advanced by those depicting "the surge" in Iraq as an epic feat of arms and keen to enshrine General David Petraeus as one of history's Great Captains—might discreetly camouflage, but cannot conceal, the irreversible collapse of George W. Bush's "Freedom Agenda," predicated on expectations that the concerted application of American military power will democratize or at least pacify the Islamic world. The conviction that "the remoralization of America at home ultimately requires the remoralization of American foreign policy"—wars waged to incorporate dark quarters of the Islamic world into the American Century fostering renewal and revitalization at home—has likewise proven baseless and even fanciful.[11] Abu Ghraib, Guantánamo, the revival of waterboarding and other forms of torture, and the policy of so-called extraordinary rendition have left the "incandescent moral clarity" that some observers attributed to U.S. policy after 9/11 more than a little worse for wear.[12]

The argument here is not to invert the American Century, fingering the United States with responsibility for every recurrence of war, famine, pestilence, and persecution that crops up on our deeply troubled planet. Nor is the argument that the United States, no longer the "almighty superpower" of yore, has entered a period of irreversible "decline," pointing ineluctably to retreat, withdrawal, passivity, and irrelevance.[13] Rather, the argument, amply sustained by the essays collected in this volume, is this: To further indulge old illusions of the United States presiding over and directing the course of history will not only impede the ability of Americans to understand the world and themselves but may well pose a positive danger to both. Faced with a reality that includes, within the last decade alone,

- *an inability to anticipate,* whether the events of 9/11, the consequences of invading Iraq, or revolutionary upheaval in Egypt and elsewhere in the Arab world;
- *an inability to control,* with wars begun in Iraq, Afghanistan, and Pakistan, along with various and sundry financial scandals, economic crises, and natural disasters, exposing the limits of American influence, power, and perspicacity;
- *an inability to afford,* as manifested by a badly overstretched military, trillion dollar annual deficits, increasingly unaffordable entitlement programs, and rapidly escalating foreign debt;
- *an inability to respond,* demonstrated by the dysfunction pervading the American political system, especially at the national level, whether in Congress, at senior levels of the executive branch, or in the bureaucracy; and
- *an inability to comprehend* what God intends or the human heart desires, with little to indicate that the wonders of the information age, however dazzling, the impact of globalization, however far-reaching, or the forces of corporate capitalism, however relentless, will provide answers to such elusive questions,

Americans today would do well to temper any claims or expectations of completing the world's redemption. In light of such sobering facts, which Americans ignore at their peril, it no longer makes sense to pretend that the United States is promoting a special message in pursuit of a special mission. Like every other country that confronts circumstances of vast complexity and pervasive uncertainty, the United

States is merely attempting to cope. Prudence and common sense should oblige Americans to admit as much.

Life magazine, Luce's foremost journalistic creation, is long defunct, having ceased weekly publication in 1972 after a brilliant run lasting several decades. In secondhand shops, used bookstores, and on eBay, it survives as a quaint artifact of another era. No one opens an old issue of *Life* today with expectations of unearthing truths that possess contemporary relevance. They do so to indulge their taste for nostalgia, resurrecting memories, real or imagined, of an America that was good and getting better, a land and people overflowing with promise. Whether the America found in *Life*'s pages ever actually existed or whether Luce and his collaborators simply conjured it up in weekly editorial meetings is pretty much beside the point.

Something of the same can be said of Luce's other great creation, albeit with a crucial distinction. Today his vision of an American Century also survives as an artifact, encapsulating an era about which some (although by no means all) Americans might wax nostalgic, a time, real or imagined, of common purpose, common values, and shared sacrifice. Yet there is this difference. The insistence that the American Century perdures—that it *does* convey truths of ongoing relevance—goes beyond nostalgia to signify something akin to a collective flight from reality. To insist that the perpetuation of the American Century (along with its corollary American Exceptionalism) offers a template for national policy is to indulge in escapism, inviting Americans to enter an alternative universe of their own invention.

Escapism makes for good box office but bad politics. Only by jettisoning the American Century and the illusions to which it gives rise will the self-knowledge and self-understanding that Americans urgently require become a possibility. Whether Americans will grasp the opportunity that beckons is another matter.

Notes

1. *Life* at the Dawn of the American Century

1. This quotation, those that precede it, and those that follow are all from *Life,* February 17, 1941.

2. Quoted in Alan Brinkley, *The Publisher: Henry Luce and His American Century* (New York, 2010), 214.

3. Barack Obama, "Renewing American Competitiveness," speech, June 16, 2008.

4. Richard Cohen, "President Obama's Afghanistan Speech Confirms America's Decline," *Washington Post,* June 22, 2011.

5. Fareed Zakaria, *The Post-American World* (New York, 2010).

2. The Origins and Uses of American Hyperpower

1. Philip Roth, *American Pastoral* (Boston, 1997), 40–41.

2. David Cannadine, ed., *Blood, Toil, Tears and Sweat: The Speeches of Winston Churchill* (Boston, 1989), 282.

3. *Historical Statistics of the United States* (Washington, D.C., 1975), 135.

4. Samuel I. Rosenman, comp., *The Public Papers and Addresses of Franklin D. Roosevelt,* vol. 2, *The Year of Crisis, 1933* (New York, 1938), 14.

5. John Keegan, *The Second World War* (New York, 1989), 240.

6. Winston S. Churchill, *The Second World War: The Grand Alliance* (Boston, 1951), 606–608.

7. Ibid., 608.

8. David Irving, *Hitler's War* (New York, 1977), 354.

9. *Reports of General MacArthur: Japanese Operations in the Southwest Pacific Area,* vol. 2, pt. 1 (Washington, D.C., 1966), 33, n. 14.

10. An English version is available as Giulio Douhet, *The Command of the Air,* trans. Dino Ferrari (New York, 1942; originally published in Italian in 1921). See also Mitchell's *Our Air Force,* published in the same year as Douhet's original volume.

11. A full account can be found in John E. Brigante, *The Feasibility Dispute: Determination of War Production Objectives for 1942 and 1943* (Washington, D.C., 1950).

12. Richard Polenberg, *War and Society: The United States, 1941–1945* (Philadelphia, 1972), 229–230.

13. See especially Maurice Matloff, "The 90-Division Gamble," in *Command Decisions*, ed. Kent Roberts Greenfield (Washington, D.C., 1960), 365–81.

14. Polenberg, *War and Society*, 221.

15. Matloff, "The 90-Division Gamble," 373.

16. Ibid.

17. Richard Overy, *Why the Allies Won* (New York, 1995), 206; Alan Milward, *War, Economy, and Society* (Berkeley, Calif., 1979), 92ff.; Bureau of the Budget, *The United States at War* (Washington, D.C., 1946), 509.

18. John Morton Blum, *V Was for Victory: Politics and American Culture during World War II* (New York, 1976), 98.

19. Robert C. Mikesh, *Japan's World War II Balloon Bomb Attacks on North America* (Washington, D.C., 1973); see also John McPhee, "Balloons of War," *The New Yorker*, January 29, 1996, 52–60.

20. Arthur S. Link, ed., *The Papers of Woodrow Wilson* (Princeton, 1966–1994), vol. 30, 251.

21. G. John Ikenberry, "Liberal Order Building," in *To Lead the World: American Strategy after the Bush Doctrine*, ed. Melvyn P. Leffler and Jeffrey W. Legro (New York, 2008), 86.

22. Truman's address to United Nations delegates, April 25, 1945, http://www.trumanlibrary.org/whistlestop/study_collections/un/large/documents/index.php?pagenumber=1&documentdate=1945-04-25&documentid=86&studycollectionid=UN.

23. Geir Lundestad, "Empire by Invitation? The United States and Western Europe, 1945–1952," *Journal of Peace Research* 23 (September 1986), pp. 263–277.

24. Robert Kagan, "End of Dreams, Return of History," in Leffler and Legro, *To Lead the World*, 40.

25. "The National Security Strategy of the United States of America," September 2002, http://www.whitehouse.gov/nsc/nss.pdf.

3. Consuming the American Century

1. Ted Steinberg, *Down to Earth: Nature's Role in American History* (New York, 2002).

2. Naomi Lamoreaux, *The Great Merger Movement in American Business, 1895–1904* (Cambridge, UK, 1985).

3. Marilyn Young, in *The Rhetoric of Empire: American China Policy, 1895–1901* (Cambridge, Mass., 1968), provides the classic examination of the "China market." On trade expansion generally, see Walter LaFeber, *The New Empire: An Interpretation of American Expansion, 1860–1898* (Ithaca, 1963). Emily S. Rosenberg, in *Spreading the American Dream: Economic and Cultural Expansion* (New York, 1982), charts the development of a "promotional state" in the late nineteenth and early twentieth centuries.

4. Peter Shergold, in *Working-Class Life: The "American Standard" in Comparative Perspective, 1899–1913* (Pittsburgh, 1982), argues that before World War I American workers did not have a higher standard of living than those in Europe. But Marina Moskowitz, in *Standard of Living: The Measure of the Middle Class in Modern America* (Baltimore, 2008), explores the larger cultural meanings of a middle-class "standard of living." On Ford's public impact, see David Lewis, *The Public Image of Henry Ford: An American Folk Hero and His Company* (Detroit, 1976).

5. Jackson Lears, *Fables of Abundance: A Cultural History of Advertising in America* (New York, 1994), 113–115.

6. Charles McGovern, *Sold American: Consumption and Citizenship, 1890–1945* (Chapel Hill, 2006); on contrasting visions of "The American Way," see Wendy Wall, *Inventing the "American Way": The Politics of Consensus from the New Deal to the Civil Rights Movement* (New York, 2008).

7. Gary Cross, *An All-Consuming Century* (New York, 2002), 38–43. On working-class immigrants and the new consumption-oriented society, see, especially, Kathy Peiss, *Cheap Amusements: Working Women and Leisure in Turn-of-the-Century New York* (Philadelphia, 1986); Steven Ross, *Working-Class Hollywood: Silent Film and the Shaping of Class in America* (Princeton, 1998); Andrew Heinze, *Adapting to Abundance: Jewish Immigrants, Mass Consumption, and the Search for American Identity* (New York, 1990); Nan Enstad, *Ladies of Labor, Girls of Adventure* (New York, 1999).

8. Daniel Boorstin, in *The Americans: The Democratic Experience* (New York, 1973), provides the classic celebratory account of consumption communities.

9. Joseph Chambers, in *Madison Avenue and the Color Line: African Americans in the Advertising Industry* (Philadelphia, 2008), 1–57, and Grace Elizabeth Hale, in *Making Whiteness: The Culture of Segregation in the South, 1890–1940* (New York, 1999), 121–195, discuss the images of African Americans in advertisements and popular culture.

10. On advertising, see William R. Leach, *Land of Desire: Merchants, Power, and the Rise of a New American Culture* (New York, 1994); Roland Marchand, *Advertising the American Dream: Making Way for Modernity, 1920–1940* (Berkeley, 1986); Stephen Fox, *The Mirror Makers: A History of American Advertising and Its Creators* (New York, 1984); Lears, *Fables of Abundance;* Cross, *An All-Consuming Century;* McGovern, *Sold American.*

11. Roland Marchand, *Creating the Corporate Soul: The Rise of Public Relations and Corporate Imagery in American Big Business* (Berkeley, 2001); Adam Arvidsson, "Brand Management and the Productivity of Consumption," in *Consuming Cultures, Global Perspectives,* ed. John Brewer and Frank Trentmann (Oxford, UK, 2006), 71–94. Al Ries and Jack Trout's *Positioning: The Battle for Your Mind* (New York, 1980) is a classic text emphasizing image, "positioning," and "branding."

12. On late twentieth-century ethnic marketing, see Marilyn Halter, *Shopping for Identity: The Marketing of Ethnicity* (New York, 2002).

13. Leigh Eric Schmidt, *Consumer Rites: The Buying and Selling of American Holidays* (Princeton, 1997); Martha Olney, *Buy Now, Pay Later: Advertising, Credit, and Consumer Demand in the 1920s* (Chapel Hill, 1991); Lendol Calder, *Financing the American Dream: A Cultural History of Consumer Credit* (Princeton, 1999); Giles Slade, *Made to Break: Technology and Obsolescence in America* (Cambridge, Mass., 2006).

14. Daniel L. Lykins, *From Total War to Total Diplomacy: The Advertising Council and the Construction of the Cold War Consensus* (Westport, 2003); Robert Griffith, "The Selling of America: The Advertising Council and American Politics," *Business History Review* 57 (1983): 388–412.

15. Jennifer Klein, *For All These Rights: Business, Labor, and the Shaping of America's Public-Private Welfare State* (Princeton, 2003); Lykins, *From Total War.*

16. Charles S. Maier, "The Politics of Productivity: Foundations of American International Economic Policy after World War II," *In Search of Stability: Explorations in Historical Political Economy* (New York, 1987), pp. 121–152; Victoria de Grazia, *Irresistible Empire: America's Advance through Twentieth-Century Europe* (Cambridge, Mass., 2005), 75–129. On the spread of Hollywood movies, see Thomas Guback, *The International Film Industry: Western Europe and America since 1945* (Bloomington, 1969); Ian C. Jarvie, *Hollywood's Overseas Campaign: The North Atlantic Movie Trade, 1920–1950* (New York, 1992); John Trumpbour, *Selling Hollywood to the World: U.S. and European Struggles for Mastery over the Global Film Industry, 1920–1950* (New York, 2002); Jens Ulff-Møller, *Hollywood's Film Wars with France: Film Trade Diplomacy and the Emergence of the French Film Quota Policy* (Rochester, 2001).

17. On the economic and cultural aspects of the Marshall Plan, see, especially, Richard Kuisel, *Seducing the French: The Dilemma of Americanization* (Berkeley, 1993); Richard H. Pells, *Not Like Us: How Europeans Have Loved, Hated, and Transformed American Culture since World War II* (New York, 1998); Brian Angus McKenzie, *Remaking France: Americanization, Public Diplomacy, and the Marshall Plan* (New York, 2005).

18. Kenneth Osgood, *Total Cold War: Eisenhower's Secret Propaganda Battle at Home and Abroad* (Lawrence, Kans., 2006); Walter L. Hixson, *Parting the Curtain: Propaganda, Culture, and the Cold War, 1945–1961* (New York, 1997), 139; Lykins, *From Total War.* On the U.S. propaganda war generally, see, especially, Scott Lucas, *Freedom's War: The US Crusade against the Soviet Union, 1945–56* (Manchester, 1999); Tony Shaw, *Hollywood's Cold War* (Amherst, 2007).

19. Robert H. Haddow, *Pavilions of Plenty: Exhibiting American Culture Abroad in the 1950s* (Washington, D.C., 1997).

20. See Laura A. Belmonte, "A Family Affair? Gender, the U.S. Information Agency, and Cold War Ideology, 1945–1960," in *Culture and International History,* ed. Jessica C. E. Gienow-Hecht and Frank Schumacher (New York, 2003), 79–93; Laura A. Belmonte, *Selling the American Way: U.S. Propaganda and the Cold War* (Philadelphia, 2008); Helen Laville, "'Our Country Endangered by Underwear': Fashion, Femininity, and the Seduction Narrative in *Ninotchka* and *Silk Stockings*," *Diplomatic History* 30 (September 2006): 623–644; and Susan Smulyan, *Popular Ideologies: Mass Culture at Mid-Century* (Philadelphia, 2007), 41–81, on gender, consumption, and the Cold War. For a review of the scholarship on gender and international relations history, see Kristin Hoganson, "What's Gender Got to Do with It? Gender History as Foreign Relations History," in *Explaining the History of American Foreign Relations,* ed. Michael J. Hogan and Thomas G. Paterson (Cambridge, UK, 2004), 304–322.

21. Richard M. Nixon, "Russia as I Saw It," *National Geographic Magazine* 116 (December 1959): 718, 723; Karal Ann Marling, *As Seen on TV: The Visual Culture of Everyday Life in the 1950s* (Cambridge, Mass., 1994), 243–283; Elaine Tyler May, *Homeward Bound: American Families in the Cold War Era* (New York, 1988), 10–13, 145–146; Greg Castillo, *Cold War on the Home Front: The Soft Power of Midcentury Design* (Minneapolis, 2010).

22. Osgood, *Total Cold War,* 312.

23. Patrick Hyder Patterson, "Truth Half Told: Finding the Perfect Pitch for Advertising and Marketing in Socialist Yugoslavia, 1950–1991," *Enterprise and Society* 4 (June 2003): 179–225.

24. For example, Mark Landsman, *Dictatorship and Demand: The Politics of Consumerism in East Germany* (Cambridge, Mass., 2005); William Taubman,

Khrushchev: The Man and His Era (New York, 2004); Susan E. Reid, "The Khrushchev Kitchen: Domesticating the Scientific-Technological Revolution," *Journal of Contemporary History* 40 (April 2005): 289–316; Katherine Pence, "The Myth of a Suspended Present: Prosperity's Painful Shadow in 1950s East Germany," in *Pain and Prosperity: Reconsidering Twentieth-Century German History,* ed. Paul Betts and Greg Eghigian (Palo Alto, 2003), 137–159.

25. Jack Masey and Conway Lloyd Morgan, *Cold War Confrontations: US Exhibitions and Their Role in the Cultural Cold War, 1950–1980* (Baden, 2008).

26. See Richard Pells, "American Culture Goes Global, or Does It?" *Chronicle of Higher Education* (April 12, 2002): B 7–9, and his *Modernist America: Art, Music, and the Globalization of American Culture* (New Haven, 2011), 400–405; Kristin Hoganson, "Stuff It: Domestic Consumption and the Americanization of the World Paradigm," *Diplomatic History* 30 (September 2006): 571–594.

27. Lisa Tiersten, *Marianne in the Market: Envisioning Consumer Society in Fin-de-Siècle* (Palo Alto, 2001); Rosalind H. Williams, *Dream Worlds: Mass Consumption in Late Nineteenth-Century France* (Berkeley, 1982); de Grazia, *Irresistible Empire;* Adam Arvidsson, "Between Fascism and the American Dream: Advertising in Interwar Italy," *Social Science History* 25 (2001): 151–186; see also the review essay by Joe Perry, "Consumer Citizenship in the Interwar Era: Gender, Race, and the State in Global-Historical Perspective," *Journal of Women's History* 18 (2006): 157–172.

28. Sheldon Garon, "Japan's Post-war 'Consumer Revolution,' or Striking a 'Balance' between Consumption and Saving," in Brewer and Trentmann, *Consuming Cultures,* 189–217; Sheldon Garon and Patricia L. MacLauchlan, eds., *The Ambivalent Consumer: Questioning Consumption in East Asia and the West* (Ithaca, 2006); de Grazia, *Irresistible Empire.*

29. Marie-Laure Djelic, *Exporting the American Model: The Postwar Transformation of European Business* (Oxford, 1998). Although some have argued that she overstates acceptance of the U.S. model in France, her discussion of national differences is suggestive. Michael Stephen Smith, in *The Emergence of Modern Business Enterprise in France, 1800–1930* (Cambridge, Mass., 2006), downplays American influences and emphasizes pre–World War II roots of large-scale enterprise in France, and essays in Dominique Barjot, ed., *Catching Up with America: Productivity Missions and the Diffusion of American Economic and Technological Influence after the Second World War* (Paris, 2002), also emphasize the complexity of internal and external influences. See also David W. Ellwood, *Rebuilding Europe: Western Europe, America, and Postwar Reconstruction* (London, 1992); Jonathan Zeitlin, "Americanization and Its Limits: Theory and Practice in the Reconstruction of Britain's Engineering Industries 1945–55," *Business and Economic History* 24, no. 1 (1995): 277–286.

30. Stephen Gundle, "Hollywood Glamour and Mass Consumption in Postwar Italy," *Journal of Cold War Studies* 4 (Summer 2002): 95–118 (quote on p. 95); Vanessa R. Schwartz, *It's So French! Hollywood, Paris, and the Making of Cosmopolitan Film Culture* (Chicago, 2007).

31. Rob Kroes, *If You've Seen One, You've Seen the Mall: Europeans and American Mass Culture* (Urbana, 1996). "New women" provide an example. See Alys Weinbaum et al., eds., *The Modern Girl around the World: Consumption, Modernity, and Modernization* (Durham, 2008); Mona L. Russell, *Creating the New Egyptian Woman: Consumerism, Education and National Identity, 1863–1922* (New York, 2004); Joanne Hershfield, *Imagining la Chica Moderna: Women, Nation, and Visual Culture in Mexico, 1917–1936* (Durham, 2008). On the Japanese *moga* and the Chinese "modern girl," see Miriam Silverberg, *Erotic Grotesque Nonsense: The Mass Culture of Japanese Modern Times* (Berkeley, 2007); Antonia Finnane, *Changing Clothes in China: Fashion, History, Nation* (New York, 2008), 167. Silverberg develops the idea of "code-switching."

32. Jing Wang, in *Brand New China: Advertising, Media, and Commercial Culture* (Cambridge, Mass., 2008), presents a suggestive discussion of advertising at the intersections of the global and local. The essays in A. G. Hopkins, ed., *Global History: Interactions between the Universal and the Local* (New York, 2006), exemplify the ways in which the "global" and "local" construct each other.

33. Geremie R. Barmé, *In the Red: On Contemporary Chinese Culture* (New York, 1999), 237.

34. Angus Maddison, in "The Nature and Functioning of European Capitalism: A Historical and Comparative Perspective," *Banca Nazionale del Lavoro Quarterly Review* (December 1997), at www.ggdc.net/maddison/, provides comparative data illustrating income growth.

35. Interpretations differ over whether to emphasize the dominance of U.S. mass cultural forms or their local adaptations. Compare, for example, James L. Watson, ed., *Golden Arches East: McDonald's in East Asia* (Palo Alto, 1997), with Joe L. Kincheloe, *The Sign of the Burger: MacDonald's and Cultural Power* (Philadelphia, 2002), which argues that Watson goes too far in stressing local adaptation.

36. Gary Cross, *An All-Consuming Century*. Emily S. Rosenberg, in "Consumer Capitalism and the End of the Cold War," in *The Cambridge History of the Cold War*, vol. 3, ed. Melvyn P. Leffler and Odd Arne Westad (Cambridge, UK, 2010), 913–956 elaborates on the ideas in this section.

37. Nayan Chanda, in *Bound Together: How Traders, Preachers, Adventurers, and Warriors Shaped Globalization* (New Haven, 2007), has a genealogy of the use of the word "globalization."

38. See Robert B. Reich, *Supercapitalism: The Transformation of Business, Democracy, and Everyday Life* (New York, 2007), 5, and his *Aftershock: The Next Economy and America's Future* (New York, 2011).

39. Charles S. Maier, *Among Empires: American Ascendancy and Its Predecessors* (Cambridge, Mass., 2007), 191–284.

40. Niall Ferguson, Charles S. Maier, Erez Manela, and Daniel J. Sargent, eds., *The Shock of the Global: The 1970s in Perspective* (Cambridge, Mass., 2010), looks broadly at a range of economic and cultural changes.

41. Speech by Ben Bernanke, 2005, at http://www.federalreserve.gov/board docs/speeches/2005/200503102/.

42. Data are from Jeffrey Rosen, "Why Brandeis Matters: The Constitution and the Crash," *New Republic,* June 29, 2010, and, generally, from Joseph E. Stiglitz, *Freefall: America, Free Markets, and the Sinking of the World Economy* (New York, 2010).

43. Net domestic savings is the sum total of the depreciation-adjusted savings of households, businesses, and the government sector. See Stephen S. Roach, "The Consumption Gap," *Foreign Policy,* July 21, 2010.

44. Thomas Friedman, a high priest of globalization, is one, among many voices, who highlights the environmental perils of an American-style consumerist order that does not seriously revamp cost structures and production processes. His *Hot, Flat, and Crowded: Why We Need a Green Revolution and How It Can Renew America* (New York, 2008) presents his environmental critique.

45. Michael T. Klare, *Rising Powers, Shrinking Planet: The New Geopolitics of Energy* (New York, 2009).

4. The Problem of Color and Democracy

Thanks to Laura Helton for her research assistance and to Andrew Bacevich and Thuy Linh Tu for comments on an earlier draft of this essay.

1. I borrow this term from Vijay Prashad, *The Darker Nations: A People's History of the Third World* (New York, 2007).

2. W. E. B. Du Bois, *Color and Democracy: The Colonies and Peace* (New York, 1944).

3. Michael Ignatieff, "The Burden," *New York Times,* January 5, 2003; "Rice, in Alabama, Draws Parallels for Democracy Everywhere," *New York Times,* October 22, 2005, A4.

4. Barack Obama, *Dreams from My Father* (New York, 2007), preface, iv.

5. "An American Century," *Time,* March 5, 2011. I have found more than thirty references to "the American Century" sprinkled throughout Obama's speeches during 2010–2011.

6. Henry Luce, *The American Century* (New York, 1941), 23.

7. Donald White, "The 'American Century' in World History," *Journal of World History* 3 (Spring 1992): 14.

8. Luce, *The American Century,* 39.

9. "Some have spoken of the American Century. I say that the century we are entering—the century which will come out of this war—can and must be the century of the common man." See Henry Wallace, *Democracy Reborn* (New York, 1944), 193. Also see Nikhil Pal Singh, "Culture/Wars: Recoding Empire in an Age of Democracy," *American Quarterly* 50 (1998): 481.

10. Carey McWilliams, *Brothers under the Skin* (New York, 1944), 24.

11. I borrow this term from Bruce Cumings, *Dominion from Sea to Sea: Pacific Ascendancy and American Power* (New Haven, 2009), 39.

12. White, "'American Century,'" 14.

13. Dwight MacDonald, *Henry Wallace: The Man and the Myth* (New York, 1947), 31. Also see Singh, "Culture/Wars," 481.

14. Cumings, *Dominion,* 391.

15. MacArthur's father, Arthur, was a general in the U.S. Philippine War, where the son also served as a captain. See General MacArthur's "Pledge to Australia," quoted in Travis Hardy, "The Consanguinity of Ideas: Race and Anticommunism in the U.S.-Australian Relationship, 1933–1953" (unpublished PhD diss., University of Tennessee–Knoxville, 2010), 124.

16. Chalmers Johnson uses the term "empire of bases," while Bruce Cumings calls this the "archipelago of empire." See Chalmers Johnson, *Sorrows of Empire: Militarism, Secrecy and the End of the Republic* (New York, 2004); Cumings, *Dominion,* 393.

17. Jay Jackson, the celebrated cartoonist at the *Defender,* produced scores of images on this theme. On Churchill, the black press, and the Atlantic Charter, see Penny Von Eschen, *Race against Empire* (Ithaca, 2001).

18. "Axis Radio Enjoys Field Day with Riot Reports," *Chicago Defender,* July 3, 1943.

19. W. E. B. Du Bois, "A Chronicle of Race Relations," *Phylon* 3, no. 4 (1942): 417; W. E. B. Du Bois, "As the Crow Flies," *New York Amsterdam News,* July 31, 1943.

20. George Padmore, "US Stalls on Colonies at UNO, Haunted by Threat of World Revolt," *Chicago Defender,* February 9, 1946.

21. W. E. B. Du Bois, *Color and Democracy: The Colonies and Peace* (New York, 1944); St. Clair Drake and Horace Cayton, *Black Metropolis: A Study of Negro Life in a Northern City*, vol. 2 (New York, 1945), 736.

22. John Robert Badger, "World View," *Chicago Defender*, May 29, 1943.

23. Ralph Ellison, "Editorial Comment," *Negro Quarterly* 3 (Fall 1942): 196; Also see Nikhil Pal Singh, *Black Is a Country: Race and the Unfinished Struggle for Democracy* (Cambridge, Mass., 2004), 131.

24. Gunnar Myrdal, *An American Dilemma: The Negro Problem and Modern Democracy*, 2 vols. (New York, 1944), 13; also see Singh, *Black Is a Country*, 48.

25. Myrdal, *An American Dilemma*, 1021.

26. Du Bois, *Color and Democracy*, 91.

27. L. S. Stavrianos, *Global Rift: The Third World Comes of Age* (New York, 1981), 459.

28. Frederick Kepel, "Foreword," in *An American Dilemma*, xlvi. Also see Singh, *Black Is a Country*, 135.

29. Singh, *Black Is a Country*, 164.

30. Carol Anderson, *Eyes off the Prize: The United Nations and the African American Struggle for Human Rights, 1944–1955* (Cambridge, UK, 2003).

31. Quoted in Manning Marable, *Race, Reform and Rebellion: The Second Reconstruction in Black America* (Oxford, 1991), 21.

32. Quoted in George Herring, *From Colony to Superpower: U.S. Foreign Relations since 1776* (Oxford, 2008), 656.

33. Quoted in Mary Dudziak, "Desegregation as a Cold War Imperative," *Stanford Law Review* (1988): 65.

34. Harold Isaacs, *The New World of American Negroes* (New York, 1963), 11; Also see Singh, *Black Is a Country*, 207.

35. Martin Luther King Jr., "My Trip to the Land of Gandhi," in *Testament of Hope: The Essential Writings of Martin Luther King, Jr.*, ed. James M. Washington (New York, 1986), 24.

36. Odd Arne Westad, *The Global Cold War* (Cambridge, UK, 2005), 5.

37. Singh, *Black Is a Country*, 187.

38. Malcolm X, *By Any Means Necessary* (New York, 1970), 153. Also see Singh, *Black Is a Country*, 188.

39. Jack O'Dell, *Climbin' Jacob's Ladder: The Black Freedom Movement Writings of Jack O'Dell* (Berkeley, 2010), 3.

40. "Linked fate" is Michael Dawson's term for understanding African American solidarity in the face of racial oppression. See Michael Dawson, *Black Visions: Roots of Contemporary African American Political Ideologies* (Chicago, 2003).

41. Martin Luther King Jr., *Where Do We Go from Here? Chaos or Community?* (New York, 1968), 221.

42. King, "The American Dream," in *Testament of Hope*, 208; King, "A Time to Break the Silence, in ibid., 234.

43. O'Dell, *Climbin' Jacob's Ladder*, 45.

44. Andrew Young, *An Easy Burden: The Civil Rights Movement and the Transformation of America* (New York, 1996), 234; also see O'Dell, *Climbin' Jacob's Ladder*, 43.

45. Mahmood Mamdani, *Good Muslim, Bad Muslim: America, the Cold War, and the Roots of Terror* (New York, 2005), 163.

46. Andrew J. Bacevich, *The New American Militarism: How Americans Are Seduced by War* (New York, 2005), 53.

47. Cumings, *Dominion*, 481.

48. Alfred McCoy, *Policing America's Empire: The United States, the Philippines, and the Rise of the Surveillance State* (Madison, 2009).

49. Robert Kaplan, "The Coming Anarchy," *The Atlantic*, February 1994.

50. John Lewis Gaddis, *Surprise, Security, and the American Experience* (Cambridge, Mass., 2003), 78.

51. Patrick Wolfe, *Settler Colonialism and the Transformation of Anthropology* (London, 1999).

52. "John McCain's New Hampshire Primary Speech," *New York Times*, January 8, 2008.

53. Nikhil Pal Singh, *Black Is a Country* (Cambridge, Mass., 2004), 57.

5. Pragmatic Realism versus the American Century

1. Given this common outlook, interventionists and imperialists will not be distinguished in this essay, except when specific circumstances require it. I also wish to thank Andrew Bacevich for inviting me to give the lecture that became this essay and for first raising the question of how to define key terms; Christopher Nichols for a timely intervention that helped me recast the direction of my argument; and Karen Parker Lears for her endlessly patient and probing advice that vastly improved the final product.

2. http://www.emersoncentral.com/amscholar.htm.

3. The classic and still unsurpassed account of modern American intellectuals' obsession with activism is in Christopher Lasch, *The New Radicalism in America: The Intellectual as a Social Type, 1889–1963* (New York, 1965).

4. The literature on upper-class masculinity at the turn of the century is huge, but see, especially, Kim Townsend, *Manhood at Harvard: William James and Others* (Cambridge and London, 1996); Kristin Hoganson, *Fighting for American Manhood: How Gender Politics Provoked the Spanish-American and Philippine-American Wars* (New Haven and London, 1998); Kevin P. Murphy, *Political Manhood: Red Bloods, Mollycoddles, and the Politics of Progressive Era Manhood* (New York, 2008).

5. Roosevelt characterized ineffectual men as "mollycoddles" in "The College Man: An Address Delivered at the Harvard Union" [1907], reprinted in Donald Wilhelm, *Theodore Roosevelt as an Undergraduate* (Boston, 1910), 78–90. For Johnson's use of "nervous Nellies," see *Time*, May 27, 1966; for Bush's, see *New York Times*, September 15, 2002.

6. Epigraph to Theodore Roosevelt, *The Strenuous Life: Essays and Addresses* (New York, 1900), n.p.; William James, "Is Life Worth Living?" in his *The Will to Believe and Other Essays* (New York, 1897), 55. James's essay "The Moral Equivalent of War [1906] is available at http://www.constitution.org/wj/meow.htm.

7. For emphasizing the link between James and Bourne, I am indebted to Christopher McKnight Nichols, "Rethinking Randolph Bourne's Trans-National America: How World War I Created an Isolationist Antiwar Pluralism," *The Journal of the Gilded Age and Progressive Era* 8 (April 2009): 217–257. His *Promise and Peril: America at the Dawn of a Global Age* (Cambridge, 2011) recasts familiar notions of internationalism and isolationism in challenging ways.

8. The image of Niebuhr at the podium is from Richard Wightman Fox, *Reinhold Niebuhr: A Biography* (New York, 1985), viii. My indebtedness to Fox's searching account will be evident throughout my discussion of Niebuhr in this essay.

9. http://etext.virginia.edu/jefferson/quotations/jeff1400.htm; www.fff.org /comment/AdamsPolicy.asp.

10. Roosevelt quoted in Michael Kazin, *A Godly Hero: The Life of William Jennings Bryan* (New York, 2006), 106. Jackson Lears, in *Rebirth of a Nation: The Making of Modern America, 1877–1920* (New York, 2009), summarizes the arguments for empire on pp. 207–215.

11. The Philippines War and its atrocities are ably documented in Stuart Creighton Miller, *"Benevolent Assimilation": The American Conquest of the Philippines, 1899–1903* (New Haven and London, 1982).

12. William James to F. C. S. Schiller, August 6, 1902, quoted in Robert F. Beisner, *Twelve against Empire* (New York, 1968), 44; William James, *A Pluralistic Universe* [1909] (New York, 1967), 20; William James, "On a Certain Blindness in Human Beings," http://www.des.emory.edu/mfp/jcertain.html.

13. Robert Richardson, *William James: In the Maelstrom of American Modernism* (Boston and New York, 2006), 385.

14. James, "A Certain Blindness."

15. Mark Twain, "The Person Sitting in Darkness" [1901], in *Mark Twain: Tales, Speeches, Essays, and Sketches*, ed. Tom Quirk (New York, 1994), 264–281.

16. See Randolph Bourne, "Trans-National America" [1916], in his *War and the Intellectuals: Collected Essays, 1915–1919*, ed. Carl Resek (New York, 1964), 110, 120, 122.

17. Randolph Bourne, "A Moral Equivalent for Universal Military Service" [1916], in ibid., 142, 146.

18. Randolph Bourne, "The War and the Intellectuals" [1917], in ibid., 8; quote on p. 6.

19. Ibid., 10, 11.

20. Ibid., 12, 13.

21. Randolph Bourne, "Twilight of Idols" [1917], in ibid., 53, 54.

22. Ibid., 60, 64.

23. Robert Westbrook, "Bourne Over Baghdad," *Raritan* 27 (Summer 2007): 105.

24. Ronald Steel, *Walter Lippmann and the American Century* (Boston and Toronto, 1980), 4, 17.

25. Walter Lippmann to Newton Baker, quoted in ibid., 11.

26. Walter Lippmann, Editorial, *New York World*, December 29, 1926, quoted in ibid., 237.

27. Reinhold Niebuhr, *Moral Man and Immoral Society* (New York, 1932), 88, 234.

28. See the probing discussion of Niebuhr, King, and the "spiritual discipline against resentment" in Christopher Lasch, *The True and Only Heaven: Progress and Its Critics* (New York, 1991), 377–390.

29. Robert Taft, "Shall the United States Enter the European War?" address of May 17, 1941, *Congressional Record*, May 19, 1941, quoted in Ronald Radosh, *Prophets on the Right: Profiles of Conservative Critics of American Globalism* (New York, 1975), 128.

30. Robert Taft, "Repeal of Neutrality Act Means War," speech to U.S. Senate, October 28, 1941, quoted in ibid., 131. Radosh discusses the background to the *Kearny* incident in *Prophets*, 48–52.

31. Charles Beard, *A Foreign Policy for the United States* (New York and London, 1940), chaps. 3, 4. Quotation at p. 44.

32. Beard discusses "Continental Americanism" in ibid., chap. 2, 5. My thinking on these matters has been shaped by Robert Westbrook's pathbreaking discussion in "Isolationism Reconsidered," *Raritan* 30 (Fall 2010): 4–36.

33. Charles Beard to Harry Elmer Barnes, January 6, 1948, quoted in Richard Hofstadter, *The Progressive Historians: Turner, Parrington, Beard* (New York,

1968), 343; Charles Beard, *President Roosevelt and the Coming of the War* (New Haven, 1948), 578.

34. In the *Christian Century*, quoted in Fox, *Reinhold Niebuhr*, 222; Niebuhr on Nazism, quoted in ibid., 199. On imaginable alternatives to military intervention against Hitler in 1941, see Westbrook, "Isolationism Reconsidered," 28–30.

35. Ibid., 166; H. Richard Niebuhr, "The Grace of Doing Nothing," *Christian Century*, March 23, 1932, 379; Niebuhr on the American Century, quoted in Fox, *Reinhold Niebuhr*, 202.

36. Niebuhr to Conant, quoted in ibid., 225.

37. Niebuhr on "faceless men" in U.S. State Department Radio Broadcast, "Ideological Special No. 256," June 30, 1953, quoted in ibid., 256; Fox on fearing war too much in ibid., 229; Luce title in ibid.

38. Niebuhr on "first use" quoted in ibid., 278; Fox on Niebuhr's changing views, ibid., 232.

39. Walter Lippmann, "Today and Tomorrow," *New York World*, September 29, 1931, quoted in Steel, *Walter Lippmann*, 327; Walter Lippmann, Speech at the Thirtieth Reunion of the Harvard Class of 1910, June 18, 1940, quoted in ibid., 384.

40. Walter Lippmann, *United States War Aims* (New York, 1944), 189; Lippmann, "Today and Tomorrow," *New York World*, December 30, 1944, quoted in Steel, *Walter Lippmann*, 415.

41. George Kennan, "The Sources of Soviet Conduct" [1947], reprinted in his *American Diplomacy: Expanded Edition* (Chicago and London, 1984), 115, 128.

42. George Kennan, "Reflections on the Walgreen Lectures," in ibid., 164.

43. George Kennan, "American Diplomacy and the Military," in ibid., 178.

44. George Kennan, *Around the Cragged Hill: A Personal and Political Philosophy* (New York and London, 1993), 27, 182, 64–65, 70–71.

45. Ibid., 183.

46. Walter Lippmann, television interview, taped April 1961, quoted in Steel, *Walter Lippmann*, 530.

47. Walter Lippmann, "Today and Tomorrow," December 29, 1964, syndicated column, quoted in ibid., 564; Walter Lippmann, interview in *Washington Post*, October, 17 1971, quoted in ibid., 586.

48. J. William Fulbright, *The Arrogance of Power* (New York, 1966), 3.

49. Ibid., 248, 13.

50. Ibid., 255.

51. Ibid., 25.

52. George Kennan, Testimony before U.S. Senate Foreign Relations Committee [1966], quoted in ibid., 17–18.

53. Ronald Reagan, "Peace: Restoring the Margin of Safety," Speech to Veterans of Foreign Wars Convention, Chicago, August 18, 1980, at http://www.reagan.utexas.edu/archives/reference/8.18.80html.

54. The best concise account is James Mann, *Rise of the Vulcans: The History of Bush's War Cabinet* (New York, 2004).

55. George Packer, "Recapturing the Flag," *New York Times Magazine,* September 30, 2001, 15.

56. See the entries for September 27, 2001, and October 3, 2001, at http://www.historycommons.org/timeline.

57. William Pfaff, "Manufacturing Insecurity: How Militarism Endangers America," *Foreign Affairs* (November/December 2010), 133–140.

58. The phrase "government in a box" is Gen. Stanley McChrystal's, quoted in Dexter Filkins, "Afghan Offensive Is New War Model," *New York Times,* February 13, 2010.

59. Ralph Waldo Emerson, "Self-Reliance," in *Selections from Ralph Waldo Emerson,* ed. Stephen E. Whicher (Boston, 1960), 158.

60. David Brooks, "Obama's Christian Realism," *New York Times,* December 14, 2009; "Obama's Nobel Remarks," *New York Times,* December 9, 2009.

6. Toward Transnationalism

1. *Asahi,* January 1, 1940, 1.

2. Josepha Laroche, *Mondialisation et Governance Mondiale* (Paris, 2003), 18.

3. Wang Gungwu, "Migration and Its Enemies," in *Conceptualizing Global History,* ed. Bruce Mazlish and Ralph Buultiens (Boulder, 1993), 131–152.

4. Jane C. Desmond, *Staging Tourism: Bodies in Display from Waikiki to Sea World* (Chicago, 1990), xvii.

5. David Held, Anthony McGraw, Davud Goildblatt, and Jonathan Perraton, *Global Transformations: Politics, Economics and Culture* (Stanford, 1999), 344.

6. Ibid., 345.

7. In 2006, for instance, 43 million people in Africa, 75 million in South America, and 457 million in Asia were reported to be connected to the Internet. They comprised more than 50 percent of the total world population, indicating that the entire globe, not just Europe and North America, was becoming "wired." *Data Book of the World,* vol. 20 (Tokyo, 2008), 121.

8. For a discussion of cultural internationalism, see Akira Iriye, *Cultural Internationalism and World Order* (Baltimore, 1997).

9. See Martin Bernal, *Black Athena* (New Brunswick, N.J., 1988).

10. Fabrizio Maccaglia and Marie-Anne Matard-Bonucci, eds., *Atlas des Mafias* (Paris, 2009), 69.

11. Pierre Beckouche and Yann Richard, eds., *Atlas d'une Nouvelle Europe* (Paris, 2008), 24.

12. Warren Cohen, *The Asian American Century* (Cambridge, Mass., 2001).

13. *The World Almanac and Book of Facts, 2007* (New York, 2007), 162.

7. From the American Century to Globalization

1. The material in this essay is largely drawn from my *Global Capitalism: Its Fall and Rise in the Twentieth Century* (New York, 2007). Except in the case of specific quotations, facts, and other particularities, original sources can be found there.

2. Dean Acheson, *Morning and Noon: A Memoir* (Boston, 1965), 267.

3. *Proceedings of the Academy of Political Science* 17, no. 1 (May 1936): 113.

4. At ftp://ftp.electionstudies.org/ftp/nes/studypages/1948prepost/nes1948.txt.

5. For a full analysis, see Karen E. Schnietz, "The Institutional Foundation of U.S. Trade Policy: Revisiting Explanations for the 1934 Reciprocal Trade Agreements Act," *Journal of Policy History* 12 (2000): 417–444.

6. Doug Irwin and Randall Kroszner, "Interests, Institutions, and Ideology in Securing Policy Change: The Republican Conversion to Trade Liberalization after Smoot-Hawley," *Journal of Law and Economics* 42 (October 1999): 643–673.

7. For an outstanding analysis of this process, see Benjamin O. Fordham, *Building the Cold War Consensus: The Political Economy of U.S. National Security Policy, 1949–1951* (Ann Arbor, 1998).

8. Illusions of an American Century

1. Obama is quoted in Jessica Opoien, "Obama Discusses Education Jobs with College Journalists," *Iowa State Daily,* September 28, 2010. Examples of analyses examining the post-2003 fate of the American Century include David S. Mason, *The End of the American Century* (Lanham, 2009), a wide-ranging analysis with extensive references; Richard Cohen, "Moralism on the Shelf," *Washington Post,* March 10, 2009, A19. An earlier, detailed critique is found in Nicholas Guyatt, *Another American Century? The United States and the World since 9/11* (London, 2003), esp. chaps. 1, 5. "Slinking" is used according to the *Webster's Collegiate Dictionary* definitions "to move or go in a furtive, abject manner, as from fear or shame," and, notably, "to walk or move in a sinuous, provocative way."

2. Francis Fukuyama, "The End of History?" *The National Interest* 16 (Summer 1989): 3–18.

3. A particularly important analysis of these private enterprise coalitions and their failure, an account based on too often overlooked European archival material as well as U.S. primary documents, is found in Frank C. Costigliola, *Awkward Dominion: American Political, Economic, and Cultural Relations with Europe, 1919–1933* (Ithaca, 1984).

4. Originally in the February 17, 1941, *Life* issue, Luce's essay has often been republished. An especially useful discussion is in *Diplomatic History* 23 (Spring 1999), which features Luce's original followed by a series of commentaries by historians. For a useful analysis of Luce's experiences in Asia and how they shaped his thinking, see Michael Hunt, "East Asia in Henry Luce's 'American Century,' " in that symposium, esp. 321–328. Andrew J. Bacevich, in *Washington Rules: America's Path to Permanent War* (New York, 2010), uses Luce's essay as a point of departure and discusses, especially on 12–15, an important sentence from the essay: Americans should "accept wholeheartedly our duty to exert upon the world the full impact of our influence for such purposes as we see fit and by such means as we see fit." This idea is integral to Luce's "Good Samaritan" reference.

5. Norman Vincent Peale, *The Power of Positive Thinking* (New York, 1952).

6. Richard Wightman Fox, *Reinhold Niebuhr: A Biography* (New York, 1985), 202.

7. An important examination of the reasons for the division is in Lloyd Gardner, *Spheres of Influence* (Chicago, 1993). For valuable insights into Truman's quest for "85 percent" and why he failed, see Arnold Offner, *Another Such Victory: President Truman and the Cold War, 1945–1953* (Stanford, 2002), esp. 70–84.

8. *Public Papers of the Presidents of the United States. Harry S. Truman. 1947* (Washington, D.C., 1963), 167–172, reprints the Baylor speech. Along with Offner's biography, Richard Freeland's *The Truman Doctrine and the Origins of McCarthyism: Foreign Policy, Domestic Politics, and Internal Security, 1946–1948* (New York, 1972) continues to be of special importance for its linking of the early Cold War's foreign and domestic policies.

9. Rosemary Foot, *The Wrong War: American Policy and the Dimensions of the Korean Conflict, 1950–1953* (Ithaca, 1985), esp. 114–118. Bruce Cumings has pioneered research on U.S.-Korean relations; note a section on the Korean War in his important overview, *Dominion from Sea to Sea: Pacific Ascendancy and American Power* (New Haven, 2009), 393–407.

10. Alan Brinkley, *The Publisher: Henry Luce and His American Century* (New York, 2010), 369; Mark H. Lytle's *The Origins of the Iranian-American Alliance, 1941–1953* (New York, 1987), 192–218, is an important account. Kermit

Roosevelt, the agent who helped lead the CIA in overthrowing Mossadegh, tells his proud and sometimes humorous story in *Countercoup: The Struggle for the Control of Iran* (New York, 1979).

11. Gary Sick, *All Fall Down: America's Tragic Encounter with Iran* (New York, 1985), esp. vii–49, 101–140, remains an important account written by a former U.S. government official critical of Carter and several of his advisers; see Bacevich, *Washington Rules,* 134–135, for Ronald Reagan's politically effective criticism of Carter's policies.

12. Keddie concludes that the roots of the errors running back to the 1950s and earlier, which were committed by the shah and the United States, proved so formative that different U.S. policies in 1979 could not have prevented the shah's overthrow. See Nikki R. Keddie, *Roots of Revolution: An Interpretive History of Modern Iran* (New Haven, 1981).

13. "Memo for President for Leaders' Meetings, May 24/53," May 22, 1954, Meetings with the President, 1954, White House Memoranda Series, Papers of John Foster Dulles, Dwight D. Eisenhower Library, Abilene, Kansas. Two leading accounts, with differing interpretations, are Richard H. Immerman, *The CIA in Guatemala: The Foreign Policy of Intervention* (Austin, 1982), and Piero Gleijeses, *Shattered Hope: The Guatemalan Revolution and the United States, 1944–1954* (Princeton, 1991).

14. Superb accounts are Greg Grandin, *The Blood of Guatemala: A History of Race and Nation* (Durham, 2001), particularly for the essential background; Grandin, *Empire's Workshop: Latin America, the United States, and the Rise of the New Imperialism* (New York, 2006), esp. 42–45, 54–55. Citations for the Guatemalan story and the secretary-general's quote are in Walter LaFeber, *Inevitable Revolutions: The United States in Central America,* 2nd ed. (New York, 1993), 108–127; chap. 5.

15. The CIA quotes are in the excellent, detailed account by Lars Schoultz, *That Infernal Little Cuban Republic: The United States and the Cuban Revolution* (Chapel Hill, 2009), 57–60; see also Raymond Dennett and Robert K. Turner, eds., *Documents on American Foreign Relations,* 10 (1948) (Princeton, 1950), 484–502.

16. Quoted in Lloyd E. Ambrosius, *Woodrow Wilson and the American Diplomatic Tradition: The Treaty Fight in Perspective* (New York, 1987), 293.

17. Schoultz, *That Infernal Little Cuban Republic,* esp. 55–56, 138, 142–169.

18. Ibid., 193–194.

19. Brinkley, *The Publisher,* 446–447. For the counterview that questioned U.S. policy assumptions by emphasizing Vietnamese nationalism and Vietnam's long conflict with China, see the account by George McT. Kahin, distinguished scholar of Southeast Asia, in his *Intervention: How America Became Involved in*

Vietnam (New York, 1986); for several U.S. attempts to come to terms with the need to reconcile American Century promises with Vietnam's realities, see Bacevich, *Washington Rules,* esp. 122–134.

20. Good background is found in Fredrik Logevall and Andrew Preston, eds., *Nixon in the World: American Foreign Relations, 1969–1977* (New York, 2008), esp. 6–8, 12–14; Tom Switzer, in "The World Today, Foretold by Nixon," *New York Times,* July 5, 2011, offers a superb, brief analysis of the Pittsburgh speech and its context. Switzer notes that if such a speech were given in 2011, the speaker would be condemned as a declinist and defeatist, but "Nixon's speech sparked no outrage in July 1971."

21. Craig K. Elwell, *Brief History of the Gold Standard in the United States* (Washington, D.C., 2011), esp. 12–14. This is a report prepared by the Congressional Research Service.

22. These and other economic trends (notably deregulation) climaxed in 2008 in the worst American economic crisis since the Great Depression of the 1930s. The immediate background is analyzed by Joseph E. Stiglitz, winner of the Nobel Prize in Economics, in *Free Fall: America, Free Markets, and the Sinking of the World Economy* (New York, 2010), esp. 1–52.

23. The *Time* quote is in Melvyn P. Leffler, *For the Soul of Mankind: The United States, the Soviet Union, and the Cold War* (New York, 2007), 455.

24. Kenton Clymer's work on the history of U.S.-Cambodian relations is standard; on Carter's role, see especially Clymer's "Jimmy Carter, Human Rights, and Cambodia," *Diplomatic History* 27 (April 2003): 245–273.

25. Speech of April 27, 1982, *Public Papers of the Presidents of the United States. Ronald Reagan. 1982,* 2 vols. (Washington, D.C., 1983), vol. 1, 523.

26. A telling analysis of the Middle East tragedy and its ramifications (and context) is found in Douglas Little, *American Orientalism: The United States and the Middle East since 1945* (Chapel Hill, NC, 2002), esp. 245–248; for Grenada and the relationships between the invasion and the Beirut killings, see Lou Cannon, *President Reagan: The Role of a Lifetime* (New York, 2000), 389–391.

27. William M. LeoGrande's *Our Own Backyard: The United States in Central America, 1977–1991* (Chapel Hill, N.C., 1998) is important on these points. For an excellent summary that deals with, among other themes, the domino theory as it does not relate to Central America, see LeoGrande's op-ed, "Salvador's [sic] No Domino," *New York Times,* March 9, 1983, A23.

28. *Washington Post,* April 23, 1987, A10; ibid., May 19, 1985, 28; ibid., April 23, 1987, A10; ibid., March 18, 1988, B1; *New York Times,* March 26, 1988, 1; ibid., August 22, 1989, D3. I am indebted to Professor William Walker and his work for the estimated drug figures.

29. George Shultz, *Turmoil and Triumph: My Years as Secretary of State* (New York, 1993), esp. 703; citations and examples for the effects of the new technologies can be found in Walter LaFeber, "Technology and U.S. Foreign Relations," *Diplomatic History* 24 (Winter 2000): 12–18. Leffler, *For the Soul of Mankind,* 425, contains the Matlock quote.

30. A persuasive account of Reagan's subordinate role to Gorbachev in the ending of the Cold War, based on newly released Soviet documents as well as Reagan's personal papers, is found in Leffler, *For the Soul of Mankind,* esp. 466.

31. An excellent overall account of the 1990s, which catches the growing dilemmas created by the expansive use of U.S. power to deal with the fragmentation that marked the initial post–Cold War decade, is found in Derek Chollet and James Goldgeier, *America between the Wars from 11/9 to 9/11: The Misunderstood Years between the Fall of the Berlin Wall and the Start of the War on Terror* (New York, 2008), esp. 176, 232–233.

32. Ibid., esp. 75–80, 95–98, 246–250.

33. An important analysis that includes an examination of the "Project for the New American Century" is found in James Mann, *The Rise of the Vulcans* (New York, 2004); the first Gates quote is in "For Gates, Caring for Troops Was Job No. 1," *Los Angeles Times,* June 28, 2011, emphasis added; the second quote is in Thom Shanker, "Gates Warns against Wars Like Iraq and Afghanistan," *New York Times,* February 26, 2011, A7.

34. Liz Sly, "U.S. Losing the Arab World as Protests Rage," *Washington Post,* February 4, 2011, A1, A17.

35. A pioneering examination of roots, policies, and early results of the post-1890s U.S. informal empire is found in Thomas J. McCormick, *The China Market* (Chicago, 1967).

36. Two notable examples are: William Pfaff, *The Irony of Manifest Destiny: The Tragedy of America's Foreign Policy* (New York, 2010), a critique of recent U.S. foreign policies that also traces the policies' historical roots; and the work of filmmaker George Lucas's documentary unit, headed by Sharon Wood, which has produced a highly instructive three-part series on the course of U.S. "Manifest Destiny" from the early nineteenth century to the foreign policies of former president George W. Bush and President Barack Obama.

9. The Heavenly City of Business

For reading and commenting on drafts of this essay, I thank Jackson Lears, Anthony Godzieba, Stanley Hauerwas, and Lauren Winner. I also extend abundant gratitude to Madeline Chera and Nicholas Morris, my research assistants, for their invaluable efforts.

1. Nancy Mitford, *The Blessing* (New York, 1951), 185–186.

2. Thomas Friedman, "A Manifesto for the Fast World," *New York Times Magazine,* March 28, 1999, 40.

3. Terry Eagleton, *After Theory* (New York, 2003), 99.

4. For my understanding of Augustinian thought, I have relied principally on Eric Gregory, *Politics and the Order of Love: An Augustinian Ethic of Democratic Citizenship* (Princeton, 2008), and Graham Ward, *Cities of God* (London, 2000).

5. Michael Saler, "Modernity and Enchantment: A Historiographic Review," *American Historical Review* 113 (June 2006): 692–716, offers a capacious and thoughtful survey of historical literature on "enchantment" and its persistence. Weber's account of "disenchantment" can be found in "Science as a Vocation" (1915), in *From Max Weber: Essays in Sociology,* ed. Hans Gerth and C. Wright Mills (New York, 1946), 129–156. On commodity fetishism, the *locus classicus* is Karl Marx, *Capital,* vol. 1 (New York, 1906 [1867]), 81–96.

6. Perry Miller, *Errand into the Wilderness* (Cambridge, Mass., 1956); Anders Stephanson, *Manifest Destiny: American Expansionism and the Empire of Right* (New York, 1995), 5.

7. John Winthrop, letter to his father, in *The Life and Letters of John Winthrop,* ed. Robert C. Winthrop (Boston, 1864), 310, 312.

8. Sacvan Bercovitch, *The American Jeremiad* (Madison, 1980), 31–61, quotes on 46, 47. Mark Valeri, *Heavenly Merchandize: How Religion Shaped Commerce in Puritan America* (Princeton, 2010), traces the relationship of piety and profit in New England over four generations of merchants.

9. Harvey G. Townsend, ed., *The Philosophy of Jonathan Edwards from His Private Notebooks* (Eugene, 1955), 207–208; "Some Thoughts Concerning the Present Revivals," in *The Great Awakening,* ed. C. C. Goen (New Haven, 1972), 353–358.

10. Joseph Warren, "Song on Liberty," cited in Richard Frothingham, *The Life and Times of Joseph Warren* (Boston, 1865), 405.

11. Ezra Stiles, *The United States Elevated to Glory and Honor* (New Haven, 1783), 7, 10, 12, 35.

12. James Madison, Federalist Paper #10, in *The Federalist Papers,* ed. Isaac Kramnick (New York, 1987), 126–127; Thomas Jefferson, letter to Madison, April 27, 1809, in *The Papers of Thomas Jefferson: Retirement Series,* ed. J. Jefferson Looney (Princeton, 2004), vol. 1, 169.

13. On the "market revolution," see Charles Sellers, *The Market Revolution: Jacksonian America, 1815–1846* (New York, 1994); on "Manifest Destiny" before the Civil War, see Stephanson, *Manifest Destiny,* 28–65. Paul Conkin, *Prophets of*

Prosperity: America's First Political Economists (Indianapolis, 1980); on evangelical economics, see Stewart Davenport, *Friends of the Unrighteous Mammon: Northern Christians and Market Capitalism, 1815–1860* (Chicago, 2008); also see Lyman Beecher, *A Plea for the West* (New York, 1835), 10, 32, 12; John L. O'Sullivan, "Annexation," *United States Magazine and Democratic Review* 17 (July–August 1845): 5. On the "white republic" and *herrenvolk* democracy, see Alexander Saxton, *The Rise and Fall of the White Republic: Class Politics and Mass Culture in Nineteenth-Century America* (New York and London, 1990).

14. John L. O'Sullivan, "The Great Nation of Futurity," *United States Magazine and Democratic Review* 6 (November 1839): 427; William H. Seward, cited in Stephanson, *Manifest Destiny*, 61–63.

15. Ralph Waldo Emerson, "The Young American" (1844), in his *Essays and Lectures* (New York, 1983), 217, 226.

16. Herman Melville, *White-Jacket, Or the World in a Man-of-War* (New York, 2000 [1850]), 153.

17. Herman Melville, *Israel Potter: His Fifty Years of Exile* (Evanston, 2000 [1855]), 120; *The Confidence-Man: His Masquerade* (Urbana-Champaign, 2007 [1857]), 203–214, quotes on 204, 205.

18. Henry Cabot Lodge is cited in Jackson Lears, *Rebirth of a Nation: The Making of Modern America, 1877–1920* (New York, 2009), 201; Walter LaFeber, *The American Search for Opportunity, 1865–1913* (New York, 1994); see also LaFeber, *The New Empire: An Interpretation of American Expansion, 1860–1898* (Ithaca, 1998 [1963]).

19. Brooks Adams, *America's Economic Supremacy* (New York, 1900), 81, 83, 25.

20. Josiah Strong, *Our Country: Its Possible Future and Its Present Crisis* (New York, 1891 [1885]), 14–15, 175; emphasis added.

21. Albert J. Beveridge, "Our Philippine Policy" (January 9, 1900), in his *The Meaning of Our Time and Other Speeches* (Indianapolis, 1908), 85, 87; "The March of the Flag" (September 16, 1898), ibid., 48, 47.

22. Alan Trachtenberg, *The Incorporation of America: Politics and Culture in the Gilded Age* (New York, 1982); Lears, *Rebirth of a Nation*, 296.

23. See Lears, *Rebirth of a Nation*, 276–326, on the "civilizing mission" and "regeneration."

24. Martin J. Sklar, *The Corporate Reconstruction of American Capitalism* (Cambridge, UK, 1988), 78–85. The notion that imperialism was a necessary phase of capitalist development was, Sklar writes, "a 'bourgeois theory' before it was a 'Marxist theory.'" Also see Charles A. Conant, "The Economic Basis of Imperialism," *North American Review* 167 (September 1898): 336.

25. Elihu Root, cited in William Appleman Williams, *Empire as a Way of Life: An Essay on the Causes and Character of America's Predicament Along with a Few Thoughts about an Alternative* (New York, 1980), 154.

26. Theodore Roosevelt, cited in Lears, *Rebirth of a Nation,* 316; on "innovative nostalgia," see Robert M. Crunden, *Ministers of Reform* (Urbana, Ill., 1985), 90–162. Also see Walter Weyl, *American World Policies* (New York, 1917), 149; Herbert Croly, *Progressive Democracy* (New York, 1914), 193, 427, 410, 353.

27. Herbert Croly, *The Promise of American Life* (New York, 1909), 300–307, quote on 302; Croly, *Progressive Democracy,* 192.

28. Walter Lippmann, *Drift and Mastery: An Attempt to Diagnose the Current Unrest* (Madison, 1985 [1914]), 35, 39, 44–45, 154–155; Lippmann, *Men of Destiny* (New Brunswick, 2003 [1927]), 26.

29. Walter Lippmann, *The Stakes of Diplomacy* (New York, 1915), 90; "What Position Shall the United States Stand for in International Relations?" *Annals of the American Society of Political and Social Science* 66 (July 1916): 61; Lippmann, *The Good Society* (New Brunswick, N.J., 2005 [1937]), 319, 320.

30. W. T. Stead, *The Americanization of the World, or, The Trend of the Twentieth Century* (New York and London, 1902), preface (n.p.), 163, 104, 9, 164; see especially 132–146 on the American economy. For other examples of European ambivalence about American ascendancy, see Andre Siegfried, *America Comes of Age: A French Analysis* (New York, 1927); G. K. Chesterton, *What I Saw in America* (New York, 1922).

31. The most insightful studies of Wilson himself are found in John Milton Cooper, *The Warrior and the Priest: Woodrow Wilson and Theodore Roosevelt* (Cambridge, Mass., 1983), and Cooper's more recent *Woodrow Wilson: A Biography* (New York, 2009). The most comprehensive study of Wilsonian "idealism" is found in David Steigerwald, *Wilsonian Idealism in America* (Ithaca, 1994).

32. Wilson's remark on Providence is cited in August Heckscher, *Woodrow Wilson* (New York, 1991), 245; Wilson, "Democracy and Efficiency," *Atlantic Monthly* 87 (March 1901): 297; "The Ideals of America," *Atlantic Monthly* 90 (December 1902): 733; Wilson's remarks to students are cited in Sklar, *Corporate Reconstruction,* 415–417.

33. Wilson, "Democracy and Efficiency," 297, 298; Wilson's remarks to the Senate are cited in Arthur S. Link, *The Higher Realism of Woodrow Wilson* (Nashville, Tenn., 1972), 20.

34. Wilson, "Wilson's Address at the Salesmanship Congress" (July 10, 1916), in *President Wilson's State Papers and Addresses,* ed. Albert Sloan (New York, 1918), 282–283.

35. Kim McQuaid, in *A Response to Industrialism: Liberal Businessmen and the Evolving Spectrum of Capitalist Reform, 1886–1960* (New York, 1986), 98–157, examines the "New Capitalism" of the 1920s. On the significance of *Forbes,* see Morrell Heald, *The Social Responsibility of Business: Company and Community, 1900–1960* (Cleveland, 1970), 48; editorial in *Forbes,* November 30, 1918, 588.

36. Edward A. Filene, *Successful Living in This Machine Age* (New York, 1931), 113, 223, 236.

37. Earnest Elmo Calkins, *Business the Civilizer* (Boston, 1928), 232–233, 272, 294–295.

38. Michael Augspurger, *An Economy of Abundant Beauty: Fortune Magazine and Depression America* (Ithaca, 2004). On the BAC and the CED, see Robert M. Collins, *The Business Response to Keynes, 1929–1964* (New York, 1981), 56–62, 81–87, 129–152.

39. Luce's prospectus is quoted in Augspurger, *Economy of Abundant Beauty,* 6; Young and Rubicam advertisement, *Fortune,* February 1930, 105. On the new "hegemonic bloc," see Thomas Ferguson, "Industrial Conflict and the Coming of the New Deal: The Triumph of Multinational Liberalism in America," in *The Rise and Fall of the New Deal Order, 1930–1980,* ed. Steve Fraser and Gary Gerstle (Princeton, 1989), 3–31.

40. Luce, "The American Century," *Life,* February 17, 1941, 65.

41. Ibid., 64, 65.

42. Ibid., 61, 63, 65.

43. Editors of *Fortune, U.S.A.: The Permanent Revolution* (New York, 1951), viii, x–xi, 30, 67–68, 198. The book was originally published as the February 1951 issue of *Fortune.*

44. Robert J. Griffith, "Dwight D. Eisenhower and the Corporate Commonwealth," *American Historical Review* 87 (February 1982): 87–122; Fraser and Gerstle, *Rise and Fall of the New Deal Order;* Michael Useem, "Revolt of the Corporate Owners and the Destabilization of Business Political Action," and Cesar J. Ayala, "Theories of Big Business in American Society," both in *Critical Sociology* 16 (Summer–Fall 1989): 7–25 and 91–119 respectively; Ralph Cordiner, *New Frontiers for Professional Managers* (New York, 1956), 31; Leo D. Welch, speech to the National Foreign Trade Convention (November 12, 1946), cited in Richard J. Barnet, *Roots of War* (New York, 1981 [1972]), 19; W. W. Rostow, "The Great Transition: Tasks of the First and Second Post-war Generations," speech at the University of Leeds, 1967, cited in Barnet, *Roots of War,* 75.

45. Peter Drucker, *Concept of the Corporation* (New York, 1946), 6–7; *The Future of Industrial Man* (New York, 1942), 99; see also *The Future of Economic Man* (New York, 1939); *The New Society: An Anatomy of the Industrial Order*

(New York, 1950); *The Practice of Management* (New York, 1954). William H. Whyte, *The Organization Man* (New York, 1956), 10, 286; Daniel Bell, *The End of Ideology: On the Exhaustion of Political Ideas in the Fifties* (Glencoe, 1961 [1960]).

46. On post-Fordism, see David Harvey, *The Condition of Postmodernity: An Enquiry into the Origins of Cultural Change* (Oxford, 1990), 141–199.

47. Marshall McLuhan, *The Mechanical Bride: The Folklore of Industrial Man* (New York, 1951), 9–11, 33; *Understanding Media: The Extensions of Man* (Cambridge, Mass., 1994 [1964]), 6, 67, 114; "The Playboy Interview: Marshall Mc-Luhan," *Playboy*, March 1969, 61. Grant Havers, in "The Right-Wing Postmodernism of Marshall McLuhan," *Media, Culture, and Society* 25 (Fall 2003): 511–525, cuts through much of the ideological fog that still surrounds McLuhan. Also see Daniel Bell, *The Cultural Contradictions of Capitalism* (New York, 1976), 73; Thomas Frank, *The Conquest of Cool: Business Culture, Counterculture, and the Rise of Hip Consumerism* (Chicago, 1997).

48. Fred Turner, *From Counterculture to Cyberculture: Stewart Brand, the Whole Earth Network, and the Rise of Digital Utopianism* (Chicago, 2006), esp. 222–232. Alvin Toffler's corpus of techno-prophecy includes *Future Shock* (New York, 1970) and *The Third Wave* (New York, 1980). Bill Gates waxes on "friction-free capitalism" in *The Road Ahead* (New York, 1995), 157–183.

49. Books in this genre include George Gilder, *Microcosm: The Quantum Revolution in Economics and Technology* (New York, 1990), and *Telecosm: How Infinite Bandwidth Will Revolutionize Our World* (New York, 2000); Kevin Kelly, *New Rules for the New Economy* (New York, 1998); Nicholas Negroponte, *Being Digital* (New York, 1995); Esther Dyson, *Release 2.0: A Guide for Living in the Digital Age* (New York, 1997); Toffler, *Future Shock*, 144, 233; Negroponte, "Being Digital: A Book (Pre)review," *Wired*, February 1995, 182.

50. Bill Gates, *Business @ the Speed of Thought: Succeeding in the Digital Economy* (New York, 2000), 6, 15–38; Gates, *The Road Ahead*, 181.

51. Esther Dyson, George Gilder, George Keyworth, and Alvin Toffler, "Cyberspace and the American Dream: A Magna Carta for the Knowledge Age (Release 1.2, August 22, 1994)," *Information Society* 12 (Summer 1996): 295–297.

52. Gingrich, interview with Dyson, "Friend and Foe," *Wired*, August 1995, 111, 160. Many of Gingrich's other books exhibit a similar conflation of religion, techno-enchantment, and militarism: see, for instance, *Window of Opportunity* (New York, 1985), and *To Renew America* (New York, 1996).

53. To borrow David Harvey's terms, I see neoliberalism as *both* "a *utopian* project to realize a theoretical design for the reorganization of international capitalism" *and* "a *political* project to re-establish the conditions for capital accumulation and to restore the power of economic elites." See Harvey, *A Brief History of*

Neo-Liberalism (New York, 2006), 19; emphasis in the original. William Finnegan's "The Economics of Empire: Notes on the Washington Consensus," *Harper's,* May 2003, 41–54, is a penetrating reflection on imperial mythology. President Bush is cited in Andrew J. Bacevich, *The Limits of Power: The End of American Exceptionalism* (New York, 2008), 53. Also see John Micklethwaite and Adrian Woolridge, *A Future Perfect: The Challenge and Hidden Promise of Globalization* (New York, 2000), 225–245, 339–342, quotes on 341, 342.

54. President Clinton and Secretary Rice are cited in Andrew J. Bacevich, *American Empire: The Realities and Consequences of U.S. Diplomacy* (Cambridge, Mass., 2002), 1, 32, 34; George W. Bush, "President's Remarks at National Day of Prayer and Remembrance," September 14, 2001. On the contemporary convergence of evangelical Protestantism and capitalist economics, see William E. Connolly, "The Evangelical-Capitalist Resonance Machine," *Political Theory* 33 (December 2005): 869–886. For an example of the Christian Right's most recent providentialist thinking, see Stephen H. Webb, *American Providence: A Nation with a Mission* (New York, 2004). Also see Ari Fleischer, White House press briefing, May 7, 2001, at www.georgewbush-whitehouse.archives.gov.

55. Francis Fukuyama, *The End of History and the Last Man* (New York, 1992), xii, 90, 98–108, 46; emphasis added. Fukuyama first propounded his thesis in "The End of History?" *National Interest* 3 (Summer 1989): 3–18.

56. "Statement of Principles," The Project for a New American Century, at www.newamericancentury.org/statementofprinciples.htm.

57. *The National Security Strategy of the United States of America,* ed. Frank Columbus (Hauppauge, 2003), 3, 5, 32. "Full spectrum dominance" was first enunciated in the Pentagon's *Joint Vision 2010,* first published in 1996 and revised in 2000 as *Joint Vision 2020*—that is, during the Clinton administration. See Bacevich's discussion of full spectrum dominance in *American Empire,* 131–133. Franks is quoted in Bacevich, *The New American Militarism: How Americans Are Seduced by War* (New York, 2005), 22.

58. Thomas Friedman, *The Lexus and the Olive Tree: Understanding Globalization* (New York, 1999), and *The World Is Flat: A Brief History of the Twentieth Century* (New York, 2005); Thomas Friedman, *Hot, Flat, and Crowded: Why We Need a Green Revolution—and How It Can Renew America* (New York, 2008).

59. Friedman, *World Is Flat,* 616, 580–604; *Lexus and the Olive Tree,* 110–111, 365.

60. Friedman, *Lexus and the Olive Tree,* 468–470, 102, 109, 368.

61. Chalmers Johnson, *The Sorrows of Empire: Militarism, Secrecy, and the End of the Republic* (New York, 2004), 23; Bacevich, *Limits of Power,* 173.

62. Nina Easton, "What Obama Means for Business," *Fortune,* June 20, 2008, 46.

63. Both speeches—"The New Way Forward" (December 1, 2009) and "Remarks by the President at the Acceptance of the Nobel Peace Prize" (December 10, 2009)—are available at www.whitehouse.gov.

64. Frank Rich, "Obama's Logic Is No Match for Afghanistan," *New York Times,* December 5, 2009, WK10; Garry Wills, *Bomb Power: The Modern Presidency and the National Security State* (New York, 2010), 239–240.

65. Slavoj Žižek, "Multiculturalism: Or, the Cultural Logic of Multinational Capitalism," *New Left Review* 1, no. 225 (September–October 1997): 28–51.

66. President Obama, "The New Way Forward," www.whitehouse.gov.

67. Williams, *Empire as a Way of Life,* 211–212.

10. Not So Different After All

1. George W. Bush, "Second Inaugural Address," January 20, 2005.

2. Woodrow Wilson, "Speech at Pueblo, Colorado," September 25, 1919.

3. Lyndon Baines Johnson, "Peace without Conquest," speech at Johns Hopkins University, April 7, 1965.

4. The capitalized phrases refer to the operational code names attached to the U.S. military interventions in Panama (1989), Somalia (1992), and Afghanistan (2001).

5. Michael Scherer, "Obama Too Is an American Exceptionalist," *Time,* April 4, 2009.

6. Mallory Factor, "American Exceptionalism—and an 'Exceptional' President," *Forbes,* August 31, 2010.

7. Richard Lowry and Ramesh Ponnuru, "An Exceptional Debate," *National Review,* March 8, 2010. The article carries this subtitle: "The Obama Administration's Assault on American Identity."

8. Jonathan Zimmerman, "U.S. Exceptionalism and the Left," *Shreveport Times,* December 28, 2010.

9. Sarah Palin, "America the Exceptional," *National Post,* December 9, 2010.

10. In his January 25, 2011, State of the Union Address, President Obama tried to recover, declaring, "America [is] not just a place on a map, but the light to the world." For his critics, it was a case of too little too late. Appearing two days later on CNN, Speaker of the House John Boehner refused to relent. "They've refused to talk about America exceptionalism," he said. "I don't know if they're afraid of it, whether they don't believe it. I don't know." See "Boehner: Obama Doesn't Believe in American Exceptionalism," http://www.examiner.com/populist-in-national/boehner-obama-doesn-t-believe-american-exceptionalism.

11. William Kristol and Robert Kagan, "Toward a Neo-Reaganite Foreign Policy," *Foreign Affairs* (July/August 1996): 31.

12. Norman Podhoretz, "In Praise of the Bush Doctrine," *Commentary,* September 2002.

13. The cover of the *New York Times Magazine,* March 28, 1999, had anointed the United States the "almighty superpower." The occasion was the publication of a new book by *Times* columnist Thomas Friedman, touting the wonders of globalization.

Acknowledgments

This book began life as a lecture series organized under the auspices of Boston University's International History Institute during the 2009–2010 academic year. I am grateful to my friends Bill Keylor and Cathal Nolan for including me in the life of the Institute that they jointly founded and so ably lead. In various important ways, Christian Estrella, Zach Fredman, and Allison Patenaude all pitched in to make that series work. My thanks to each of them. Without the resources made available by David Campbell, then serving as university provost, the project would have never made it past the how-about-this-idea stage. I thank David for his support in this endeavor and for the many kindnesses he extended to me over the years. I won't forget.

In converting lectures into a book, John Wright offered his usual sage advice and counsel. John, my debt to you grows apace. At Harvard University Press, Joyce Seltzer lost no time in demonstrating why she is such a renowned editor of history. The book is notably better as a result. Her colleagues at the Press, including Brian Distelberg, did an exemplary job of ushering the manuscript through to completion. Thanks also to Barbara Goodhouse and Michele Lansing for their excellent assistance.

Here at home, just the two of us (plus Archie) remain. Almost without our noticing it, our life together has moved into a different phase. Watching me sitting hunched over my books and computer for hours on end, I know that Nancy wonders at times what exactly I think I'm doing. Watching her as she stands in front of her easel, I don't have to wrestle with such questions: She makes things of beauty. To be her husband is a great gift.

Contributors

Andrew J. Bacevich is professor of history and international relations at Boston University. His books include *The New American Militarism: How Americans Are Seduced by War; The Limits of Power: The End of American Exceptionalism;* and *Washington Rules: America's Path to Permanent War.*

Jeffry A. Frieden, professor of government at Harvard University, specializes in the politics of international monetary and financial relations. His books include *Global Capitalism: Its Fall and Rise in the Twentieth Century* and (with Menzie Chinn) *Lost Decades: The Making of America's Debt Crisis and the Long Recovery.* He has contributed to a wide variety of scholarly journals, among them *International Organization* and the *Journal of Economic History.*

Akira Iriye, Charles Warren Professor of American History, Emeritus at Harvard University, has written widely on U.S. diplomatic history and modern international relations. Among his recent books are *The Globalizing of America, Cultural Internationalism and World Order,* and *Global Community.* He is a past president of both the American Historical Association and the Society for Historians of American Foreign Relations (SHAFR).

David M. Kennedy is Donald J. McLachlan Professor of History, Emeritus at Stanford University. His book *Birth Control in America: The Career of Margaret Sanger* won the Bancroft Prize. He also won the Pulitzer Prize for History for his 1999 book *Freedom from Fear: The American People in Depression and War, 1929–1945.* He is a Fellow of the American Academy of Arts and Sciences and the American Philosophical Society.

Walter LaFeber, Andrew H. and James S. Tisch Distinguished University Professor at Cornell, served as president of SHAFR, has been a Guggenheim Fellow, and is a member of the American Academy of Arts and Sciences. His many books, beginning with *The New Empire: An Interpretation of American Expansion, 1860–1898,* have earned a variety of awards, among them the Albert J. Beveridge Prize, the Bancroft Prize, and the Ellis Hawley Prize of the Organization of American Historians.

T. J. Jackson Lears is Board of Governors Professor of History at Rutgers, where he also edits the quarterly journal *Raritan*. His books include *Rebirth of a Nation: The Making of Modern America, 1877–1920*; *Fables of Abundance: A Cultural History of Advertising in America* (winner of the *Los Angeles Times* Book Award); and *No Place of Grace: Antimodernism and the Transformation of American Culture, 1880–1920*. In 2009 he was elected a Fellow of the American Academy of Arts and Sciences.

Eugene McCarraher is associate professor of humanities and history at Villanova University. He is the author of *Christian Critics: Religion and the Impasse in Modern American Social Thought* and *The Enchantments of Mammon: Corporate Capitalism and the American Moral Imagination,* scheduled to appear in 2012. He is a frequent contributor to *Books & Culture, Commonweal,* and *In These Times.*

Emily S. Rosenberg is professor of history at the University of California, Irvine, and a past president of SHAFR. Her books include *Spreading the American Dream: American Economic and Cultural Expansion, 1890–1945; The Day Which Will Live: Pearl Harbor in American Memory;* and *Financial Missionaries to the World: The Politics and Culture of Dollar Diplomacy, 1900–1930,* which received the Robert Ferrell Book Award.

Nikhil Pal Singh is associate professor of social and cultural analysis at New York University, where he also directs the graduate program in American studies. He is the author of *Climbin' Jacob's Ladder: The Black Freedom Movement Writings of Jack O'Dell* and *Black Is a Country: Race and the Unfinished Struggle for Democracy,* winner of the Liberty Legacy Foundation Award of the Organization of American Historians and the Norris and Carol Hundley Award, sponsored by the Pacific Coast Branch of the American Historical Association.

Index